Mertz · Arab Aid to Sub-Saharan Africa

Entwicklung und Frieden · Wissenschaftliche Reihe 29

Edited by the Scientific Commission of the Catholic Working Group on Development and Peace

Herausgegeben von der Wissenschaftlichen Kommission des Katholischen Arbeitskreises Entwicklung und Frieden

* Studien zum Konflikt im Südlichen Afrika

ROBERT ANTON MERTZ
PAMELA MacDONALD MERTZ

Arab Aid to Sub-Saharan Africa

KAISER • GRÜNEWALD

Distributed by WESTVIEW PRESS

For Cadence, Christopher and Alicia

Distributed throughout the world,
except in Germany, Austria, and Switzerland, by
    Westview Press, Inc.
    5500 Central Avenue
    Boulder, Colorado 80301
    U.S.A.

Library of Congress Catalog Card Number: 83-61022

ISBN 0-86531-646-5

CIP-Kurztitelaufnahme der Deutschen Bibliothek

Mertz, Robert Anton:
Arab Aid to Sub-Saharan Africa / Robert Anton
Mertz ; Pamela MacDonald Mertz. – München :
Kaiser ; Mainz : Matthias-Grünewald-Verlag, 1983. –
    (Entwicklung und Frieden : Wiss. Reihe ; 29)
    ISBN 3-7867-1048-1 (Matthias-Grünewald-Verl.)
    ISBN 3-459-01499-7 (Kaiser)
NE: Mertz, Pamela MacDonald; Entwicklung und
Frieden / Wissenschaftliche Reihe

© 1983 Chr. Kaiser Verlag, München
© 1983 Matthias-Grünewald-Verlag, Mainz
Umschlag: Kroehl Design Gruppe
Satz: Satzstudio Ingrid Ehrle, Ober-Olm
Druck und Bindung: Druckhaus Darmstadt

Table of Contents

List of Tables

8

Introduction

Oil wealth since 1973 has enabled the Arab oil producing countries to embark on a concentrated period of rapid economic development unparalleled in modern history. It has also provided certain countries with surplus financial resources on an unprecedented scale. A considerable portion of this wealth has been passed on to less fortunately endowed countries in the Arab world, Asia and Africa in the form of financial assistance.

This report sets forth the results of our analysis of the flows of bilateral and multilateral financial assistance from Algeria, Iraq, Kuwait, Libya, Qatar, Saudi Arabia and the United Arab Emirates (UAE) to Sub-Saharan Africa. The fundamental purpose of our investigation has been to assess the content, motives and objectives of bilateral and multilateral Arab aid programs. We have concentrated our analysis on the influence of national political and economic interests, Islam and humanitarian concerns as they shape and determine the amount, direction and types of aid awarded to Sub-Saharan Africa by the individual donor nations and Arab-sponsored multilateral institutions.

Our investigation has been based, in the first instance, on a statistical analysis of Arab financial flows contained in the various bilateral and multilateral aid programs. Additionally, we reviewed the publications of the various lending agencies and the written works of other analysts. We supplemented these sources with an extensive series of interviews with aid officials and independent observers in Europe and the Middle East.

In an economic and financial analysis such as this the quality of the data base is of utmost concern. Unfortunately, aside from most institutional lenders which document their activities well, details concerning the bulk of Arab aid provided by governments are published in haphazard fashion, if at all. Such data as are available are often contradictory and difficult, if not impossible, to reconcile. Rather than rely on partial and largely asymmetrical data, we have chosen to utilize a single statistical source in order to ensure consistency. The most thorough compilation of Arab aid statistics was the UNCTAD study, but it covered only the period 1973–1976. Therefore, we have utilized the annual review of OPEC aid flows published by the OECD, which is supplemented by topical analyses and occasional statistical annexes. This work offers an excellent and consistent source of information on Arab aid flows and has the added virtue of annual updating and revision. It also has limitations. First, the breadth and comprehensiveness of the OECD data appear to have declined somewhat after 1976 as statistics on government and institutional assistance have become more difficult to obtain. Second, the definition of "official development assistance" and "total official flows" utilized by OECD exclude certain important sources of Arab aid including transfers of military and Islamic assistance (with the exception of educational programs), short term financial resources and contributions to the IMF Oil and Supplementary Financing Facilities. With the exception of the IMF, these transfers are rarely documented publicly and are, thus, exceedingly difficult to report accurately.

We have accepted the parameters of aid established by the OECD and have only supplemented their statistics with information derived from a variety of other sources in a few areas of deficiency. We have done this with regard to assistance from Islamic organizations such as the Islamic Solidarity Fund and the Muslim World League, aid for Islamic social and religious purposes and aid from countries such as Algeria, Iraq and Libya which choose not to report in detail on their aid programs. Due to its classified nature, we were unable to obtain any information concerning Arab military assistance to Sub-Saharan Africa, although we expect that it follows patterns similar to the non-military assistance described in this study.

A further difficulty in utilizing OECD material is the question of what constitutes "aid" or "financial assistance". The OECD distinguishes carefully between concessional and non-concessional flows of financial resources. The former are designated "official development assistance" (ODA) and referred to as "aid", while the latter are included in "total official flows" (TOF). ODA includes grants and loans undertaken by the official sector at concessional financial terms (i.e. with a "grant element" of at least 25 %) with the promotion of economic development and welfare as the main objective, but excludes loans or credits with a maturity of less than one year and assistance for military or religious purposes. In addition to ODA, total official flows encompass grants from the private sector, transactions on commercial terms, direct investments and purchases of securities of international organizations active in development. Most of this assistance is on non-concessional terms.

A final difficulty arising from the use of OECD statistics is caused by the debate among aid specialists as to whether commitments or disbursements are the more accurate indicator of aid policies and trends. The OECD monitors both but focuses on disbursements in its publications, arguing logically that only disbursements constitute real resource transfers and that many commitments, particularly those from Algeria and Libya, are never translated into disbursements.

We recognize the importance of these distinctions, but we have chosen to utilize "commitments" of "total official flows" as the most appropriate measure of Arab financial assistance for our analysis and to highlight substantial discrepancies between concessional and non-concessional flows and between commitments and disbursements as appropriate in the text.[1]

(Where we discuss other types of financial assistance we have so designated it).

Our reasons for focusing primarily on commitments are several. First, the main purpose of this study is to assess the motives and objectives of Arab financial assistance to Sub-Saharan Africa. Commitments generally represent accurately donor policy interests and intentions at the time of an agreement to provide aid. Second, commitments are an indication of future aid flows. With the exception of bilateral general support grants or emergency assistance which may be transferred immediately to a recipient's account, disbursements invariably lag commitments. In some cases, circumstances do change and donors subsequently reassess the value of political and economic relations with a recipient leading them to cancel or reduce aid commitments. But, far more important, there has been a steadily growing preference among Arab donors for "project" instead of "program" or general support lending, particularly in geographic areas outside the Arab world. This preference alone frequently results in an extended disbursement period geared to the financing of each project and considerable asymmetry between the annual level of commitments and disbursements. In Africa, most commitments are in the process of disbursement, with the exception of countries (such as Uganda) where there has been a fundamental shift in political relations or a change in economic and financial circumstances. Third, commitments are easier to monitor than disbursements. Characteristically, publicity attends the announcement of a new aid commitment, while disbursements or the cancellation or withdrawal of commitments are largely unrecorded. Consequently, while our reliance on commitments may result in some distortion of the level of Arab aid to Sub-Saharan Africa, it will not substantially distort the overall trend of that assistance.

We have chosen to concentrate on total official flows, not official development assistance in our analysis, for several other reasons. First, Arab donors distinguish carefully between aid and investment. With rare and decreasingly frequent exceptions, all Arab concessional and non-concessional assistance to Sub-Saharan Africa — whatever its form — has been intended as aid, not investment. Second, many Arab donors extend both concessional and non-concessional assistance and vary their terms to accommodate the particular financial and economic circumstances of each project and each recipient. Thus, a project which may be financed on concessional terms in a relatively poor country may be financed on "harder" or even non-concessional terms in a wealthier country. Both should properly be recorded among the donor's aid commitments. Finally, the

---

1 As a result, although our statistics are drawn largely from OECD sources, readers should bear in mind the differences in terminology employed when making comparisons.

increasing emphasis on "project finance" has resulted in a slight "hardening" of the terms of some Arab financial assistance since 1973, although there are considerable differences between national aid programs and between aid extended to various geographic regions on this point. Indeed, some of the Arab multilateral institutions which were capitalized with concessional assistance in the form of equity subscriptions lend these funds on variable and even non-concessional terms, yet this support is intended as aid no matter what the terms.

We would like to thank many friends and acquaintances in the Arab world, especially in Saudi Arabia, Kuwait and Abu Dhabi, and Europe and the United States for their assistance and encouragement. Individuals from the private sector, government and the several national and international funds generously shared their views on the subject of aid and helped us collect statistical information without which this study would have been less complete and less well-informed. Because our interviews were all conducted "off the record" we owe them each a debt of silent gratitude.

We would like to pay special tribute to Mr. Jürgen Bartsch and Mrs. Ruth Stock of the OECD in Paris who annually compile the excellent and thorough analysis of OPEC aid published as part of the OECD's annual review, *Development Cooperation*. They willingly and generously shared their research and insights with us and provided us with the statistical foundation for our analysis. We could not have carried out this work without the gracious hospitality of Dr. Anton Gelli and the staff of the superb library on developing countries at the IFO Institut in Munich. We are also grateful to Dr. Udo Steinbach and Dr. Detlev Khalid of the Deutsches Orient-Institut in Hamburg who willingly gave us access to their excellent library. In equal manner, we wish to thank Dr. Dieter Braun and Dr. Albrecht Zunker for making available to us the considerable resources of the Stiftung für Wissenschaft and Politik in Ebenhausen, Bavaria. We would also like to thank Mr. Izzat Farahat, Head of the External Relations Division at BADEA for helping us fill in several statistical lacunae.

We would like to extend a word of special gratitude to Dr. Theodor Hanf of the Arnold Bergstraesser Institute in Freiburg im Breisgau, West Germany. Dr. Hanf originally suggested that we undertake this study, and he and his wife provided continued intellectual encouragement and gastronomic sustenance. Through their sympathetic indulgence and hard work under pressure his associates — Angela Herrmann, Irene von Strachwitz, Gisela Wunderle, Anngret Weyand and Bernhild Josten — made a marked contribution to this study. In the United States, Giselle Fox-Little and Christine Momot helped turn the original study completed in October 1980 into what we hope is an improved and updated manuscript. We owe them all our thanks. However, the views expressed in this study are ours alone.

A. General Trends in Arab Aid

The quadrupling of oil prices in 1973 and early 1974 and further sharp increases in 1979—1980 have provided the oil-producing countries with unprecedented wealth. The principal Arab recipients of this bonanza — Algeria, Iraq, Kuwait, Libya, Qatar, Saudi Arabia and the United Arab Emirates — have become major sources of financial assistance to developing countries. Total official flows of assistance committed by this group of nations rose from less than $ 500 million in 1972 to an annual average of $ 7 billion during the period from 1973 to 1980, totalling over $ 56 billion (see Table 1).

Of the amount committed since 1974, $ 44 billion had been disbursed by the end of 1980. Indeed, disbursements of Arab aid as a percentage of total net resource receipts of developing countries from all sources increased from 1.7 % in 1972 to an annual average of 8.5 % between 1974 and 1979.[1]

Saudi Arabia alone committed almost $ 22 billion (about 40 %) of the Arab total. During 1976 and 1977, the Kingdom became the second largest donor of "official development assistance" in the world after the United States, although it slipped to number six by 1979. Together, Kuwait and Abu Dhabi committed another $ 23 billion of the Arab total.

There are substantial differences among the aid programs of the seven Arab donor nations and the Arab-sponsored multilateral institutions. However, there are several general trends which have characterized Arab aid since 1973. A preliminary analysis of these trends will provide important background to understanding the individual bilateral and multilateral Arab aid programs directed toward Sub-Saharan Africa which are discussed in the following chapters. The most important of these general trends are discussed in this chapter and include the following:

1. the declining level of total aid flows since 1976;
2. donor preference for bilateral assistance;
3. the institutionalization of aid;
4. the increased emphasis on "project" in contrast to "program" lending;
5. the continued geographic concentration of Arab aid in Arab countries.

---

1   OECD, *Development Cooperation, 1980 Review,* Paris, 1980, p. 177.

1. Level of Total Aid Flows

As indicated in Table 1, Arab aid commitments rose rapidly from $ 2.7 billion in 1973 to $ 9.6 billion in 1976. In both nominal and real terms, however, commitments have been in a downward trend thereafter, falling 44 % to $ 5.4 billion in 1979, the lowest level since 1973. As would be expected, disbursements initially rose more slowly but have consistently averaged over $ 6 billion annually since 1975.

Several reasons account for the fluctuations in the level of commitments since 1973. First, and most important, the level of aid flows, particularly of new commitments, has been highly dependent on changes in the level of the current account surplus enjoyed by the oil-exporting nations. The level of the combined OPEC surplus has influenced particularly the establishment and capital replenishment of some multilateral agencies, while the overall level of resources allocated to foreign aid by the major surplus countries − Saudi Arabia, Kuwait, Abu Dhabi, Iraq and Qatar − have normally mirrored changes in the level of their respective current account surpluses. The combined OPEC surplus (earned largely by Arab members of the cartel) peaked at $ 65 billion in 1974, then declined to $ 4.3 billion in 1978.[2] This trend was the result of the much larger-than-anticipated absorptive capacity of OPEC members due to accelerating private and public consumption and investment, to world wide inflation, as well as to a slowing in the growth of oil consumption in the oil-importing nations. Together, these factors caused a steady decline in the "real" price of oil during the 1973−78 period and account, in large part, for the OPEC decision to raise prices significantly in 1979−80. The latest round of oil price increases resulted in a combined OPEC current account surplus before official transfers of $ 69 billion in 1979 and $ 103 billion in 1980.[3] This surplus too is expected to diminish during the early 1980's as the expenditures contained in the development plans of the OPEC countries continue at an extraordinary rate. The increase in aid which would have been expected following the 1979−80 price increases has been slower to materialize than was the case in 1973−74. According to OECD statistics, commitments of official assistance actually declined 35 % in 1979 from the previous year, from $ 8.3 billion to $ 5.4 billion.[4] Current indications are that a substantial increase in aid will be forthcoming eventually. Indeed, preliminary data show that commitments rose 36 % in 1980 to $ 7.3 billion and that commitments in 1981 are running at a higher level.

---

2   Morgan Guaranty Trust, *World Financial Markets*, September 1976, p. 4, and September 1980, p. 2.
3   Information on OPEC current account levels is from *World Financial Markets*, September 1980, p. 2, and May 1981, p. 4.
4   OECD, *op. cit.*, p. 229.

14

Secondly, as the real price of oil declined during the mid-1970s and as oil-importing countries adjusted to the higher nominal prices, the crisis atmosphere of 1974 faded and the oil exporters felt themselves to be under less intense pressure to provide compensatory financial assistance. The successful "recycling" effort of the private commercial banking system contributed to the easier environment, although not all LDC's enjoyed equal access to private capital markets. Drawing in part on oil-derived OPEC deposits, commercial bank loans outstanding to non-OPEC developing countries rose from $35 billion at the end of 1974 to an estimated $150 billion at year end 1979.[5] These banks provided almost two thirds of the "net" external financing requirements of the non-OPEC LDC's in 1979 compared to less than one third in the early 1970s. Official institutional sources of finance, especially the World Bank and the IMF, increased the absolute volume of their assistance as well. However, the share of the combined non-OPEC LDC deficit financing provided by official transfers from all bilateral and multilateral sources including the IMF fell from 48% in 1974 to 39% in 1978. With other sources sharing the burden and internal adjustments beginning to deflect the political pressure, the Arab OPEC share of ODA, as measured by the OECD, fell from 23% of total bilateral ODA in 1975 to 16% in 1979.[6] The increased aid committed in 1980 and anticipated for 1981 is in part compensation for the heightened financial burden on the oil importing LDC's in the wake of the higher oil prices of 1979 and 1980.

Thirdly, after 1973 the Arab countries embarked on an era of rapid institution-building with the establishment and capitalization of numerous bilateral and multilateral Arab-sponsored development institutions.[7] These commitments drained resources temporarily from non-institutional bilateral aid programs. Virtually all of the original capital subscribed in these institutions and, particularly, those in the latter category, was committed before the end of 1977. A second phase of recapitalization began in 1980–1981.

After 1976–77, a substantial share of official aid, especially to countries outside the Arab world, has been provided by these development agencies. The most significant effect of the establishment of these institutional channels has been to increase the emphasis on "project" lending for economic and social development purposes. This in turn has led to much

---

5 The following information is from *World Financial Markets*, December 1978, pp. 2–3.

6 OECD, *op. cit.*, p. 125.

7 Neither Arab OPEC contributions of $3.0 billion to the $6.9 billion IMF oil Facility in 1974 and 1975, nor the $2 billion contribution of Saudi Arabia and the UAE to the Supplementary Financing Facility are included in our study. Both provided oil-importing countries with substantial additional resources, subject to the IMF's normal terms and conditions, during the past 7 years.

15

longer lead times in project development than was the case with earlier bilateral grants. This shift in emphasis has caused not only a reduction in the amount of aid committed because of the application of more stringent project lending standards, but has also protracted the period over which funds are disbursed. The net effect has been to slow down the commitment and disbursement of institutional funds considerably.

A further reason which contributed to a generally declining trend of Arab aid during the latter half of the 1970s may well have been disappointment among donor countries over the utility of foreign aid in achieving their foreign policy objectives, particularly in compelling countries to change their policies in return for aid. Egypt might be cited as an example of a country which, though dependent on massive transfusions of Arab capital after 1973, nevertheless broke ranks and violated a cardinal Arab political conviction by signing a separate peace treaty with Israel which subordinates a solution to the Palestine question. Uganda might be cited as a Sub-Saharan example. For political and religious reasons, Arab states committed more money to Uganda under President Idi Amin than to any other African nation outside the Arab League, yet were apparently powerless to influence the policies of his regime or to block his overthrow. While there have been instances of countervailing success, Arab governments have undoubtedly learned since 1974 what other governments have also learned through experience; that unless there are compelling mutual interests, the expenditure of foreign aid alone will, at best, only rent, not purchase international allegiances.

Finally, both the level and trend of Arab aid commitments have been sharply affected in the short term by the financial flows resulting from major political events in the Middle East. For example, a consequence of Egypt's peace agreement with Israel was the commitment of a further $ 3.5 billion in aid from Arab oil-producers to the "Rejectionist Front" (Syria, Jordan and the Palestine Liberation Organization) at the Baghdad Summit in November 1978. Without this commitment the trend toward lower annual levels of Arab aid would have been far steeper. Civil war in Lebanon and war between Iran and Iraq have also resulted in promises of sizeable future assistance. Arab Gulf states have reportedly pledged $ 2 billion for reconstruction in Lebanon over 5 years.[8] There are unconfirmed reports of as much as $ 10 billion in financial assistance to Iraq in order to prosecute the war with Iran and to rebuild the country in the event of peace.

---

8   OECD, *op. cit.*, p. 130.

2. Bilateral Aid

Arab financial assistance may be divided into two categories: bilateral flows between governments, including aid from national development funds and financial institutions, and assistance through multilateral institutions. Bilateral aid has averaged over 85 % of total annual commitments since 1973 (see Table 2). Even for an area such as Sub-Saharan Africa, for which several specialized Arab institutions have been established, Arab aid continues to emphasize bilateral channels. Fully 85 % ($ 1,227 million) of the $ 1,454 million pledged to Sub-Saharan Africa between 1977–1982 by Saudi Arabia, Kuwait, Qatar and the UAE is to be disbursed bilaterally.[9]

The preference for bilateral aid derives primarily from the fact that aid is a key element of foreign policy. Indeed, for the Arab donor states, financial assistance is relatively a far more important instrument of foreign policy than is the case among Western or Communist nations. The Arab states have little else they can or wish to offer as assistance. Accordingly, many Arab donors desire to maximize their political and administrative control over the allocation of their financial assistance, particularly in areas of geographic priority. Bilateral assistance usually affords a donor greater specificity and leverage to further national interests than comparable support for a multilateral institution. At the same time, bilateral channels allow maximum exposure and public relations impact of aid if that is an objective, yet provide complete discretion should that be preferred.

The emphasis on bilateral aid has been one reason why total disbursements have lagged total commitments by an aggregate $ 12.5 billion during the period from 1973 to 1980 (see Tables 1, 2 and 3). Although the phased capitalization of multilateral institutions has been a contributing factor, most of the lag ($ 11 billion) has been in bilateral disbursements. Changes in bilateral political relations such as occurred following the signature of the Egyptian-Israeli peace treaty or the overthrow of Idi Amin in Uganda affect the final disbursement of bilateral commitments. In such circumstances, it seems highly doubtful that considerable portions of the bilateral aid committed ever will be disbursed. Even more important than political factors is the normal delay experienced in the disbursement of project loans.

Table 2 demonstrates that the emphasis on bilateral aid varies substantially among donors. The principal reason for these differences is the extent to which individual donors have institutionalized their respective bilateral aid programs. In the case of Algeria, Libya and Qatar, none of these

---

9 Ahmad Yousef Ahmad, *Arab-African Relations and their Implications for the Red Sea Region*, (unpublished), Al-Ahram Center for Political and Strategic Studies, Cairo, May 1980, p. 87.

states has created a national development fund or other institution concerned with bilateral aid.[10] Consequently, these countries will occasionally utilize multilateral institutions in situations where the larger Arab donors can rely on their own funds. In addition, the aid programs of these countries are among the smallest of the seven donor states. As a result, they have had to commit a greater proportion of their aid resources to subscribe capital in Arab-sponsored multilateral institutions in order to ensure a sufficient degree of influence over institutional decision-making relative to the larger Arab countries. In the case of Saudi Arabia, its very wealth (which to date has allowed it the luxury of not having to be too selective), the diversity of its foreign political, economic and financial interests relative to most other Arab donors, its active participation in established international institutions and its desire and ability to play a significant role in the institutions it supports account for a relatively high percentage of multilateral aid. In all four cases, however, bilateral aid can be expected to comprise an even greater percentage of total aid flows in future years once the latest period of institutional recapitalization is past.

3. Institutionalization of Aid

From its establishment in 1961 until 1974, the Kuwait Fund for Arab Economic Development was the only Arab development institution in existence (see Table 4). Until 1974, Arab aid was awarded almost exclusively on a case-by-case basis to other Arab governments in the form of grants or loans for balance-of-payments or budgetary support or as oil credits. Such credits did not require an elaborate administrative structure as there was seldom any expectation of repayment. Requests for aid were rarely scrutinized closely for their financial or economic merits, so there was little need for appraisal and analysis. Authority to award aid was closely held but informal, shared by the Ruler and senior members of the Royal family and government, especially the Ministers of Foreign Affairs and Treasury, who were often influenced by foreign advisers, officials and other members of the political elite. With the partial exception of the Kuwait Fund, aid was given primarily for the purpose of furthering bilateral political relations and awarded either to traditionally friendly states or to countries where the donor perceived immediate or potential national

---

10 The Libyan Arab Foreign Bank is regarded by the Libyan government as a development institution in part but its activities are primarily those of a commercial bank. It also has some investments in Africa and elsewhere in banking and non-financial sectors. In early 1980, Libya announced its intention to establish a fund capitalized at $ 675 million to help LDC's pay higher oil bills. (OECD, *op. cit.*, p. 131).

18

interests. Occasionally aid was extended on purely humanitarian grounds to neighboring Arab or Muslim countries suffering from natural catastrophes.

Since the mid-1970s, a considerable portion of Arab aid has become "institutionalized," by which we mean both the commitment of a substantial percentage of aid through bilateral and multilateral, Arab and international development institutions and the tendency to subject requests for aid to analysis based on comparative economic and social criteria, economic and financial rates of return, conformity to national development priorities and so forth. Institutionalization has been an outgrowth of the expansion of Arab aid programs, of a shift in the composition of the assistance granted, of a redirection of aid to include non-Arab countries and of the requirement for a mechanism to appraise, select and supervise the most appropriate means to dispense funds.

Institutionalization has progressed to the point where one third ($18.6 billion) of all aid committed between 1973 and 1980 passed through institutional channels. These channels include the national funds of Abu Dhabi, Iraq, Kuwait and Saudi Arabia, which together extended $7.5 billion in aid through 1980. These funds accounted for about 20% of the combined bilateral aid of their four countries during the period since they were respectively established and a far higher proportion of bilateral assistance to non-Arab countries.[11]

About 60% of total institutional assistance through 1980, amounting to about $11.1 billion, has been directed through multilateral agencies. As Table 3 demonstrates, commitments to multilateral institutions reached a peak of almost 38% of total Arab aid in 1976, the climax of a period of intense institutional establishment, before declining to an average annual level of about 10% between 1978 and 1980.

Arab multilateral commitments have been made to two different categories of institution: international organizations, including the UN, IMF, World Bank and regional development banks; and "Arab-sponsored" institutions in which Arab nations have subscribed at least 51% of the share capital. The latter category includes several Arab and African regional development agencies, Islamic institutions and the OPEC Fund (see Table 4). The amounts committed to institutions in either category have tended to fluctuate from year to year influenced strongly by the establishment or recapitalization of a gradually increasing number of agencies. At the outset in 1973 when there were no Arab institutional alternatives, the established international organizations received 95% of all multilateral commitments (see Table 5). During the mid-1970s, while the Arab-spon-

---

11 Excluding most of the politically motivated assistance committed to the Arab "Confrontation States" (Egypt, Jordan and Syria) after 1973 would probably raise this total to over 50%.

sored institutions were being created, funds were diverted to capitalize these new organs at the expense of the international agencies. However, once that period had been essentially completed in 1977, an equilibrium of financial support for institutions in both categories was established.

Although they have fostered the establishment of Arab institutions as well, several of the Arab donors, but most importantly Saudi Arabia which alone has contributed 60% of the Arab total (see Table 6), have continued to support the international organizations for several important reasons. First, support for the structural and project lending programs of the major international agencies — the IMF, World Bank and UN — is a key element of the Arab/OPEC aid strategy which developed during the mid-1970s, a strategy heralded by the establishment of the OPEC Special Fund in 1976. The principal objective of this strategy is to shift a substantial portion of the political, financial and administrative burden of assisting the oil-importing developing countries from the individual members of OPEC and the cartel as a group to multilateral institutions. OPEC has argued that these countries suffer from a spate of worldwide inflation which has raised the cost of their manufactured and non-manufactured imports, of which higher oil prices are but one example. Consequently, OPEC argues, the burden of adjustment assistance should be shared between OPEC and the OECD. Massive Saudi support for the structural lending program of the IMF — which is designed to remedy the cause of energy deficits and not just the effects of higher oil prices on the oil-importing countries — is a prominent example of this strategy.

A second reason for continued Arab support for the international agencies is recognition of the value of cooperation between them and Arab-sponsored institutions at a time when many are predicting the advent of a period of unprecedented economic and financial hardship for oil-importing developing countries following the 1979–80 oil price increases. This last point is confirmed by the extent of "co-financings" between Arab and international agencies. According to recent OECD statistics, "co-financed" projects increased from 108 in early 1978 to 251 by the end of 1979, and the amounts involved nearly doubled from $ 7.6 billion to $ 14.4 billion.[12]

A third reason is the enhanced leverage over institutional policies such contributions may be expected to purchase. For just as Arab donors contribute financially to the resources of these organizations, so they will expect a concomitant share in the power to shape organizational programs and objectives. In particular, Saudi Arabia has become an increasingly active participant in the finance and management of these institutions. The Saudis took the lead in creating and funding the UN-sponsored Inter-

---

12 OECD, "The Co-Financing of Development Projects by DAC and OPEC Members and International Financial Institutions," Paris, 1980, p. 1.

national Fund for Agricultural Development (IFAD). The country's role in the establishment of IFAD was symbolized by the election of a Saudi national as that agency's first managing director. Further evidence of Saudi Arabia's enhanced importance in the function of these agencies was confirmed by the election of the Kingdom to a permanent seat of the IMF Board of Governors. Through participation at the executive level, Arab donors may also be able to influence the policies of these institutions in a manner consistent with their respective national or regional interests.[13]

A fourth reason is that the Arab donor countries, and particularly Saudi Arabia, continue to benefit from the independent and substantial technical resources of these institutions. For example, Saudi Arabia currently has a 30-man technical assistance team from the World Bank resident in the country. The Saudis also rely on the IMF for training and advice for their national institutions and for analysis and monitoring of national economic, financial and fiscal policies of countries such as Egypt and the Sudan to which they have or are giving substantial financial assistance. Where appropriate, Saudi aid has been coordinated with IMF programs to lend added weight to both parties' terms and conditions.

A final reason undoubtedly is that some of the debt instruments of the World Bank offer Arab donors a unique opportunity, a financial asset which combines support for worthwhile development objectives with a good yield and triple "A" security. The OPEC nations (principally Arab countries) hold directly or indirectly an estimated $ 6.5 billion of the Bank's $ 31 billion of outstanding obligations. Of this amount, about $ 4.4 billion has been placed directly with OPEC member governments and central banks.[14]

During the past year there has been a significant increase in the amount of Arab financial support for international organizations. In March 1981, the IMF announced that Saudi Arabia had agreed to lend it the equivalent of $ 9.5 billion over the next two years in the form of direct quota subscriptions and supplemental lending. In addition, Saudi Arabia committed itself to provide a further $ 4 billion in 1983, balance of payments and international reserves permitting. This agreement is the first and most important fruit of a round of negotiations between the IMF and surplus countries which began in 1979 aimed at enhancing the Fund's resources.[15] It is hoped that similar bilateral loans may be granted soon by Kuwait and the UAE.

Despite the continued support for international organizations, Arab-

---

13 The unsuccessful Arab effort to admit representatives of the Palestine Liberation Organization to the Annual IMF/World Bank meeting in September 1980 as observers may be an initial indication of such future actions.
14 Associated Press – Dow Jones News Service, June 4, 1981.
15 IMF, *IMF Survey*, April 6, 1981, pp. 97–101.

sponsored institutions received 60 % ($ 6.2 billion) of all multilateral commitments between 1973–1979. This development is the logical consequence of a desire to extend Arab control over multilateral institutions in order to make their commitments generally as consistent as possible with Arab interests.

However, the Arab-sponsored multilateral institutions serve a variety of other purposes as well. All of these institutions have been founded to meet specific political, geographic, religious or functional objectives (see Table 4). First, as multilateral agencies, they allow even the larger donor nations to aggregate human and financial resources to focus on these objectives in a manner which both highlights areas of special concern and augments the impact of the aid being provided, yet complements and supplements bilateral interests, aid programs and institutions. As such, they serve as repositories of technical, analytical and administrative skills related to economic development which are in short supply in a region still struggling to build institutional capabilities simultaneously in most fields. Second, they offer a particularly cost-effective means of broadening the reach of the bilateral aid programs of countries, such as Algeria, Libya and Qatar without national funds, while allowing participation in institutional policy-making. Third, through the application of objective, comparative criteria and analysis to project selection, the multilateral institutions should minimize the risks in project lending, while occasionally serving as a foil to deflect requests for assistance which bilateral agencies and governments find difficult or embarrassing to refuse. Both bilateral and multilateral institutions create a mechanism to supervise the disbursement of financial assistance. Before these agencies were established, there were cases in which aid funds were not expended as anticipated, were utilized for frivolous or prestige projects which did not promote social or economic development, or were altogether unaccountable, instances which heightened donor concern about the wastage of aid transfers. While these situations will recur even with institutional surveillance, such abuses have diminished as a result of stricter supervision and reporting standards established by the institutions. In sum, these positive features have, in most cases, been sufficient to offset the loss of a certain degree of national political control over the policies and activities of the Arab-sponsored multilateral institutions, thereby ensuring considerable and continuing donor support to date.

The current recapitalization of bilateral and multilateral Arab-sponsored institutions, in addition to recent Saudi commitments to the IMF, suggests that the proportion of Arab aid extended through institutional channels in the future may be greater than in the past decade. Since late 1979, over $ 12 billion has been committed to augment the capital of four of the most important Arab-sponsored institutions. The directors of the OPEC Fund for International Development have voted to increase its capital by

150 % to $ 4 billion. The subscribed capital of the Islamic Development Bank was raised by 130 % to just over $ 2 billion, and the capital of the Kuwait Fund for Arab Economic Development has been doubled to $ 7.4 billion. Finally, the capital of the Saudi Fund for Development was increased by 167 % in two stages from $ 3 billion to $ 8 billion.[16]

4. Project and Program Aid

An important consquence of the institutionalization of Arab aid has been the increased emphasis given to lending for specific projects. Project lending includes both project finance – i.e. projects linked to repayment from an identifiable revenue stream, as well as commitments of a specific nature for infrastructural projects and transfers for emergency relief, health, educational, cultural and Islamic purposes. In contrast, program aid provides general financial support to countries, though it may be classified specifically as general, budgetary or balance-of-payments support and may take the form of the purchase of government obligations, central bank deposits, or oil, trade or other credits.

The distinction between project and program aid is not only one of nomenclature. It usually involves fundamental differences in the analysis and selection of requests for assistance, the terms on which it is extended, the period of disbursement, expectations of repayment, the degree of post-commitment supervision expected and, often, the amounts awarded. The distinction is also likely to reflect the relative degree of importance which the donor attaches to political and economic relations with the recipient.

Generally, project aid is given by institutional lenders on the basis of an analysis of specific economic, financial and social criteria, often including conformity to national development priorities, to further economic and social development. Although the selection of recipient countries and the determination of the amount of aid to be extended may be subject to political calculus, the actual selection of projects to finance is often not politically motivated. Because it is usually paid out according to schedule during the construction period of the project, this type of aid is disbursed gradually over several years. In comparison, most program aid is transferred in the form of bilateral grants without expectation of repayment to friendly countries of immediate national political importance, without application to specific projects. It is usually disbursed quickly.

Because of the increased emphasis on project aid, the terms on which Arab aid is extended tend to be highly variable. Most bilateral project assistance is awarded at concessional rates of between 1.5 % – 8 % and over such long periods of time (up to 40 years) as to heavily discount the value of future

16 *Middle East Economic Survey*, May 25, 1981.

repayments. In effect, the most concessional project aid is virtually a grant. In other cases, financial assistance is only forthcoming on non-concessional terms or in the form of equity investments, as is the case with much of the aid from Kuwait and Libya and the Abu Dhabi Fund (see Table 7). In contrast, the financial terms of the aid extended by Arab multilateral institutions have usually been considerably "harder" — though still concessional — than the terms of aid provided by bilateral Arab donors. One reason for this highly variable practice is that differences in financial terms are one of the few means by which Arab donors can distinguish with varying degrees of preference between recipients of their aid. Contributing to the latitude of financial terms is the highly dissimilar nature of the many types of projects financed by Arab bilateral and multilateral lenders.

The OECD argues with good reason that the terms of Arab aid are marginally less concessional than the terms of aid granted by other donors, principally of the OECD nations.[17] However, OECD donors often "tie" assistance to the purchase of nationally produced goods and services, thereby earning an economic profit in addition to a financial return. Arab donors rarely enjoy this double barreled advantage.

A further characteristic which distinguishes project aid is its administrative complexity. Whereas program aid may still be accomplished by a single bank transfer, project assistance usually involves substantial bureaucratic involvement on the part of donor and recipient. Donors normally scrutinize capital budgets closely, insist on competitive bidding and monitor disbursements, project implementation and management. Although such practices are designed specifically to prevent the misuse of financial resources — a major concern of lenders — they may also prolong the initial development period of a project, adding to costs in an inflationary environment. Such procedures also tend to favor well organized recipients and pose an extra obstacle to the poorer, least developed countries seeking financial assistance. Partly in recognition of this complicating aspect of project lending and partly in recognition of the fact that some developing countries urgently require general financial support, there has been a growing awareness among development institutions that reliance solely on project aid may not be appropriate in some situations. Accordingly the World Bank, for example, has initiated a program of Structural Adjustment Lending to assist countries which face medium-term balance of payments difficulties with "program" loans.[18]

Despite the institutional emphasis on project aid discussed above, the majority of Arab aid still consists of program assistance, due to the considerable financial support from the Gulf states for the Arab "Confronta-

---

17 OECD, *Development Cooperation, 1979 Review,* Paris, 1979, p. 135.
18 World Bank, *Annual Report, 1980,* pp. 67—68 and 111—112.

tion States". Outside of the Middle East, however, the majority of Arab aid takes the form of project lending. This is so because of the direct relationship between the ratio of project and program aid received by a country (or a region) and its relative political importance to the donor. In other words, the percentage of project aid as a share of total aid received by a country is likely to vary inversely with the donor country's geo-political interests in the recipient.

5. Geographic Distribution of Aid Flows

Aid is an integral component and any nation's foreign policy, but it takes on added significance for countries such as the Arab donors with relatively few alternative means of achieving their foreign policy objectives. Despite their wealth, the Arab oil-producers have limited financial resources to place at the disposal of their foreign policies. Logically, they concentrate those resources in regions and countries of paramount national interest, extending diminishing amounts of aid as countries descend the scale of national priority. Consequently, the geographic distribution of aid is a highly sensitive gauge of donor national interests and the relative importance of bilateral relations with various countries. An analysis of the geographic distribution of Arab aid will, therefore, enable us to establish the relative importance accorded by donor countries to Sub-Saharan Africa and to the development of Afro-Arab relations within the context of overall Arab and individual donor country foreign policy interests and priorities.

Prior to 1973, Arab aid was reserved almost exclusively for Arab nations with the exception of occasional contributions to international organizations. This narrow focus was the result of what were then the relatively modest financial means of the donor countries, their preoccupation with regional Arab issues and the absence of national or pan-Arab institutions with an extra-regional focus. As its name manifests, even the pioneering Kuwait Fund for Arab Economic Development concerned itself solely with Arab nations until its charter was amended in 1974 to allow the extension of its operations to non-Arab developing countries.

Since 1973, other Arab countries have remained the prime beneficiaries of the Arab donors, receiving 69 % ($ 34 billion) of all aid between 1973—1979 (see Table 8). Expressive of the paramount importance of inter-Arab relations to individual donor countries, Arab nations received 76 % of total bilateral aid during the same period (see Table 9). As a further indication of the priority given to bilateral Arab relations, perhaps as much as 75 %—80 % of inter-Arab aid has been in the form of support grants (program aid) of one type or another.

Despite the continuing Arab concentration, there has been a noticeable geographic diversification of Arab aid since 1973. While there have been significant annual fluctuations in the geographic distribution of this aid, all other regions generally benefitted from this diversification. During the period 1973–1979, the proportion of total aid received by non-Arab countries rose as high as 44 % in 1974 and more than doubled from 11 % to 24 % as a percentage of bilateral assistance. Non-Arab countries received commitments averaging $ 2.2 billion annually between 1973 and 1979, a total of $ 15.2 billion.

As a region, Asia appears to have been the principal non-Arab beneficiary of this largesse, receiving 10 % of total aid during the period and over 11 % of bilateral aid, a total of about $ 4.9 billion through 1979.[19] Asia also has received just over one quarter of all funds committed by national funds. India, Pakistan and Bangladesh have received the largest portion of this aid. The reasons for this interest on the part of donors are not hard to discern. Aside from geographic proximity, these countries, but particularly Pakistan and India, share traditionally close religious, economic and cultural relations with the Arab Gulf states. Since 1974, mutually beneficial economic links have drawn them even closer, while Saudi Arabia has become deeply involved politically in these and other Asian countries as far east as Taiwan.[20] Additionally, these nations have large populations and, correspondingly, large absorptive capacities for aid. Table 10 illustrates the importance of Arab and Asian countries as primary and secondary beneficiaries of disbursements of Arab aid during the years 1976–1980.

Despite the high level of aid, Asia as a whole has not been singled out for special concern by the donor nations. Although it has received a sizeable proportion of the aid provided by some Arab-sponsored funds – 39 % and 34 % respectively from the OPEC Fund and the Islamic Development Bank – no multilateral institution has been established to focus exclusively on Asian problems. Furthermore, while it has received only 43 % more aid than Sub-Saharan Africa between 1973 and 1979, it is 300 % more populous (excluding the People's Republic of China) and is equally as poor when measured on the basis of per capita Gross National Product.[21] Thus, when weighted according to population, Asia received a fraction of the aid extended to Africa.

---

19 These figures have been calculated on the basis of regional commitments by bilateral and multilateral aid programs for which the geographic distribution of commitments has been reported.

20 Dr. Detlev H. Khalid, "The Phenomenon of Re-Islamization", *Aussenpolitik*, Vol. 29, 4/78, pp. 433–453.

21 World Bank, *1980 World Bank Atlas*.

6. Importance of Sub-Saharan Africa

Africa has not only received a higher per capita level of aid than Asia, but also total Arab aid amounting to more than $ 2.8 billion since 1973, including substantial amounts of bilateral and multilateral assistance. Moreover, Africa is the only non-Arab region to have been favored with the establishment of Arab institutions — the Special Arab Aid Fund for Africa (SAAFA) and its successor, the Arab Bank for Economic Development in Africa (ABEDA) — concerned, respectively, with alleviating the continent's balance of payments deficits and realizing its economic potential through project financing.

However, Africa received only a modest share of Arab assistance between 1973—1979: 5.8 % of total Arab aid, 4.1 % of total bilateral aid, and 8.9 % of total multilateral aid (see Tables 8, 9 and 6, respectively). Furthermore, despite the offsetting effects of multilateral aid commitments from 1974 through 1977 — first to SAAFA and then to ABEDA — the nominal and real amounts of Arab aid extended to Africa have been in a downward trend since 1974, from $ 571 million in that year to $ 403 million in 1979 (Table 8). Aid to Africa has even declined faster in those years, such as 1975, 1976 and 1978, when Arab aid was increasing overall.

The decline in Arab assistance to Sub-Saharan Africa is all the more apparent when one contrasts the amount of aid extended to the 40 nations which comprise the Sub-Saharan area with the aid granted to four other Sub-Saharan African countries — Djibouti, Mauritania, Somalia and Sudan — which are members of the Arab League.[22] These four countries of what we will call "Arab League Africa" to distinguish them from "Sub-Saharan Africa" are ethnically, historically and geographically transitional between the continent's Arab North (which includes Egypt, Libya, Tunisia, Algeria and Morocco) and its African South. Aside from their transitional character, an important factor itself, the principal difference between them and the other 40 nations south of the Sahara is membership in the Arab League.

Analysis of comparative aid flows to these two groups of countries suggests that a nation's "Arab" identity, as confirmed by membership in the Arab League, is the single most influential factor for Arab donors in selecting African recipients for their aid. Although Sub-Saharan Africa contains ten times as many countries and is ten times more populous than Arab League Africa, the four Arab League members received almost two thirds ($ 3,636 million) of the $ 5,526 million of bilateral aid committed to these 44 countries between 1973 and 1980 (see Table 11).[23] The 40

22 For a variety of reasons, we have not included Namibia, Nigeria, Reunion or South Africa in our analysis.
23 The recent edition of the *World Bank Atlas* (1980 edition, p. 12) includes the fol-

countries of Sub-Saharan Africa received only 34 % ($ 1,891 million) of the total. On a per capita basis, Arab donors have committed $ 234 to Arab League Africa and $ 7 to Sub-Saharan Africa. An indication of the priority given to other Arab nations is the reported agreement of the 5 Arab Gulf donors to establish a fund to benefit the 5 least developed Arab countries including Mauritania, Somalia and Sudan, as well as the 2 Yemens, over a 10-year period. To be capitalized at $ 5 billion, this fund will provide soft, 30-year loans for economic and social development projects.

One final manifestation of the apparent differing importance accorded the two African regions by the donor countries is the dissimilar proportion of program and project aid extended.[24] Table 12 summarizes the type of bilateral aid extended to all 44 countries. Arab League Africa received 46 % ($ 1,469 million) of its bilateral aid in the form of program assistance, whereas Sub-Saharan Africa received only 29 % ($ 420 million) as program aid.

The comparative record of Arab aid to Africa may appear surprising in view of the factors which reputedly draw the two regions together and which have been frequently proclaimed as the "foundations" of "Afro-Arab cooperation" and "solidarity". Among these factors are the following: (1) geographic proximity − 9 Arab states (including the 5 along the Mediterranean littoral) are members of both the Arab League and the Organization for African Uniy (OAU); (2) shared bonds of Islamic brotherhood − 11 African nations are members of the Islamic Conference; (3) dependence on the export of primary products and thus a mutual interest in establishing the "New International Economic Order"; (4) stated hostility to Israeli and southern African "racism"; (5) varying degrees of devotion to common third world shibboleths: "anti-colonialism", "non-alignment" and "anti-imperialism". The existance of apparently important common interests contrasts so sharply with the record of Arab aid to Africa that one is forced to inquire about the reasons for this divergence. Moreover, one is moved to ask whether or not the establishment of joint Afro-Arab Standing Committees, the triennial Afro-Arab Summit, or the founding of ABEDA − unique among Arab institutions for its exclusive, non-Arab

---

lowing statistical evidence:

Area	No. of Countries	Population (mid-1979 estimates)
Arab League Africa	4	23.6 million
Sub-Saharan Africa	40	239.2 million

Bilateral aid is the most appropriate basis of comparison because while the Arab League States are eligible for aid from numerous Arab regional institutions, Sub-Saharan Africa benefits from the more modest programs of SAAFA and ABEDA.

24 Amounts not identifiable as either program or project aid have been excluded from the calculations.

geographic focus — signify something more substantive than merely the formal institutionalization of Afro-Arab "solidarity" since 1973.

Our analysis to this point has focused on general trends in Arab aid since 1973. We have stressed throughout that aid flows are essentially a function of bilateral policies and interests and must ultimately be assessed in those contexts. Consistent with divergent national interests and dissimilar foreign policy objectives, the geographic distribution of aid differs markedly between individual donor states. Table 13 underlines the differences in the distribution of bilateral aid since 1973 among Arab donors. While the relative importance of bilateral relations with Africa suggested by these statistics might be expected of neighboring states such as Algeria and Libya, both Kuwait and Saudi Arabia have committed substantial amounts to Africa. In order to understand the significance of these differences, we turn, in the following sections of this report, first to an analysis of the programs of several of the multilateral institutions dealing with Africa and, then, to an assessment of the bilateral aid programs for Africa of the seven Arab donor nations.

B. Aid from Multilateral Institutions

Aid flows are motivated primarily by considerations of national interest. Arab national interests are rarely enunciated by government officials and there are no fora for public articulation of these interests. Nevertheless, scrutiny of the foreign policies of individual donor nations suggests certain interests, some idiosyncratic, others shared generally by Arab donors. For analytical purposes, Arab national interests in Africa can be grouped in four categories: political, economic, humanitarian and religious, although it is rare in practice that one interest will be pursued in isolation.

As the subsequent analysis of bilateral aid programs will demonstrate, political interests and the political dimension of other interests generally take precedence over all other considerations in motivating the commitment of financial assistance. Most important among these political interests have been the following:

1. enhancement of an individual donor country's national security, political and economic influence and power;
2. preservation of regional political stability or, conversely, encouragement of change in order to make the regional political status quo congenial to a donor country's aspirations;
3. diplomatic isolation of Israel by winning and retaining support for the Arab position on Palestine;
4. "solidarity" with other Third World nations on issues such as "non-alignment", the "North-South dialogue", the "New International Economic Order" and "anti-colonialism".

Among economic interests, the following have been important:

1. acquiescence in continued oil price increases;
2. acceptance of support for primary commodity producer cartel practices and organizations;
3. improved ability to influence the policies of key African producers of oil, alternative energy sources and strategic raw materials;
4. ownership of profitable and significant African mineral resources.

Additionally, the oil-exporting nations as a group have been motivated by the following concerns which are in part humanitarian but which have had a critical political dimension:

1. amelioration of the adverse social and economic impact of the rising cost of imported oil;
2. furtherance of the economic and social development of other "developing" countries.

Finally, several Arab nations have been motivated by interests which are primarily of a religious nature:

30

1. enhancement of the political and economic power of the Islamic bloc of nations, individually and collectively;
2. improvement of the spiritual, social, economic and political status of Muslim communities in Africa;
3. conversion;
4. reassertion of Islamic pride and power.

The extent to which any of these specific interests motivates the foreign policy and the foreign aid program of each donor country differs markedly. The manner in which countries seek to achieve their foreign policy goals through their aid programs is also disparate. Whether to utilize bilateral or multilateral channels is an essential consideration and depends, fundamentally, on the circumstances and nature of the national interest(s) being served.

While the major portion of Arab aid since 1973 has been committed on a bilateral basis, there have been occasions when the donor nations as a group have determined that a multilateral framework would be more appropriate for the pursuit of certain interests. In those instances, they have often established multilateral institutions to further their common purposes.

In Section A.3., we described in general the reasons which prompted Arab donor countries to contribute to multilateral institutions. In this section, we analyze in specific terms the common interests, motives and objectives which led to the establishment or revitalization of four secular and three religiously oriented Arab sponsored multilateral institutions which provide aid to Africa (see Table 14). We also investigate the status of the operations of these institutions individually and their role in the context of overall Arab aid. Three of the secular institutions focus exclusively on Africa; the others include the continent within broader geographic terms of reference, generally according it a high priority.

1. Secular Financial Institutions

a. Origins of Afro-Arab Solidarity

The decision to establish the three secular institutions focusing on Africa — the Special Arab Aid Fund for Africa (SAAFA), the Arab Fund for Technical Assistance to Arab and African countries (AFTAAAC) and the Arab Bank for Economic Development in Africa (ABEDA) was a product of the political and economic environment in the aftermath of the Arab-Israeli war in October 1973 and the subsequent 300% increase in oil prices. In the immediate post-war period, two important and related political interests united Arab oil producers in their policies toward Africa: first, to retain the newly won African political support for the

Arab position in the conflict with Israel; second, to provide immediate financial assistance to African oil-importing countries to ameliorate the impact of the sharp rise in oil prices and mute the strong criticism of these prices emanating from Third World capitals.

Although most Sub-Saharan countries were seriously affected by rising oil prices, the principal Arab motive for the establishment of these specialized institutions was the need to express what was referred to as "political solidarity" with Africa in gratitude for the dramatic and nearly unanimous African support of the Arab countries in the latest round of the Middle East conflict. This support was the climax of political trends apparent in Afro-Israeli relations on the one hand and Afro-Arab relations on the other hand, which had caused eight African nations to sever relations with Israel in the years after the previous Arab-Israeli war in 1967.[1] In the days and weeks immediately following the outbreak of the 1973 war, 20 Sub-Saharan nations dramatically announced the formal rupture of diplomatic relations with Israel. By the end of October 1973, all but four African countries — Lesotho, Malawi, Swaziland and Mauritius (which broke relations in July 1976) — formally turned their backs on Israel to side with the Arabs. The importance of this action in Arab eyes is underlined by the fact that of the nine countries which severed relations before the outbreak of the war, four — Uganda, Guinea, Zaire and Mali — rank first, second, third and fourth, respectively among the Sub-Saharan recipients of bilateral Arab aid since 1973 (see Table 15). Although common religious bonds and bilateral considerations have been important contributing factors in some cases, this result is testimony to the extraordinary significance of this particular political dimension of Afro-Arab relations.

In mid-November 1973, there was a flurry of diplomatic activity aimed at institutionalizing the new spirit of Afro-Arab solidarity. The Ministerial Council of the OAU meeting in mid-November entrusted a commission of seven member states with the task of establishing links and initiating economic cooperation with Arab countries through the Arab League.[2] One week later, in response to African diplomatic and political support since early October, the participants at the Sixth Arab Summit Conference agreed to establish two institutions to provide long-term economic assis-

---

1 The following chronology indicates the dates when African nations broke formal diplomatic relations with Israel: 1967 — Guinea; 1972 — Uganda, Chad, Congo; pre-war 1973 — Niger, Mali, Burundi, Togo and Zaire; October 1973 — Rwanda, Benin, Upper Volta, Cameroon, Eq. Guinea, Tanzania, Madagascar, CAR, Ethiopia, Nigeria, Gambia, Zambia, Ghana, Senegal, Gabon, Sierra Leone; November 1973 — Kenya, Liberia, Ivory Coast and Botswana; 1976 — Mauritius (Kühlein, *op. cit.*, p. 98 and press accounts).

2 ABEDA, "Afro-Arab Cooperation: Main Landmarks of Progress", Khartoum (no date).

tance to Africa.[3] With initial capital of $ 125 million, ABEDA was to be a specialized bank supporting long-term agricultural and industrial development. With capital of $ 15 million, AFTAAAC was to replace the technical assistance which had been the most useful and distinctive aspect of Israel's cost-effective aid program in Sub-Saharan Africa.[4]

Shortly after this announcement, however, in December 1973 oil prices were more than doubled and it became obvious to African leaders that the impact on Sub-Sahara's fragile economies would be devastating. As 1974 wore on, the enormity of Africa's problems became even more apparent.[5] Despite a 2.2 % decline in oil consumption (see Table 16), the aggregate cost of oil imports for 15 reporting countries rose at least 220 % or some $ 560 million from 1973 to 1974 (see Table 17). These countries represented 58 % of Sub-Saharan oil consumption in 1974. By extrapolation the cost of imported oil for all 40 countries rose an estimated $ 960 million in 1974.[6] While by no means the single causal factor, oil prices were largely responsible for converting an overall near trade balance for Africa in 1973 into a deficit which reached an estimated $ 2.7 billion by 1975.[7]

It is certainly true that the soaring price of oil was but one among several important external and internal factors which combined to depress Sub-Saharan economies during the 1970s. Moreover, it is also true, as an OAPEC study has argued, that not all oil importing developing countries were affected equally by rising oil prices. Many, including a large number in Sub-Saharan Africa, have not reached levels of development which require heavy petroleum consumption and, therefore, have been relatively less seriously affected than the more advanced "industrializing" developing countries.[8] But the relative impact on Sub-Saharan nations individual-

---

3 For a description of the establishment and operation of these institutions, see Aziz Alkazaz, *Arabische Entwicklungshilfe-Institutionen,* Deutsches Orient-Institut, Hamburg, 1977, pp. 105–124; E.C. Chibwe, *Afro-Arab Relations in the New World Order,* Julien Friedman Publisher, Ltd., London, 1977, pp. 68–78; Hartmut Neitzel and Renate Nötzel, *Afrika und die arabischen Staaten,* Institut für Afrikakunde, Hamburg, 1979, pp. 284–331; and *Middle East Economic Survey,* February 20, 1978 and October 16, 1978.

4 For a description of the Israeli aid program, see Moshe Decter, *To Serve, to Teach, to Leave,* American Jewish Congress, New York, 1977, and Amir, *Israel's Development Cooperation with Africa, Asia and Latin America,* Praeger, New York, 1974.

5 As confirmation of Africa's special plight, 21 of the 33 countries designated by the UN as "most seriously affected", primarily by the increased oil prices, were Sub-Saharan states.

6 This figure compares with the estimate published by the Economist Intelligence Unit (*Saudi Arabia,* II 1974) that 30 non-oil producing African states would spend an additional $ 1.3 billion for oil in 1974.

7 IMF, *Direction of Trade Yearbook,* 1973–1979.

8 Organization of Arab Petroleum Exporting Countries, *Bulletin,* (Vol. 5, no. 10) October 1979, pp. 11–18.

ly and as a whole was severe. Kenya is but one example of the depressing impact of higher oil prices on a nation which has enjoyed an above average rate of economic growth and which might be somewhat better able to absorb the financial shock of these increases. Despite the need for increased energy consumption and with limited indigenous alternative energy resources available immediately, oil consumption in Kenya declined 22% from 1973 to 1978. Yet, even with decreased consumption, the cost of oil imports rose over 300% from $ 47 million in 1973 to $ 191 million in 1974 alone and continued to increase. In aggregate through 1978 before the second shock of oil price increases hit, higher oil prices added $ 1.1 billion to Kenya's import bill. Partly, as a result, the balance-of-payments deficit rose from $ 24 million in 1973 to $ 253 million in 1974 before declining gradually until 1978, when it again increased.

African countries tried to deal with the financial and economic crises confronting them in several ways. The first reaction at the risk of slowing the pace of economic growth was to curtail petroleum consumption. Table 16 indicates that the "apparent" consumption of crude oil and refined petroleum products for 40 Sub-Saharan countries declined from 262,000 barrels per day (b/d) in 1973 to a low of 248,000 b/d in 1976, before recovering to 276,000 b/d in 1978; a barely perceptible increase of 1% per annum in petroleum consumption and an actual decrease in real, per capita terms. While these figures confirm buyer sensitivity to higher oil prices, they also reflect the deflationary effects of the 1974–75 worldwide recession and internal economic troubles, among other factors. However, as these figures suggest there was a level below which oil imports could not fall without risking even further economic contraction until such time as such alternative forms of energy as were available could be exploited.

In the interim, Sub-Saharan nations had no alternative but to tap additional sources of foreign capital to finance their continuing oil imports and growing balance of payments deficits as best they could. A few countries with adequate credit ratings turned to the international capital markets. Most, however, had to rely on the largesse of sympathetic international aid agencies and bilateral OECD assistance programs. As a result of heavy borrowings, the debt service ratio of countries such as Ivory Coast and Senegal rose 122% and 174%, respectively between 1973–1978.[9] For Sub-Saharan Africa as a whole, debt service increased from $ 651 million in 1972 to $ 2,479 million in 1978.[10] Debt service amounted to one-third, on average, of net resource transfers during the 1972–1978 period. Although this amount was more than adequately covered by net external resource flows, a not insignificant portion went to service debt contracted to pay for oil imports.

---

9 World Bank, *Debt Service Tables*, 1980.
10 World Bank, *Annual Report*, 1980, Washington, D.C. 1980, p. 140.

34

An important alternative for Sub-Saharan Africa was a concerted effort to extract more aid from the oil-producing countries. Initial efforts focused on winning assurances of secure oil supplies and concessional prices. After the oil embargo ended in 1974, the former ceased to be a problem.

Oil prices were a different matter. Beginning in late 1973, Ethiopia, Gabon, Ghana, Kenya, Liberia, Tanzania and Uganda (states which together accounted for 41% of Sub-Saharan oil consumption in 1973) among others spoke sharply in criticism of the scale and speed of Arab financial relief, alleging an Arab political "obligation" and calling for compassion for their African and Third World "brothers".[11] Idi Amin put the case plainly in a cable to OPEC Heads of State warning that Africa expected a "reciprocal gesture" for the break of relations with Israel. He left no doubt that that meant subsidized oil.[12] Although individual nations may have cut the price of oil selectively to certain favored nations, OPEC, as a body, strongly resisted any initiative to supply oil at concessional rates, preferring to extend long-term credits for oil purchases. In 1975, Nigeria finally offered to supply needy African countries with oil at concessional prices "in order to demonstrate African solidarity and ensure that the momentum of economic development is not slowed . . . because of the oil situation". The Algerian-led OPEC refusal to sanction this offer was a particularly poignant example of OPEC solidarity for Africa and effectively terminated the effort to extract oil at concessional prices.[13]

From the beginning, African nations sought to increase the level of Arab financial assistance directed to them. In early 1974, a Tanzanian government delegation visited Arab capitals to put the case directly about the lack of concrete and appropriate assistance.[14] The Africans argued that while they did not expect the Arabs to fully compensate them for higher oil prices, the scale of assistance represented by ABEDA and AFTAAAC was not remotely compatible with the added economic and financial burdens of oil imports. Moreover, the aid envisaged through these funds would take years to disburse, even after they became operational.

b. *Special Arab Aid Fund for Africa (SAAFA)*

The Africans must have carried their dissatisfaction into the First Conference of Afro-Arab Cooperation which met in Cairo on January 22–23, 1974, for the ten Arab Oil Ministers present agreed to provide immediate

---

11 E.I.U., *Liberia*, I 1974; *Ghana*, IV 1973 and *Tanzania*, I 1974. See also *Revue Française d'Etudes Politiques Africaines*, no. 1 & 4 August 1974.

12 E.I.U., *Uganda*, II 1974.

13 E.I.U., *Algeria*, I 1975.

14 E.I.U., *Tanzania*, I 1974.

financial relief through the Special Arab Aid Fund for Africa (SAAFA). Initially capitalized at $ 200 million, SAAFA was conceived not as a new development fund, but as a means of disbursing a fixed sum rapidly in amounts to be determined by the Africans themselves through the Organization for African Unity (OAU). By March, the Arab states had also agreed to increase the capital of ABEDA to $ 231 million and in October the capital of AFTAAAC was raised to $ 25 million.[15]

Despite protestations to the contrary, by such actions the Arab donors recognized their political obligation to Africa and accepted an added share of responsibility for the continent's adjustment to rising oil prices. They may also have awakened expectations that SAAFA would become, in fact, a permanent institution and that there would be further infusions of Arab capital for Africa. Indeed, the establishment of ABEDA and AFTAAAC had already set a precedent linking African support on Palestine, rising oil prices and compensatory financial assistance which has plagued Afro-Arab relations since. The subsequent creation of SAAFA confirmed this relationship. Nevertheless, the Arab nations have consistently refused to acknowledge such a precedent, the existence of any substantive linkage between these three factors or any responsibility to compensate for oil price increases. Claiming that oil prices alone are not the cause of Africa's economic problems, they have argued that others, including the OECD nations, should share the financial burden. Since 1973, they have consistently characterized their aid as "economic assistance" and as an expression of "political solidarity with the Third World" and have rigorously sought to avoid any implication of "compensation".

After several months of internal debate, the OAU finally prepared and transmitted to the Arab League the criteria by which the capital of SAAFA was to be allocated to 31 recipients. These criteria emphasized the impact of higher oil prices, as well as national income, geography and exceptional circumstances such as the drought in the West African Sahel. The Arab League agreed to the OAU's proposed allocations but reserved the right to refuse payment to any state which took an "anti-Arab" position of the Middle East conflict.[16] On this basis, the $ 7.5 million allocated to Malawi was blocked, although Lesotho and Swaziland each received their full entitlements. Other states received their allotments in two tranches, with the exception of Ivory Coast, beginning in October 1974 (see Table 18). Most payments were completed in 1975. In 1976, the capital was increased by a further $ 150 million to $ 350 million and some uncharacteristically large sums were disbursed to five newly independent nations in 1976 and 1977.

---

15 Alkazaz, *op. cit.*, pp. 107—122.
16 *ibid.*, p. 117.

Algeria chose to participate in spirit but independently and established a $ 20 million Algerian Trust Fund (ATF) nominally administered by the African Development Bank — a specific OAU request for all of SAAFA's capital which was rejected by the Arab donors. Aid disbursed by the ATF conformed largely to the criteria established by the OAU, but Algeria reserved the right to select the recipients of these funds itself. Those designated were West African countries and the newly-independent, radical governments in Angola and Mozambique which were important to Algeria's foreign policy interests. For unaccountable reasons, the amount earmarked for Ivory Coast was withdrawn.

On December 15, 1976, the Board of Governors of ABEDA voted to merge SAAFA, its loans of $ 221.74 million and its undisbursed capital into ABEDA in March 1977. While this step had been anticipated, the effect was to fully consolidate control over the distribution of Arab aid to Africa in Arab hands.

c. Arab Fund for Technical Assistance to Arab and African Countries (AFTAAAC)

Intended to provide technical assistance to the poorest Arab and African states, AFTAAAC was a step toward filling the gap left by the withdrawal of the Israeli aid program in Africa. With the Arab world itself in desperate need of technical assistance, the Fund was severely constrained from the outset. It did not become fully operational under the administration of the Arab League in Cairo until 1976 due to organizational problems including staff recruitment.[17]

AFTAAAC's program was modest, handicapped by a shortage of skilled people to send abroad. The Fund concentrated on sending experts and organizing training programs to supplement the aid provided by other Arab institutions and countries. It gave priority to newly-independent and "least developed" countries. In its first year, it sent ten Arabic teachers, an Arabic printing unit and an educational expert to the Comoros and 12 teachers to Burundi. Both programs were continued in 1978. In that same year, the program was expanded to include 18 Sub-Saharan nations. With AFTAAAC assistance about 35 teachers went to Burundi and Senegal, 14 doctors were dispatched to Uganda and Niger, well over 70 experts were provided to Uganda, Mali, Niger, Guinea, Zambia, Kenya and Mauritius, and scholarships were made available to students from 11 Sub-Saharan countries.

The ultimate fate of AFTAAAC is unclear. No details of its program have been published by ABEDA or the Fund since 1978, nor has there been an

---

17 UNCTAD, *Financial Solidarity for Development*, Vol. I, pp. 90–91.

announcement of its dissolution. Rather, it seems to have quietly disappeared. Although its aid was well intended, Africa was a marginal beneficiary during the Fund's first two years of operation. While Arab League African countries and Yemen received 65 % of the $ 12.4 million committed, African nations received a total of just $ 4.3 million (see Table 19).

d. Arab Bank for Economic Development in Africa (ABEDA)

ABEDA has been the standard bearer of the Arab donors' effort to build a multilateral institution to aid Africa. With the participation of Iraq and Libya in 1973 and 1974, and supplemental subscriptions by the original participants, its initial capital was increased from $ 125 million to $ 231 million. Following the incorporation of SAAFA in 1977, ABEDA was also charged with the administration of AFTAAAC, effectively consolidating all Arab development efforts for Africa in one institution. ABEDA's capital was further increased in late 1977 by an additional $ 157.25 million to be paid in three annual installments. By year end 1980, its subscribed capital amounted to $ 738.25 million, of which $ 350 million was capital originally committed or pledged to SAAFA.[18]

According to its 1979 Annual Report, ABEDA was set up "to strengthen economic, financial and technical cooperation between African and Arab countries."[19] It is to accomplish this task by financing development projects, providing technical assistance and promoting and stimulating private Arab investment in Africa. Despite strong African representations to continue the balance of payments support lending of SAAFA, ABEDA's Board has required the Bank to focus on project lending. It is not empowered, with rare exception, to provide program aid or emergency assistance.

Since its first year of operation in 1975 when it committed $ 72 million, the Bank has had an uneven record which reached a low point in 1979 when it allocated just $ 44 million (see Table 20). In 1980, commitments returned to the nominal level of the peak year in 1975, although in real terms this amount represents a considerable decline from 1975.[20] By the end of 1980, it had committed $ 384 million. This amount is equal to 74 % of the Bank's subscribed capital. However, it had disbursed only $ 165 million for loans, an amount equal to 43 % of its commitments. This six-year record has disappointed donors and recipients alike.

Arab aid officials interviewed who are familiar with ABEDA's operations admit that the Bank has "not lived up to its potential", although they

---

18 ABEDA, *Annual Report*, 1980.
19 ABEDA, *Annual Report*, 1979, p. 2.
20 *Annual Report*, 1980, p. 8.

acknowledge the Bank's difficult operating environment. The *Annual Report* for 1979 suggests as much but offers a contradictory and unsatisfying explanation. In part, it attributes the sharp decline in 1979 commitments (down one-third from 1978) to the "relative exhaustion of project possibilities", in part to the "relatively slow gestation period of certain projects" and to "political upheavals".[21] While these problems affect all development agencies operating in Africa to a greater or lesser extent, the Bank admits that this is not the whole story without identifying the other causes of its declining performance.[22] More recently the Bank hinted at managerial and administrative difficulties in its lending program. The possibility also exists that ABEDA's lending activities from 1978 to 1980 were slowed by the deteriorating environment of Afro-Arab cooperation.[23] Indeed, the problems appear to be substantial enough to have raised questions about the viability of the Afro-Arab financial cooperation that ABEDA represents in its current form.

According to Arab aid officials, the Bank's problems have been essentially political. It appears itself to have become an unwitting victim of the political forces which created it and the high degree of politicization which characterizes the operations of most other Arab funds. Several specific factors can be called to account. First, the Bank's management has apparently found it difficult and distracting to reconcile the divergent policy interests of its most prominent shareholders. Second, set against the declining level of project aid in 1979, the impressive number of studies, brochures and documents publicizing the increasing level of Arab aid to Africa issued by ABEDA suggest that the Bank may have recently emphasized its public relations role as "a coordinating body between the African and Arab worlds" at the expense of its primary objective as a development agency.[24] Third, statements by Bank officials have occasionally made explicit that the Bank would refuse to aid countries which have political or economic relations with Israel. The geographic distribution of the Bank's commitments (see Table 20) suggests that its lending policy follows closely Arab political interests. For example, Ivory Coast, Malawi and Swaziland have not received ABEDA funds, although Lesotho has received $ 9.9 million for infrastructural projects despite openly maintaining relations with Israel. Such outspokeness by officials of an avowedly development institution may be viewed by African countries as unwarranted interference in their affairs. Finally, ABEDA's performance

21 *Annual Report*, 1979.
22 *Annual Report*, 1979, p. 7.
23 *Annual Report*, 1980, pp. 10 & 25 and ABEDA, "Fifth Meeting of the Coordination Committee for Afro-Arab Cooperation", (Khartoum March 13, 1981), *passim*.
24 *Annual Report*, 1978, p. 7.

may very well be regarded by Africans as further confirmation that the Arab donors, individually and through their chosen vehicle of Afro-Arab financial solidarity, have failed to honor their pledge to commit additional aid of $ 1,454 million to Africa by 1982, signalling both a decline of interest in the continent's difficulties and an unwillingness to adhere to previous commitments to help solve them.

Apparently aware of the criticism being directed at ABEDA on these grounds, the Bank's Board of Governors reportedly reprimanded management at the annual meeting in early 1980. Nevertheless, the Board expressed continued faith in management and the Chairman, Mr. Chedly Ayari, won election to a second five-year term by a narrow margin over the opposition of Arab radicals led by Libya.

It is hoped that with the election campaign finished, the improvement in the level of operations demonstrated in 1980 will continue. However, there is little reason to believe that the level of future commitments will increase substantially. The Bank itself does not appear to anticipate a significantly higher level of future operations. At the current level of operations ABEDA will commit the remainder of its subscribed capital before 1983. The 1979 *Annual Report* stated that the Bank's present financial resources are sufficient to permit it to operate for the "following five years (i.e. through 1984) without bringing in additional capital", although to date, the $ 180 million in additional capital necessary to do so pledged to ABEDA at the Cairo Summit in March 1977 has yet to be paid in.[25] This suggests that future commitments will be limited to a maximum level of less than $ 80 million per annum.

Many Arab aid officials appear skeptical that ABEDA will receive a fresh capital infusion, but the completion of a new institutional headquarters in Khartoum and work on an institutional ten-year plan suggest longevity. In the absence of further capital, the factors cited above and the general trend toward bilateral aid could lead to a gradual decline in the relative importance of ABEDA, signalling further negative implications for Afro-Arab political and financial relations.

e. OPEC Fund for International Development (OFID)

The establishment of the OPEC Special Fund on January 28, 1976, by the 13 member countries of the Organization of Petroleum Exporting Countries (OPEC) represented a new departure in the strategy of Arab aid to non-Arab countries. Although the Fund is legally an international organization representing the interests of all OPEC members, Arab countries

---

25 *Annual Report*, 1979, pp. 8–9.

number 7 of the 13 OPEC members. They have contributed just over 51 % of the Fund's capital resources and hold a comparable share of votes. In principle, decisions of the Board of Governors are taken by a two-thirds majority of the members representing 70 % of the contributions to the Fund's resources. In practice, however, decisions are arrived at by consensus whereby the interests of the individual members and the Arab bloc as a group are given adequate protection but may not dominate.

While the OPEC Fund represents a new source of financial assistance with considerable resources, its establishment has potentially far-reaching implications for the type of special relationship which Africa enjoyed with the Arab states in the immediate post-war years. These implications can be deduced from an analysis of the objectives and operations of the OPEC Fund and from changes in the pace and substance of developments in the sphere of Afro-Arab financial and political relations in the period subsequent to its establishment.

Political and economic interests common to all members of the OPEC cartel motivated the foundation of the OPEC Fund in 1976. As a collection of nations, the OPEC members sought to establish a vehicle which could help offset the burden of rising oil prices on the developing countries. As a cartel, OPEC sought to ease the anger and frustration of the Third World caused by the price rises. Although the linkage of political self-interest and financial generosity was never acknowledged officially, the relationship was never privately disavowed. OPEC had to be seen to be doing something to aid fellow developing countries: the OPEC Fund was simultaneously the cartel's public relations agency and its "window" for a transfer of resources and a partial "redistribution" of the oil wealth.

While it may not have been perceived at the outset, the multilateral nature of the OPEC Fund was quickly recognized as a unique asset that took on a special significance for the oil producers. For the Arab members of OPEC, the Fund's establishment reflected an opportunity to turn away from the geographic favoritism of the years immediately following 1973 which gave birth to what was heralded as "Afro-Arab Solidarity", but which in fact remained an attempt to "institutionalize" the linkage between political support and financial compensation. As an independent, international organization representing OPEC as a unit in Third World meetings dealing with financial and economic assistance, the Fund would disassociate the individual oil-producing nations from the issue of oil price-linked compensation. This, it was hoped, would reduce the pressure of special interest groups, including Africa, on individual nations and the Arab countries as a bloc and deflect the criticism levelled against them for failing to provide adequate compensation for rising oil prices. This it was hoped would free bilateral aid programs to pursue national foreign policy objectives independent of this linkage. In practice, most OPEC members have never been able to entirely divorce their aid programs from this issue.

The importance which the OPEC members have attached to the success of the OPEC Fund can be measured by the financial resources they have been willing to commit to it. Initially capitalized at $ 800 million, that amount was doubled in 1977. In September 1979, OPEC Finance Ministers approved in principle a further increase of $ 800 million. Even before that commitment had received final consent, however, a further capital increase of $ 1,600 million was voted in May 1980. Both replenishments have now been approved officially, and the Fund's financial resources will increase to $ 4,000 million, thereby making it the largest Arab-sponsored multilateral institution.

The scale of that financial commitment is testimony to the central importance of the Fund to future OPEC member aid strategy. While increasing the financial resources at its disposal, the Fund is to become a more orthodox development institution than has been the case hitherto. Among the policy recommendations of OPEC's Long-Term Strategy Committee was a proposal advanced by Algeria and Venezuela to convert the OPEC Fund into a development bank. Indicative of this change in its fundamental purpose was the decision in January 1981 to change its name to the OPEC Fund for International Development (OFID).

At its outset, the Fund devoted its resources exclusively to a "Balance of Payments Support Program" targeted to assist the 45 developing countries designated as "most seriously affected" (MSA's) by the UN because of the economic crisis resulting primarily from the higher oil prices of 1973 – 1974. A total of $ 197 million was committed by May 1977 to 43 MSA's and 6 other developing countries with particularly serious payments problems.[26] During the middle 1970's, however, the Fund did not escape the general trend toward project lending among Arab and non-Arab development agencies. Project loans accounted for 65 % – 70 % of its loan commitments from 1978 through 1980. Nevertheless, the Fund still committed the remaining 30 % – 35 % of its resources annually for balance of payments support in response to the needs of the recipient countries.

Henceforth, according to the committee's recommendation, the principal function of the Fund will be to finance general economic development, with emphasis on projects that foster trade among developing countries. A secondary function will be to aid countries to develop indigenous energy resources through an augmented commitment of project loans to the energy sector.[27] The emphasis on balance of payments support, which had been a distinguishing characteristic of the Fund's operations in the past, is to be transferred to another agency. Just which agency is presently unclear and the subject of considerable political maneuver. On the initia-

---

26 OPEC Special Fund, *First Annual Report, 1976*, pp. 18–22.
27 E.I.U., *Saudi Arabia*, I, 1980 and communication with the OPEC Fund dated March 31, 1981.

tive of Iraq, the OPEC Long-Term Strategy Committee recommended the establishment of a joint fund with the industrial countries to compensate developing countries for imported inflation and any increases in crude oil prices. However, the function (of balance of payments adjustment) proposed is the primary responsibility of the IMF. Given the promising results of recent negotiations between the IMF and some surplus industrial and oil-producing countries to increase its resources, the creation of a new and functionally redundant institution may not be necessary. Still to be resolved, however, is the degree to which the political authority of the surplus countries within the IMF will be augmented to match their increased financial contribution. Until that time, the OPEC Fund may continue its policy of program lending.

As Table 21 indicates, Sub-Saharan Africa has been a primary beneficiary of OPEC Fund assistance, receiving 34 % of total commitments under its lending programs. Moreover, as Table 22 suggests, that aid has been distributed broadly throughout the continent. As befits the Fund's international status, that assistance has been distributed with less evidence of political bias than is the case for most other donors studied in this report. However, the Fund is apparently not insensitive to the political concerns of its members. Although it is the sole bilateral or Arab-sponsored multilateral donor to extend any assistance to Malawi — a $ 1.8 million tranche of the First Lending Program in 1977 — it has not assisted Malawi since then and has yet to make a commitment to Swaziland or Ivory Coast.

The recent addition of $ 2.4 billion to the Fund's capital signifies a substantial increase in the future financial resources available to Sub-Saharan Africa. If the Fund's previous pattern of geographic distribution continues, the capital replenishment could amount to an additional $ 800 million, surpassing the capital already subscribed to the three Arab institutions headquartered in Khartoum under the aegis of ABEDA and suggesting that Arab multilateral aid for Africa in the future may be more likely to originate from Vienna than from Khartoum.

f. Subsequent Development of Afro-Arab Relations

1. The Arab Viewpoint

The contrast between the sense of malaise noted in the operations of ABEDA and the optimism engendered by the massive capital infusion approved for OFID confirms the shift in aid strategy of the Arab donor countries and reflects the stall in Afro-Arab relations which developed during the late 1970s as a result. Between December 1978 and March 1980, the formal institutions established to nurture Afro-Arab solidarity failed to meet. According to both Arab and African officials, Afro-Arab cooperation sank into a state of lethargy.[28]

Several factors may be called to account for the apparent loss of Arab interest in extending the horizons of Afro-Arab "solidarity" in the period after 1976. First, from the Arab point of view, the establishment of three specialized institutions dealing with Africa mitigated any fellings of urgency and further obligations to provide special assistance to African states. The decline of real oil prices after 1974 and the fact that Africa's nominal oil import bill remained stable through 1976 further reduced the sense of urgency. By the time the effect of the initial adjustment to higher prices through reduced consumption had run its course and oil import costs had begun to increase once again in 1977 because of rising consumption, and later of rising prices, the OPEC Fund had been established with the specific responsibility to ease the financial consequences for the oil-importing developing countries as a group. Thus, one of the two fundamental motives for establishing three institutions to aid Sub-Saharan Africa had been transferred to OFID.

Second, and simultaneously, the force of the other motive for establishing those special institutions — African political support — began to attenuate. Politically, as economically, the interests of the Arab donor countries began to broaden geographically after the 1973 war. On no issue was this more apparent than the settlement of the Arab-Israeli conflict. In the period after the 1967 war, but especially after 1973, the Arab states were generally successful in depicting Israel as a "racist", Zionist state in the UN and before Third World gatherings, politically isolating Israel from most of the developing countries. During this phase of the political struggle, Africa's diplomatic support and the suddenness and near unanimity of its dramatic break with Israel in October 1973 were particularly gratifying to the Arabs. However, having severed relations with Israel, there were no further practical initiatives which Africa could offer. While retaining the diplomatic support of the 37-vote Sub-Saharan bloc remained important as a form of continued moral pressure, the Arabs came to realize quickly that the political leverage to effect a settlement lay not with the Third World but with the United States. As the focus of Arab strategy and attention was drawn away by Kissinger's "shuttle diplomacy" and finally by the Camp David negotiations, the Arab nations felt a diminished financial obligation to reciprocate Africa's diplomatic support.

This sense of diminished obligation gave way, however, to a sense of anger and betrayal in 1979 and 1980 as several African states publicly began to make tentative overtures to reestablish formal relations with Israel and when the OAU repeatedly refused to condemn the Camp David Agreement.

---

28 ABEDA, "Fifth Meeting of the Coordination Committee for Afro-Arab Cooperation", (Khartoum, March 13, 1981), pp. 6 & 30.

The Secretary General of the Arab League made known these sentiments publicly in a speech to the fifth meeting of the Coordination Committee for Afro-Arab Cooperation in March 1981.[29]

Third, the re-emergence of cracks in the facade of Arab unity, forged so dramatically in 1973, further distracted the attention of the donor nations. Afro-Arab political solidarity was only one victim of the rapidly diminishing Arab capacity for cooperative action. The temporary unanimity with which the Egyptian-Israeli peace treaty was rejected faded quickly and fundamental cleavages reappeared. Political cross-currents in the Arab world were transferred to Africa and undermined the unity of purpose of organizations such as ABEDA, reducing their effectiveness. Even the Islamic institutions (discussed in the following section) were occasionally denied the unanimous and non-partisan financial commitment appropriate to their status and necessary to carry out their programs by the secular political nature of the rivalry between the two leading proponents of Islam, Libya and Saudi Arabia. While these trends opened up profitable opportunities for African nations so inclined to exploit that rivalry to advantage on a bilateral plane, it fractured further the impulse for cooperative Arab action on Africa.

As the capacity and will for multilateral Arab action in Africa ebbed in the late 1970s, there was a noticeable re-emphasis of bilateral relations reflecting the renewed primacy of national interests in donor foreign policy and foreign aid programs. The $ 1,454 million of aid pledged to Africa between 1977 and 1982 in March 1977 by Saudi Arabia, Kuwait, the UAE and Qatar was indicative of this mood. As Table 23 illustrates, fully 85 % ($ 1,231 million) of this amount was to be committed on a bilateral basis. The remaining 15 % ($ 223 million) was promised as additional capital for existing institutions, primarily ABEDA ($ 180 million) and the African Development Bank ($ 37 million).

A further factor has been the failure of Afro-Arab "solidarity" to develop naturally beyond the financial dimension.[30] Shorn of much of the political impetus by the middle of the decade, Arab-African commercial and economic relations enjoyed only a brief period of flirtation which lasted from 1974 until approximately 1976–1977. For reasons common to many developing countries, trade between the two broad geographic areas failed to grow. In fact, it appears to have declined steadily from 1975 through 1978 before rising sharply in 1979. Yet it has remained marginal

---

29 *ibid.*, p. 13.
30 Several of the speeches and documents collectively published by ABEDA as a record of the fifth meeting of the Coordination Committee for Afro-Arab Cooperation in March 1981 admit for the first time publicly to the failures of Afro-Arab cooperation substantially in terms of our analysis in these 2 paragraphs (see especially pp. 20 and 30–39).

to both Arabs and Africans. As Table 24 indicates, while there was a modest improvement in Africa's largely agricultural exports to the Middle East and North Africa, Arab exports (primarily of petroleum) to Sub-Saharan Africa appear surprisingly to have fallen in each succeeding year through 1978. Although there was a sudden and substantial increase in the volume of Afro-Arab trade in 1979, both exports and imports continued to decline as a percentage of total African trade. To be sure, there have been notable regional exceptions, including Algeria's efforts to develop two-way commercial relations with West and Central African Trans-Saharan states and Saudi Arabia's agricultural purchases from neighboring Somalia, Sudan and Ethiopia. But even these represent a fraction of total trade and, as the experience of the Arab world since 1960 and the member states of the Islamic Development Bank have shown, these trade patterns are unlikely to change until the respective national economies develop a far greater degree of complementarity.[31]

Even in the non-official financial sector, there was a noticeable decline in the level of interest in Africa on the part of private Arab financial institutions and individual investors after the initial enthusiasm and exploratory activities of the immediate post-war years. Companies and banks established during that period to invest in African projects and develop trade and commercial relations include the African-Arab Company for Trade and Development (AFARCO) and the Arab-African Bank, among others. Citing problems with existing loan portfolios, incompatible business practices, unreliable quality control and an uncertain investment climate, AFARCO and other Kuwaiti and Arab investment and commercial groups have reduced their African operations to a very low level. After a few small initial loans, usually amounting to no more than several million dollars, institutions such as the Arab-African Bank and Kuwait Foreign Trading, Contracting and Investment Company have frozen their African exposure and realigned their banking priorities to emphasize indigenous development in the Arab world or investment in Asia and the developed capital markets of the OECD nations. Additionally, Arab commercial banking consortia, such as Union de Banques Arabes et Françaises (UBAF) and Banque Arabe et Internationale d'Investissement (BAII), which syndicated or participated in sporadic loans ranging up to $15 million to

---

31 See Mohammed Diab's study of inter-Arab trade following the establishment of the Arab Common Market, *Inter-Arab Economic Cooperation, 1951–1960*, Economic Research Institute, A.U.B., Beirut, 1963. For a review of the potential for trade development among Islamic countries, see a study published by the Statistical Economic and Social Research and Training Center for Islamic Countries, *Foreign Trade of Islamic Countries: The Present State and Problems*, Ankara, August 1980. See also the *Annual Report (1979)* of the Islamic Development Bank, p. 29.

African countries including Ivory Coast, Liberia and Senegal, have apparently made relatively few new loans since 1977.[32]

2. The African Perspective

Afro-Arab relations on the political plane are long standing. As far back as the early 1960s, Arab states, particularly Algeria and Egypt under Gamal Abdel Nasser gave material and moral support to African national liberation movements, particularly those fighting against minority governments in southern Africa.[33] Following the 1973 war, the Arab Summit Conference in November 1973, which resolved to establish SAAFA as "a contribution to the economic and social development of the African countries", called on all Arab states to perfect their opposition to white minority regimes. The Conference resolved that all Arab states break remaining diplomatic, consular, economic and cultural relations with South Africa, Rhodesia and the Portuguese colonies, embargo oil deliveries and increase moral and diplomatic backing for those African national liberation movements recognized by the OAU.[34]

If there has been general satisfaction at the constancy of Arab political backing from the African perspective, there has been strong disappointment and criticism that the level of tangible financial support forthcoming as a result of Afro-Arab "solidarity" has been less than expected. This disappointment is composed of three principal elements. In the first place, there has been a natural difference in perception between donor and recipient on the amount of Arab aid to be committed to Africa. Africans may have hoped for a good deal more aid than the Arabs intended, although it is unlikely that the Arab donors, individually or collectively ever conceived an aid strategy with target levels for Africa. This difference in perception grew more acute as the Arabs grew richer and as the level of aid increased to African members of the Arab League such as Sudan, Somalia and Mauritania, and to Uganda for reasons discussed elsewhere in this report. African dissatisfaction was made more intense by the flourish and imprecision of Arab pronouncements on aid to Africa. Potentially the most important was the $ 1.45 billion of aid pledged in March 1977 at the Afro-Arab Summit Conference. Whether this was intended by the donors to be the total aid extended over the five-year period or to be additional assistance is unclear from the Conference proceedings and the subsequent

---

32 E.I.U., *Liberia*, I, 1976; *Senegal*, II, 1976; and *Ivory Coast*, III, 1977.

33 Ali Mazrui, *Africa's International Relations*, Westview Press, Boulder, Colorado, 1977, pp. 134—142, and Ahmad Yousef Ahmad, *op. cit.*, pp. 47—50.

34 "Declaration on Africa" cited by *Jeune Afrique*, Nov. 29, 1973 and quoted by Kaczynski, "African-Arab Cooperation and the Evolution in the Position of the O.A.U. on the Middle East Conflict", *Studies on the Developing Countries* (Polish Institute of International Affairs), No. 9, 1978, Warsaw, pp. 29—47.

communiques. However, that Africans assumed it was to be additional assistance seems understandable. In either case, the promise has not been fulfilled. The average level of bilateral aid from these 4 states in the two years preceding the Summit amounted to $ 162 million; in the three years from 1977—1979 just $ 161 million. On the basis of commitments through 1979, only Kuwait seems likely to fulfill its pledge.

A second factor is that the African requirement for external financial assistance has continued to increase, even as the ardor of the Arab donor nations for Africa has cooled and the amount of financial resources allocated to the Sub-Saharan area has declined. Although Africa's oil import bill was almost flat from 1974 through 1976, it rose at an annual compounded rate of 10 % during 1977 and 1978, reflecting a slight upturn in consumption. The effect of higher oil prices during the five-year period ending in 1978 was substantial. Although the 15 countries included in Table 16 experienced a marginal drop in the level of aggregate consumption (from 153,000 b/d in 1973 to 151,200 b/d in 1978), they paid an additional $ 3 billion (over and above the pre-embargo price in 1973) in scarce foreign exchange for petroleum imports during that period (Table 17) as a result of the higher prices alone. Extrapolation from the base represented by those countries suggests that the additional cost of oil imports for all 40 Sub-Saharan countries may have approached $ 5 billion over the five-year period.

Against that added financial burden, Africa received commitments of external financial assistance of $ 31.4 billion from all sources (and disbursements of $ 21.9 billion), of which slightly more than $ 2.45 billion was committed by Arab donors through bilateral and multilateral channels (Table 8).[35] These Arab commitments represented just under 50 % of the estimated added cost of imported oil between 1973 and 1978. (The sum of Arab commitments is exclusive of Arab contributions to the IMF Oil Facility, from which African drawings amounted to SDR 464 (approximately $ 560 million) or assistance provided by international organizations supported in part by Arab contributions).[36]

The latest surge in oil prices in 1979—80 has caused another massive jump in the cost of imported oil and another sharp deterioration in Africa's balance of payments position, requiring costly adjustment. Based on an extrapolation from partial data reported in Table 17, oil imports rose 47 % ($ 853 million) from 1978 to $ 2.67 billion in 1979 and were projected to increase a further $ 1.4 billion (58 %) to $ 4.1 billion in 1980. Partially as a consequence thereof, the overall Sub-Saharan balance of payments deficit increased by $ 1.9 billion in 1979 and will have widened further in 1980.

---

35 World Bank, *Annual Report, 1980*, pp. 140—141.
36 IMF, *IMF Survey*, May 4, 1981, pp. 137—138.

Finally, increasing African disappointment stemmed undoubtedly from the growing realization that by the late 1970s Arab interest had shifted away from Africa and that Africa was powerless to refocus that interest or arrest the commensurate decline in the level of Arab aid. Partly out of a sense of frustration at their inability to influence Arab donors, partly due to anxiety over their worsening economic predicament and partly because of impatience at the level and quality of aid forthcoming (largely slowly disbursed project loans), African statements on Afro-Arab relations have frequently criticized Arab aid as modest compared to the financial resources of the oil producers and inadequate compared to the financial and economic hardships caused by higher oil prices.

More recently, some African nations have begun to pressure the Arabs at their most sensitive point — relations with Israel. It is doubtful that several African states, including the Central African Republic, Ghana, Ivory Coast, Kenya and Zaire ever completely severed non-diplomatic relations with Israel in 1973. While it is true that the activities of Israel's formal technical assistance and aid programs dropped off sharply after 1973, many Israeli specialists and commercial firms remained in place.[37] Furthermore, there is evidence to suggest that the level of Israeli aid to Africa has begun to recover and that Afro-Israeli trade (excluding trade with South Africa) may have more than doubled to over $100 million per annum since 1973.[38] Finally, since 1978–1979 there have been indications of private efforts to reestablish informal links. There have also been official statements calling for the formal reestablishment of diplomatic relations with Israel. Zaire was reportedly the first African country to announce its intention to resume diplomatic links.[39] Apparently dissuaded from this course of action by other members of the OAU, Zaire was, nevertheless, one of a group of several nations — reportedly including Ivory Coast, Senegal, Kenya and Ghana — which tried unsuccessfully to introduce a formal resolution recommending the resumption of diplomatic relations with Israel at the OAU Summit Conference in July 1979. Although this resolution was withdrawn, the OAU refused to condemn the Camp David Agreement or censure Egypt and gave President Sadat a standing ovation.[40]

---

37 For an Israeli comparison of Israel's aid program in Africa before and after the 1973 war, see Shimeon Amir, *Israel's Development Cooperation with Africa, Asia and Latin America*, Praeger, New York, 1974. See also Victor LeVine and Timothy W. Luke, *The Arab-African Connection: Political and Economic Realities*, Westview Press, Boulder, Colorado, 1979, p. 143, and Africa *Research Bulletin (Political, Social and Cultural Series)*, vol. 16, no. 7, pp. 5326–5330, cited by Ahmad Y. Ahmad, *op. cit.*, pp. 74–75.

38 *African Business*, December 1979 (no. 16), pp. 16–18.

39 *Financial Times*, August 31, 1979.

40 *ibid.*, and *African Business*, December 1979 (no. 16), pp. 16–18.

Is the trend toward the rejuvenation of Afro-Israeli relations merely a tactic to extract more Arab financial assistance or the expression of a serious change in Afro-Arab relations? Most probably, it is a mixture of both. On the one hand, this group includes nations which received relatively little Arab aid during the 1970s, such as C. A. R., Ghana, Zaire, Ivory Coast and Kenya. These countries may have concluded that they have little to lose financially from a resumption of ties with Israel. However, for a close friend of Saudi Arabia and member of the Islamic Conference such as Senegal, the motive may lie in the personal stature of its President Leopold Senghor and his desire to try and bridge the gap between Arab and Israeli positions. Some of these nations may also have decided that the opportunity cost of relations with both parties to the Arab-Israeli conflict is modest and, if this does not immediately justify closer ties to Israel, it has reduced their concern for Arab sensitivities.

On the other hand, the Arab countries are still a significant source of assistance. Even if short of technical expertise, Arab donors committed an average of about $ 400 million in aid annually to Africa between 1973— 1979 (see Table 8). Israel's aid program was modest by comparison. According to one Israeli source, Israel spent only $ 60 million on bilateral aid to Africa during the decade 1961—1971.[41] Even if Israeli aid was cost-effective and well targeted, many Sub-Saharan African nations, particularly those members of the Islamic Conference which receive the bulk of Arab financial assistance, seem unlikely to re-establish formal relations with Israel, if to do so will deprive them of even the reduced level of Arab aid available through 1979. They are not likely to alter their position unless Arab aid falls again below the 1979 level. Politically, Israel's close cooperation with South Africa on security and other matters is an added irritant.

What could prove to be the decisive factor in the future course of Afro-Arab relations is the present unequal standing of the two parties in the one-dimensional Afro-Arab financial relationship which developed after 1973. Both parties recognize African dependence and, according to Arab aid officials, it has produced a sense of bitter resentment among many African recipients. In such an environment, the threat of renewed relations with Israel may be seen as a gamble against long odds to raise the level of Arab aid and as a public admission of the failure of Afro-Arab solidarity to endure past the stage of financial compensation for political support and, most importantly, as a means by which African nations can re-establish a sense of balance, proportion and mutual respect to what has been a seriously lopsided relationship.

---

41 Amir, *op. cit.*, p. 96.

2. Islamic Financial Institutions

The three institutions analyzed in this section share a common focus on the Islamic nations as a group. There are, however, fundamental differences between them in their objectives, the scope and scale of their aid programs and the style and structure of their operations. The Islamic Development Bank (IDB) — by far the largest of the three — finances economic and social development projects and foreign trade. The Islamic Solidarity Fund (ISF) supports social welfare programs and Islamic educational and cultural activities. The Muslim World League (MWL) funds the construction of mosques and other religious buildings, Islamic education and missionary activities. Recently, there have been reports of the creation of a new fund to assist social and economic development in the poorer Islamic countries. To be capitalized at $ 3 billion, this fund would operate through the established bilateral aid agencies of the donors: Kuwait, Qatar, Saudi Arabia and the UAE.

In addition to assistance from official sources, the announcement of the foundation of the Islamic Finance House (Dar al-Mal al-Islami) foreshadows the introduction of private capital into developing Islamic nations. This new institution is an outgrowth of the movement to create financial institutions based on Islamic economic and financial principles in several Arab and non-Arab countries, a desire which, in part, motivated the foundation of the IDB. The new bank is seeking equity capital of $ 1 billion by offering its shares in 44 Islamic countries and 5 states with large Muslim communities. According to the bank's chairman, Prince Mohamed al-Faysal al-Saud, its main purpose will be to promote profitable investments, chiefly from individual Muslims, in developing countries, especially Islamic nations.[1]

Considerable resources have already been placed at the disposal of Islamic institutions by the donor governments. As the figures in Table 4 indicate, at least $ 2.6 billion has been subscribed to the three institutions described in the following pages, with the prospect of substantial additional public and private capital for Islamic purposes in the future. Nevertheless, the sum allocated to date is modest in comparison with the resources already committed to the bilateral funds, Arab regional institutions or even the OPEC Fund.

Although it has been advanced through Islamic institutions, the focus of this aid has been primarily the promotion of social and economic development in Islamic countries and foreign trade among Islamic nations. Virtually all (97 %) of the capital subscribed has gone to the Islamic Development Bank. Probably no more than $ 100—150 million since 1973 has been dedicated to truly Islamic educational, cultural, religious or missionary

---

1 *Financial Times,* June 11, 1981.

activities through the Islamic Solidarity Fund and the Muslim World League. The possible creation of a new fund managed by four established development funds suggests an augmented future emphasis on development projects; a tendency likely to be enhanced by the availability of private capital to finance productive private enterprise.

This is not, however, to minimize the importance of Islam in providing a community of interest between donor and recipient nations and a focus for financial assistance. For example, the IDB provided almost twice as much aid ($ 265 million) to the Sub-Saharan members of the Islamic Congress between 1976 and 1980 as ABEDA ($ 146 million). Moreover, Islamic aid has remained independent of the lethargy apparent in Afro-Arab relations on the secular political and financial planes since the late 1970s.

a. Islamic Development Bank

Under the impetus of the late King Faisal, establishment of the Islamic Development Bank (IDB) was agreed by the Conference of Finance Ministers of Islamic Countries in December 1973. The Bank became operational in Jeddah, Saudi Arabia on October 20, 1975. Its President and Chairman is Dr. Ahmed Mohamed Ali, formerly a senior employee of the Saudi Arabian Monetary Agency and Deputy Minister of Education.

Capitalized at 2 billion Islamic Dinars (equivalent to 2 billion Special Drawing Rights of the IMF), the initial subscribed capital was set at 750 million ID (approximately $ 860 million). Since then the capital has been raised gradually with the addition of new members. In March 1981, in part as a result of persistent lobbying by the recipient countries, the Board of Governors ratified a proposal to fully subscribe the Bank's authorized capital of 2 billion Dinars (about $ 2.55 billion).

The IDB's stated objective is to foster the economic development and social progress of member countries and Muslim communities in non-member countries through loans and equity investments in accordance with the principles of the *Shari'a* (Islamic law)[2]. It is also required to promote economic and financial cooperation and complementarity among member countries through foreign trade, joint ventures and other measures. Additional objectives include the provision of technical assistance and training, particularly for persons engaged in development, and research on how best to enable economic, financial and banking activities in Muslim countries to conform with the *Shari'a*. Finally, the IDB is to give special consideration to its less developed members. Unstated, but reportedly the

---

2 Islamic Development Bank, *Articles of Agreement,* p. 6, and the *Fourth Annual Report,* 1399 Hijri (1979), p. 4.

primary motive for the Bank's establishment, was King Faisal's determination to prove the Islamic economic and financial principles could be made to work for the economic and social development and progress of the Islamic world.

One of the FOB's most controversial and political objectives — its commitment to assist Muslim communities in non-member countries — has foundered on the unwillingness of national governments to allow it to favor these particular communities with outside assistance that does not conform to national development priorities.

Membership in the IDB is restricted to countries which are members of the Islamic Conference and which are willing to accept such terms and conditions as may be decided upon by the Board of Governors. Among those terms and conditions is agreement to implement Islamic economic and financial principles, including the prohibition on interest. However, no member nation yet abides fully by that commitment and it is acknowledged that it will be difficult to require orthodoxy until such time as these principles have been proven to be realistic and practical in the modern world.

Among major Arab-sponsored multilateral institutions, the IDB is unique in combining representatives of donor and recipient countries at all levels from staff up through Executive Directors. In this manner, the interests of the recipient countries are represented on a daily basis. Undoubtedly as a result, the Bank's level of activity has grown at an annual compound rate in excess of 50 % since 1977 (see Table 25).

A review of the Bank's activities highlights the IDB's emphasis on economic development and the promotion of economic cooperation and complementarity largely through foreign trade financing. In order to conform to the *Shari'a* as well as to ensure both an adequate return and a rapid turnover of its capital, financing trade in oil and industrial intermediate goods and materials has become the Bank's most important activity, accounting for 72 % of operations in FY 1980.[3] Trade finance (where the Bank buys the goods and marks them up for resale) is, in fact, a form of program finance required urgently by the IDB's less developed members. The Bank's concentration in this area makes it unusual among Arab institutional donors. While project related financings increased from $ 150 million in 1979 to $ 171 million in the most recent financial year ending November 8, 1980, trade finance rose from $ 338 million to $ 476 million, largely promoting trade between member countries. Total operations during the first five years (through November 8, 1980) amounted to over ID 1,243 million, including ID 445 million and ID 798 million of project and trade finance, respectively.[4]

---

3 IDB, *Fifth Annual Report,* 1400 Hijra, Jeddah, 1981.
4 IDB, *Fifth Annual Report.*

In addition to trade finance, the IDB seeks to emphasize those aspects of project finance — equity, investment, leasing and profit sharing — which can be linked to project profitability and to de-emphasize loans bearing interest. Although inherently a practise subject to greater risk, the Bank has continued to reduce lending. In the past fiscal year, loans fell to only 38% of total project financing and only 10% of total financing in the year.

The IDB's project finance activities are concentrated in the same basic economic sectors as other development banks: agriculture, industry, mining, transport, communications and utilities.[5] Through year end 1980, the sectoral breakdown was as follows:

Sector	Amount (million ID)	Percentage
Agriculture	52.1	11.7
Industry and Mining	189.6	42.6
Transport and Communications	115.7	27.0
Utilities	57.5	12.9
Social Services	23.3	5.2
Other	7.3	1.6
Total	445.5	100.0%

Most of the Bank's projects are co-financed with Arab, European and international development agencies and commercial banks. The only notably "Islamic" aspect of its project financing activities in the past 2 years — aside from its mode of operation and the limitation of its commitments to member countries — was three minor financings, totalling $ 9.1 million, for specifically Islamic projects in Arab countries:

1. $ 3.9 million equity in the Bahrain Islamic Bank;
2. $ 5.1 million profit-sharing in a housing project in Dubai;
3. a $ 100,000 grant to the P.L.O. for the design of an Islamic university in Gaza.

In Africa, the IDB has concentrated exclusively on traditional economic development projects and trade financings. The $ 103 million of project financings through September 1980 were divided among the following sectors:

 Industry — $ 39.8 million;
 Agriculture — $ 18.4 million;
 Power — $ 15.9 million;
 Transport and Communications — $ 16.0 million;
 Utilities — $ 5.8 million;
 Minerals — $ 4.2 million;
 Development Bank — $ 2.6 million.

---

5 IDB, *Fourth Annual Report*, pp. 55—75.

The Bank has no formal project selection criteria but responds to official requests for assistance from recipient governments on an *ad hoc* basis. Individual projects must meet certain financial and economic standards and further the country's economic and social development. Furthermore, a project must have the explicit national development priority of the recipient. Once a project has been selected, the IDB may finance its capital cost with a loan, equity investment or lease of equipment and support its operations with trade financing for the import of intermediate goods. An example is the Soprociment clinker grinding plant in Guinea. The IDB has taken equity of $ 4.7 million in the project, leased to it $ 8 million of capital equipment and financed $ 7 million of clinker imports.

Trade financings in Africa from 1976 through November 1980 have amounted to $ 140 million, of which 69 % ($ 96 million) has been for crude oil and refined product imports from Arab oil producers. However, in 1980 alone, reflecting rising oil prices, 78 % of African trade financings have been for oil imports.

The high cost of financing petroleum imports and the tendency to commit resources to large scale development projects accounts, in part, for the concentration of Bank financings in relatively few African member countries. Of the $ 257 million committed to Africa, almost 75 % ($ 170 million) has been given to Senegal ($ 67 million), Niger ($ 53 million) and Guinea ($ 51 million) (Table 25).[6] The presence of representatives of the latter 2 countries on the Bank's Board of Executive Directors may also account in part for the favor shown to these nations. Cameroon and Guinea Bissau have received $ 18 million each, with minor amounts to the six other African members. Finally, it is noteworthy that the four nations of Arab League Africa have received an amount of total IDB assistance identical to the aid provided to the more numerous Sub-Saharan member countries.

The IDB plans two steps which may spread its resources more evenly in the future. Currently, it is beginning to try and direct a greater share of its resources to those of its members on the list of LLDC's, although these countries had received only 40 % of total commitments through 1980. In a few years' time, the Bank expects to institute a system of annual national allocations, but it is still in the process of developing an appropriate formula.

While political considerations are supposed not to play a role in the Bank's operations according to its Articles of Agreement, the selection of recipient countries and the level of aid to them is apparently sensitive to political factors. For example, although the Egyptian Executive Director of the IDB remains active, Egypt has received no assistance from the Bank since

---

6 A slightly larger amount ($ 264 million) has been committed to the four Arab League members of Sub-Saharan Africa.

it was expelled from the Islamic Conference in early 1979 and its membership in the IDB suspended following signature of its peace treaty with Israel. In March 1981, Afghanistan's membership was suspended. On the other hand, aid to Uganda has not been frozen officially since Idi Amin was overthrown in May 1979 although no new aid has been approved by the Bank since January of that year.

Although the IDB is an independent organization, Saudi Arabia has an influential voice in its management and operations. This influence, and the Islamic emphasis of Saudi foreign aid, have resulted in a similarity between the geographic distribution of IDB and Saudi assistance. Three Asian countries which have been priority targets of Saudi aid – Bangladesh, Pakistan and Turkey – and Sudan and Somalia in the Horn of Africa, have received 30 % and 15 % of total commitments, respectively, from the IDB while conservative governments in Morocco and Senegal have also received considerable support.

b. Islamic Solidarity Fund

Before analyzing the operations of the Islamic Solidarity Fund (ISF), it may be instructive first to describe the structure and objectives of the Organization of the Islamic Conference (OIC) since it is the Conference Secretariat which administers the ISF and determines its policies and which also maintains close links with the Islamic Development Bank.

1. Organization of the Islamic Conference

The Islamic Conference was first proposed by the late King Faisal in the mid-1960s as an organizational vehicle to mobilize a conservative, Islamic bloc of nations headed by Saudi Arabia. But its actual establishment took place in 1967, after Islamic resentment crystallized in reaction to the burning of the Al-Aqsa Mosque in Jerusalem. Headquartered in Jeddah and largely financed by Saudi Arabia, the Conference serves both as a moral forum and as a political organization.[7]

The Conference has 41 members presently. According to OIC officials, membership is limited to states with a Muslim majority among the population, but they admit that, in practice, the organization is willing to accept virtually any state that has a significant Muslim population and/or professes to share the organization's ideals. The case of Africa illustrates this

---

7 Saudi contributions to the Islamic Conference and its programs and subsidiary organizations reportedly amounted to $ 38 million in 1977, $ 35 million in 1978, $ 34 million in 1979 and $ 65 million in 1980. *Middle East Economic Survey*, 5/15/78 and 7/24/78 and *Saudi Economic Survey*, 5/21/80.

flexibility. Twelve Sub-Saharan nations are members: Cameroon, Chad, Comoros, Gabon, Gambia, Guinea, Guinea-Bissau, Mali, Niger, Senegal, Uganda and Upper Volta. Nigeria has long enjoyed observer status, but has refused to join the organization to avoid antagonizing Nigeria's non-Muslim inhabitants. Among the 12 African members are seven states with a demographic Muslim majority: Chad, Comoros, Gambia, Guinea, Mali, Niger and Senegal; two with a small Muslim community but Muslim Presidents at the time of admission: Gabon and Uganda; and three where Islamic organizations claim a Muslim majority but most estimates indicate that, while substantial, Muslims probably constitute a minority: Cameroon, Guinea-Bissau and Upper Volta (see Table 26). Not yet members, but countries where accession to the Islamic Conference and the Islamic Development Bank are reportedly under consideration are Madagascar, Sierra Leone and Tanzania. With the recent conversion to Islam of President Kekourou of Benin that country too may apply for membership.[8]

The objectives of the Islamic Conference are both religious and political and reflect that special blend of support for Islam and anti-Communism which is the hallmark of Saudi foreign policy. On the one hand, the OIC seeks to defend the interests of Muslim communities, propagate Islam through missionary activities, fight atheism and pursue other objectives of religious interest to Muslims.[9] On the other hand, through the Islamic Conference of Foreign Ministers and the Islamic Summit Conference, the OIC serves as an organizational vehicle to rally Islamic nations for common political ends; for example, the liberation of Palestine and Jerusalem and opposition to the Soviet invasion of Afghanistan. In Africa, especially in non-Arab member countries, it supports Arabic language instruction, promotes Islamic education and culture and aids Muslim minorities. It also supports African liberation movements and opposes "racism" in southern Africa.

2. Operations of the Fund

The Islamic Solidarity Fund (ISF) was established by the Islamic Summit Conference in 1974. Its headquarters are in Jeddah. Relatively small for an Arab world accustomed to think in billions of dollars, the Fund is supported by voluntary contributions from members of the Islamic Conference. Although reports are often conflicting and precise figures are difficult to obtain, the Fund appears to have received contributions totalling no less than $ 75 million in the six years since it was founded. At least

---

8 With the exception of Madagascar, the religious affiliation of the majority of the population in the latter 3 countries is a matter of disagreement (see Table 25).
9 For a review of the Islamic Conference's objectives, see *Journal of the Muslim World League*, (hereinafter *JMWL*), July 1979, p. 24.

$ 30 million – or 40 % – has been donated by Saudi Arabia. An additional $ 14 million each has been donated by Libya and the UAE, with $ 5.5 million from Kuwait.[10] Additionally, there have been many small donations, primarily from African and Asian countries (see Table 27).

The annual budget of the ISF has fluctuated between $ 10 – $ 14 million since 1974 without increase. Although the Chairman has repeatedly sought a minimum annual budget of $ 50 million since 1975, the year of King Faisal's death, such an amount has never been approved by the donors.[11] The failure of the donors to agree to an increased budget may indicate policy differences among the contributors and an unwillingness to expand the scope of the Fund's activities beyond a symbolic level.

The ISF seems to have been beset by financial troubles almost since its inception, possibly as a result of policy disagreements as well as rivalry between donor governments for control of the institution itself. It may also be that disagreement over fundamental issues of program content and direction led to the independent decisions of Kuwait, Libya and Saudi Arabia to halt contributions to the Fund in 1977/78 and 1978/79 (see Table 27), contributions which Kuwait and Libya apparently have not resumed. An additional motive in the case of Libya was probably the strong competition between Qaddafi and the Saudis for Islamic leadership and their decreasing ability to cooperate within an institutional framework. The financial result of this disagreement has been to leave the ISF dependent on support from Saudi Arabia, the UAE and Iraq since 1978, with Saudi Arabia alone contributing 70 % of the budget in the 1979/80 fiscal year.

Continued reliance on Saudi Arabia for financial support of this magnitude is probably not in the best interest of the ISF if its contributors wish it to survive as a genuine multilateral institution. It is reportedly the intention of the shareholders in the Islamic Development Bank that the Bank's recently agreed capital increase will enable it to attain a level of profitability whereby it will use a portion of its annual earnings to support the Islamic Solidarity Fund's activities, permitting dependence on Saudi finance to be replaced by multilateral support once again.

3. Program of ISF Assistance

The objective of the ISF is to initiate and aid religious, cultural and charitable organizations in the Muslim world and to assist Muslim com-

---

10 Saudi Arabia has also been reported to have given up to $ 20–30 million to a Trust Fund of the ISF, although this may be intended to build an organizational headquarters.

11 *JMWL*, July 1979, pp. 22–24.

munities elsewhere.[12] In its charitable, cultural and religious focus, the Fund complements the economic and social development objectives of the IDB. But as the Fund's Chairman has observed, the financial resources of the Fund are modest compared to the number of Muslims or their needs. It is, however, a "symbol" of a collective effort to help Muslims "everywhere".[13]

The ISF's activities include donations to educational, religious and charitable institutions and programs, as well as to political organizations. Among the educational projects are those which combine education and proselytism, including two Islamic universities: one at Say, Niger; the other to have been at Arua, in Muslim northwest Uganda. The decision to build an Islamic university in Niger brought into the open a sharp conflict between two of the Fund's principal backers: Saudi Arabia and Libya. Apparently progress on the project was blocked after it was first funded with an initial grant of $ 1.5 million in 1976 by the donors' inability to agree on a common set of objectives, particularly the doctrinal leaning of the university and the nationality and, thus, the presumed political loyalty of its rector. According to observers, donors and recipients alike feared that the clash between political interest groups aligned with Saudi Arabia's Islamic conservatism and Libya's Islamic radicalism could disrupt the university were the project to proceed. Ultimately, the Fund was to contribute $ 5 million to each in addition to the bilateral grants of several donor countries. With the advent of a less favorable political environment in Uganda, the ISF decided to cancel the university in Arua and allocate those funds to the project in Niger. Tenders for construction were finally announced in early 1981 and it appears that the issues which obstructed the project for 5 years have been resolved.[14]

In addition to the university, the ISF had funded Higher Institutes of Islamic Studies, usually coupled with mosques or schools, in Gabon ($ 500,000), Gambia ($ 200,000), Guinea ($ 600,000) and Senegal ($ 250,000); a technical institute in Gabon at a cost of $ 300,000; and Islamic Research Institutes in Mali and Pakistan.

The ISF focuses on support for Islamic cultural centers, especially in Africa, Asia and the West where local governments, according to the Fund, may not cater sufficiently to the needs of Muslim minorities.[15] Reportedly, 36 centers have been assisted around the world, from Australia to Ireland and the United States, including those in Guinea Bissau, Came-

---

12 *ibid.*
13 *ibid.*
14 According to BADEA, $ 10 million was finally committed to the university at Say by the Islamic Solidarity Fund in June 1980 (letter to the Authors, July 1981).
15 JMWL, *loc. cit.*

roon, Chad, Ghana, Congo, Mauritius, Sierra Leone, Tanzania and Upper Volta (see Table 28).

Charitable projects have included hospitals in Mali, Indonesia and Jordan, a maternity and pediatric clinic in Senegal and an orphanage in Somalia. In addition, the ISF has donated emergency cash grants to Muslims in the Comoros Islands, Cyprus, Guinea Bissau and the Philippines. In several instances, emergency relief is highly political, as, for example, in Guinea Bissau and the Philippines. So too, is the Fund's assistance to Arab and Islamic liberation movements in Palestine, Eritrea and the Philippines, and to the Jerusalem Fund.

The donor dissatisfaction which has been discerned in the ISF's financial performance may also be a consequence of the wide geographic dispersion of its limited resources. With so many target countries, the Fund is capable of undertaking only one or two small projects in each country. While the average commitment in member countries has been about $ 1 million over 3 years (1976/77 − 1978/79), the Fund's many contributions in non-Muslim countries range between $ 10,000 and $ 50,000, rarely exceeding $ 100,000 per country.[16]

African member countries received $ 11.4 million during the 3-year period 1976/77 − 1978/79 (32 % of total commitments), primarily for the 2 university projects. Non-member African countries have received a total of only $ 854,000, or 7 % of total commitments. However, almost half of this amount was contributed to Eritrea (and the Eritrean Liberation Front) which is considered "Arab" by the donor countries.

The weight of available evidence suggests that the donor governments of the ISF have been very cautious in expanding its activities in Africa. In the first place, the scale of the ISF's resources has remained small in comparison to the funds available to the Islamic Development Bank or the national funds whose programs focus on economic development projects. Second, the Fund's leadership has concentrated its resources in those member states which are receptive to ISF assistance for the indigenous Muslim communities, such as Niger, Mali, Senegal, Gambia and Guinea, as well as Uganda under Amin. By contrast, they have extended relatively modest sums to non-member African states or to those, such as Cameroon, Upper Volta and Chad, where the question of religious communal balance is a far more sensitive political issue. Finally, indications that Uganda has become a "marginal" participant in the activities of the Islamic Conference and no longer a recipient of ISF aid since the fall of Amin suggest that the leadership of the ISF may be aware of the conflict potential inherent in external financial assistance which favors only one religious community in pluralistic African societies.

---

16 See General Secretariat of the Organization of the Islamic Conference, "Islamic Solidarity Fund", pp. 219 and 224−225 (Jeddah, July 1980).

c. Muslim World League

Headquartered in Mecca, the Muslim World League (MWL) was established in 1961 pursuant to a decision of the First Islamic Summit which met that year. It was conceived by King Saud as an organizational vehicle under Saudi leadership to mobilize political opposition to the policy of Arab Unity sponsored by President Nasser of Egypt. Based on the common bond of Islam, it was designed to transcend the narrower basis of Arab Nationalism. The League was supposed to supercede the Islamic Congress which had been established jointly with Egyptian and Pakistani support in 1955. Although never very effective politically, the MWL remains an active international organization under Saudi leadership and with Saudi financial support.

The League is the most conservative and religious of the three Islamic institutions providing assistance to Africa. It may also be the smallest. Unlike the Islamic Development Bank, the League's aid program focuses on religious and cultural activities. Although details of its program of assistance to Africa are difficult to obtain and incomplete, it is important to investigate the League's activities in Africa for three reasons. The League's significance lies first in its stated objectives. These represent a public expression of a "fundamentalist" Islamic world view of dichotomous relations between Muslim and non-Muslim countries and of the role of Muslim minorities in non-Muslim states. As such, they are of interest in and of themselves. Second, the League's public statements are full of missionary zeal and denunciations of anti-Islamic elements and outline a strategy to "win Africa for Islam". Third, while impossible to measure precisely, there is evidence to suggest that the League, if not an actual instrument of Saudi government policy, represents the views of a portion of the Saudi leadership and may have a hand in shaping the attitudes and policies of the Saudi Arabian government toward Africa. Moreover, the League cooperates closely with the Saudi government in carrying out its aid program in Sub-Saharan Africa.

1. Objectives of the League

The primary purpose of the League is religious, both missionary and defensive; to spread the message of Islam, to win new adherents, to protect Muslim communities, and to publicize awareness of the problems which they face.

According to resolutions adopted by the International Islamic Conference meeting in Sri Lanka in January 1980, the League's religious objectives are fivefold:

1. propagate Islam in Muslim and non-Muslim countries;
2. explain Islamic teachings and principles;

3. confront those trying to attack Islam or convert Muslims;
4. eliminate the "special position" of Christian missionaries in Islamic countries where they enjoy such status;
5. assure fair treatment and respect for certain rights of Muslim minorities in non-Muslim countries.[17]

As the resolutions suggest and various articles in the *Journal of the Muslim World League* (JMWL) since 1974 elucidate, the League's objectives differ between "Islamic" and "non-Islamic" countries. Islamic states are those which the League considers to have a demographic Muslim majority. Non-Islamic states are those with significant Muslim minorities or where few Muslims live. The League concentrates its activities in what it deems to be Islamic countries and those where conversion may succeed in tipping the demographic scales in favor of Islam. Countries in these two categories include several where the League claims a Muslim majority, but where most other estimates (see Table 25) suggest that the Muslim community remains a minority. These disputed countries include Benin (whose President recently converted to Islam), Cameroon, the Central African Republic, Ethiopia, Ivory Coast, Tanzania, Togo, and possibly Guinea-Bissau, Sierra Leone and Upper Volta where the broad range of demographic estimates is inconclusive.[18]

In "Islamic" states, the League seeks to revive the faith and practice of the Muslim community, individually and collectively, through the revitalization of Islam and to encourage the introduction of the *Shari'a.*

In non-Islamic states, its goals are defense of the Muslim community and missionary activity to "eliminate the minority status of Muslim minorities by teaching and conversion". It pointedly attempts to Islamicize the ruling elites, particularly to convert leaders.[19] But in nations with few Muslims the League seems more concerned with ensuring that the Muslim community is not subject to persecution than with the propagation of Islam.

---

17 *JMWL,* April 1980, pp. 42—47 and 60—63.
18 Cameroon, Guinea Bissau and Upper Volta are the only members of this group in the Islamic Conference. For the League's demographic estimates see the following issues of the *JMWL:*
   - Tanzania, December 1973, p. 53
   - Cameroon, April 1974, p. 55
   - Benin, June 1974, p. 52
   - Madagascar, July 1974, p. 43
   - Ghana, September 1974, p. 31
   - Ethiopia, December 1974, p. 55
   - Sierra Leone, January 1975, p. 54
   - Togo, November 1974, p. 68 and November 1975, p. 31.
19 Dr. Ali Kettani, "Dawah among Muslim Minorities", *JMWL,* March 1980, pp. 31—39. For a further example of this point and a discussion of its implications for non-Muslim minorities see Dr. Said Ramadan, *Islamic Law, Its Scope and Equity,* (no publisher), 1970, pp. 113—170.

The League's strategy toward states with significant Muslim minorities is of particular interest because in these countries the potential for conflict between religious communities is greatest. The League seeks first to guarantee the survival of the local Muslim community as a "separate entity" through four measures: first, effective organization of the Muslim community; second, establishment of a mosque — considered a vital spring-board of proselytization — as a social and religious center; third, establishment of Islamic schools — as a separate, independent Islamic education is considered the only way to "safeguard" children from "assimilation"; fourth, establishment of Islamic media to inculcate a spirit of Islamic solidarity and distinctness from the rest of the national community.[20]

To implement these goals, the League calls on Islamic nations to make full use of their political, economic and diplomatic leverage to ensure that only non-Muslim states which treat their Muslim communities "correctly" will be considered as "friendly". The message is made more explicit by a definition of "correct" treatment: guarantees that the Muslim minority receive full local government recognition; support for Islamic education (including segregation of the sexes, Arabic language and religious instruction in Arabic and local languages); modification of existing legislation and regulations, if need be, to enable Muslim businessmen to conduct their affairs in accordance with the Shari'a; introduction of the Shari'a as the law of personal status for the Muslim community; and finally, freedom for Islamic missionary activity.[21]

Once defense of the Muslim minority has been assured, the second phase of the League's strategy is aimed at transforming that minority into a dominant, ruling majority through proselytization.[22] For Africa, the League is candid about the goal of its missionary activities and openly describes the strategy by which it will attain its ends. Fully conscious of the "political significance of the spread of Islam", articles in its Journal denounce Christianity for having "enslaved" Africa during the colonial period and state that Africa is the crucial battleground where Islam will "triumph" over Christianity, offering "freedom" from Christian colonialism and, thereby "securing" (often "winning") Africa for Islam.[23]

A further element of this strategy is to clear the field of any competitive forces by denying to Christian communities and schismatic Muslim sects (such as the Ahmadiya and Bahai) many of the same freedoms and rights

20 *JMWL*, March 1980, pp. 31–39.
21 *JMWL*, June 1976, pp. 11–13 and June 1980, pp. 60–63.
22 *JMWL*, March 1980, pp. 31–39.
23 *JMWL*, May 1974, pp. 58–59 and July 1974, p. 44.

which the League claims for Islam.[24] Specifically, the League calls for the elimination of schools, hospitals and charitable organizations run by Christian missionaries and the banning of all Christian missionary activities in Islamic countries, while calling for the establishment of identical Islamic missionary activities and institutions to replace them. It also urges withholding financial aid from countries which allow Christian missionary activities or which prohibit comparable Islamic proselytization.

2. Implications of the League's Objectives for Africa

The final stage of the League's strategy is the most sensitive and critical for Muslim and non-Muslim communities in Africa for it poses a fundamental question which is the quintessence of Islam: can a Muslim community enjoy the full exercise of its rights in a secular, pluralistic state or does it require the reestablishment of a traditional Islamic state as propounded by Islamic political theory? A no less vital corollary to this question is: in the event of the reestablishment of an Islamic state, what would be the role of non-Muslim communities and what would be their rights and obligations? Ultimately, this stage of the League's strategy raises the spectre of potential religious conflict in pursuit of political domination.

In fact, a definitive answer to these questions is probably not possible. Indeed, over the past 1,400 years much of the political history of Islam reflects the conflict and the compromises between Islamic theory and practical reality posed by these issues. Arab Muslim leaders with experience in Africa acknowledge privately that the conflict between what might be called "de jure" and "de facto" Islamic objectives – between legal theory and accommodation with reality – is the greatest source of debate within African Muslim communities and an important cause of tension between Muslim and non-Muslim communities. African countries are thus concerned about the religious motivations and objectives of the aid programs of conservative Islamic organizations such as the League and the Islamic Solidarity Fund and of countries such as Saudi Arabia and Libya. In the absence of a clear statement of governmental policy objectives to the contrary, the enunciated religious program of a "fundamentalist" organization supported by Saudi Arabia, such as the League, is given particular attention and credence, possibly exaggerated out of all proportion to the size of the organization's program, its impact on Arab governmental policies toward Africa, or the extent to which it is representative of those policy objectives.

The reason for African concern stems directly from the absence of any articulated compromise Muslim position, short of the complete reestablish-

---

24 See the *JMWL*, May 1974, pp. 58—59; July 1974, p. 44; June 1976, p. 35; and August 1980, p. 60.

ment of the traditional Islamic society and state of Islamic political theory and the explicit, subordinate status of non-Muslim minorities in that state, which could accommodate Africa's current socio-political institutions based on the nation-state. In modern Africa, tribalism remains the basis of personal identity, the foundation of society and state and the major source of conflict.[25] As J.S. Trimingham explains, tolerance of pluralism in Africa is a necessity; even religious practice is syncretistic. In such circumstances, there is no room for a return to a state based on communal exclusivism, no matter what the source.

In theory, both Islam and Christianity could provide a structure of universalist moral values and norms for African society to supercede tribalism and serve, therefore, as a potentially effective source of intertribal conflict resolution. In practice, however, while tribes are often split by different religious affiliations, there are few examples of religious unity across tribal lines in times of stress (Christian officers and soldiers of the Federal Nigerian army fighting to end Ibo separation being the most frequently cited example). According to African specialists, the actions of even those who convert to a monotheistic religion are motivated primarily by tribal considerations when forced to choose between loyalty to the tribal or religious communitiy.

Consequently, Africans fear the conflict potential from religious competition in the pluralistic societies of most African countries. There is a strong feeling that the introduction of a state system based on religion or the existence of competitive missionary activities aimed at changing the demographic status quo would add another serious line of cleavage to already fractured societies, widening existing cleavages with serious conflicts between universalist religions supplementing and intensifying tribal conflicts. As examples of states where tribal conflicts have recently been aggravated by religious differences, one could point to Uganda, Nigeria, Ethiopia and the Sudan.

The caution of Africans is best exemplified by Nigeria, a state with the largest Muslim community in Africa. Despite considerable internal and external pressure, the majority of the Constituent Assembly, though Muslim, has voted consistently against both the introduction of the *Shari'a* as a source of legislation and membership in the Islamic Conference. Nigeria is the Conference's only "observer". The government remains of the belief that secularism is the best melting pot for all tribal and religious interest groups in Nigeria and a safer foundation for national identity than religion. Other African leaders apparently share this view and there are, reportedly, strict controls over Muslim (and, in some cases, Christian) missionary activities, close scrutiny of Arab aid for any evidence

---

25 For an analysis of Islam in Africa, see the landmark works of Professor J. Spencer Trimingham listed in the Bibliography.

of Islamic proselytization and frequently outright refusal to allow organizations such as the Islamic Development Bank or the Muslim World League to direct aid exclusively to Muslim communities.

3. Relationship of the League and the Saudi Government

With 50 national and institutional members, the League is a legally independent, international organization and has no official links with the Saudi Arabian government. However, if not formally part of the Saudi foreign policy structure, the League cooperates so closely with Saudi Arabia in its aid program for Islamic purposes and so faithfully echoes the position of the Saudi government on many political and religious matters as to seem virtually an instrument of Saudi policy. Moreover, although the annual budget is not published, the League's activities appear to be largely financed by Saudi Arabia.

The relationship between the League and the Saudi government, however, appears to be one of complementarity rather than of direct control. On the one hand, the League benefits the Saudi government in many ways. The League represents a distinctly traditional Islamic world view and expresses deep public concern for those Islamic issues that were fundamental elements of government policy and personal interest during the reign of King Faisal. The present Saudi leadership probably finds itself thrust into a seemingly more complex international environment where other foreign policy considerations, such as anti-Communism, Great Power politics, world financial stability and local political and economic issues conflict with the stark simplicity of a dichotomous Islamic view of the world. For those who share this view of an earlier era, the League may seem an ideologically congenial refuge. To some, the League's outspoken fundamentalism may seem a useful tool to combat schismatic Islamic sects, such as the Ahmadiya, and Libya's rival brand of Islamic radicalism. Others may sense an opportunity to be seen to be doing something tangible and visible for Islam, possibly in the belief that this support will help stem foreign and internal criticism of the occasional incompatibility between public orthodoxy and private life style. To others, the League may offer the benefit of being a practical organization to raise sensitive issues, such as the treatment of Muslim communities in various lands, which the Saudi government may wish to avoid handling directly on a bilateral basis. For example, the League has attacked the "persecution" of Ugandan Muslims and called on Islamic countries to take measures, such as withholding recognition from the new government. On other issues, the League's position may be a useful supplement to an explicit Saudi governmental policy.

On the other hand, the Saudi government appears to rely on the League and its field offices in several ways which suggest that the League plays a direct role in the execution of the religious component of the Saudi foreign aid program and may even have some influence on the shaping of Saudi foreign policy and in determining the level and direction of Saudi foreign aid. First, League officials devote considerable effort to investigating the status of Muslim communities throughout the world, reporting and publicizing "cases" of apparent persecution or ill treatment. These reports to member governments, pointing out instances of "Communist influence" in Mozambique, "persecution" of Muslims in Uganda and Ethiopia, and "educational discrimination" in Ghana undoubtedly influence the attitudes of key Saudi decision makers and the policies of the Saudi government to some extent. They may also affect decisions regarding the level and type of aid provided to certain countries.[26] For example, the League's charge that the new Ugandan government was "massacring" Muslims on the basis of religious affiliation found echo in a more measured statement by the Saudi Foreign Minister that noted a fear of Muslim "repression" and called on the new government to accord the Muslim community equal treatment and full enjoyment of their rights.[27]

Second, by its pronouncements on the religious composition of various societies, the League determines which countries are deemed "Islamic". This designation carries considerable weight in determining eligibility for aid from Islamic institutional sources, as well as the level of interest and assistance likely to be forthcoming from countries such as Saudi Arabia or the Gulf states. Designation as an "Islamic" state also certainly changes Saudi perceptions of the role Islam is supposed to play in a society and raises expectations of "positive" changes for that purpose.

Third, as a respected religious leader and former Saudi Minister of Justice under King Faisal, the League's Secretary General, Sheikh Mohamed Ali al-Harakan probably retains considerable influence in government circles. Sheikh al-Harakan reportedly discussed Saudi government aid for reconstruction in Zimbabwe while leading a large delegation of the Muslim World League to southern Africa in June 1980.[28] His analysis of the political leanings of the new Zimbabwean leadership and, secondarily, of the country's financial requirements can be expected to influence the Saudi government's decision on whether or not to provide assistance for this purpose.

Finally, in addition to its own program, the League cooperates closely with the Saudi government in extending aid for Islamic purposes. On occasion, the League and its affiliate, the Higher World Council for Mosques, rely on the assistance and logistical support of local Saudi diplomatic personnel for the identification and supervision of worthwhile projects to

---

26 The *JMWL* (June 1976) reported that Mozambique has banned all religions and "nationalized" all children under the age of 5.
27 *JMWL*, April 1979 and *Deutsche Monitor Dienst*, May 14, 1979.
28 *Foreign Broadcast Information Service*, June 26, 1980.

finance, as well as for the correct disbursement of funds. At other times, the League acts as a conduit for funds donated by the Saudi government. Disbursed in amounts ranging broadly up to several $ 100,000, the League may provide $ 2—3 million or more annually on behalf of Saudi Arabia for schools, mosques, Islamic cultural centers, hospitals and Islamic organizations in various African countries. While the amounts usually are modest in countries where Muslims constitute a minority, this program seems aimed principally at propagating Islam and expanding Islamic educational opportunities through the construction and support of mosques and Islamic universities, institutes and schools.

4. Program of Assistance

In addition to its cooperation with the Saudi government, the Muslim World League has developed its own aid program. This program is elaborate in its diversity but apparently modest in the amounts allocated to achieve the League's objectives. The amount of resources applied to this program are not publicly recorded so it is impossible to describe the full scope of its aid program or the relative importance of Africa. However, several articles published in the *Journal of the Muslim World League* during the past seven years suggest the scale of the aid program, its priorities and the purposes of this aid.[29]

The League's aid program concentrates on the construction of an infrastructure of Islamic educational and religious facilities and on the provision of supporting services. While the League has encountered obstacles occasionally to the implementation of its projects from governments in Africa, such as Sierra Leone and Ivory Coast, its program seems to be spread widely throughout Sub-Saharan Africa. If there is a geographic focus, it would appear to be West Africa in the countries covered by the League's regional office in Dakar, Senegal which cooperates with the Islamic Coordinating Council for Africa (also in Dakar) to organize Islamic activities at the popular level.

During the past few years, the League and the Higher World Council of Mosques have helped local Muslim communities construct or finish mosques in Botswana, Chad, Ghana, Guinea, Liberia, Mali, Nigeria, Senegal, Sierra Leone, Togo, Upper Volta and Zimbabwe, all at a cost of less than $ 1 million per annum. The League places great emphasis on the construction of Islamic cultural centers which often, like the one in Kenya, include a mosque, school, library, dispensary and auditorium. Centers have been

---

29 The information in this section has been gleaned primarily from the following issues of the *JWML:* January 1974; June 1976; April 1980; and June 1980. Additionally, the *Journal* frequently announces specific items of assistance and there are spot articles in local publications.

built in the CAR, Comoros, Ethiopia, Ivory Coast, Kenya, Mali, Mauritius, Niger, Senegal, South Africa, Tanzania and Zimbabwe. As much as a further $ 1 million may be spent on such projects annually. Additionally, the League has helped build — and provides ongoing annual financial support for — several dozen Islamic schools from the primary through secondary level in countries as diverse as Benin, the CAR, Cameroon, Ethiopia, Ghana, Ivory Coast, Kenya, Liberia, Mauritius, Sierra Leone, Tanzania and Upper Volta. Amounts range upwards from several $ 1000 annually per school. The League has also financed the construction of 2 hospitals in Niger.

Equally as important as facilities are trained personnel to staff them. The League has established several centers to train Africans in Islamic subjects. For this purpose a center was opened in the early 1970s in Nouakchott, Mauritania to train imams, preachers, reciters of the Qur'an and missionaries. A similar center has been established at King Abdul Aziz University in Jeddah and several dozen scholarships are provided annually to Africans for higher studies. In the period before these centers can begin to graduate enough African specialists, the League plans to provide several hundred teachers, missionaries, preachers and reciters of the Qur'an annually to staff these facilities.

The League translates and prints hundreds of thousands of copies of the Qur'an in local African languages and distributes them throughout Africa along with literature and audio-visual materials on Islam. According to a recent report, the League has established a "Voice of Islam" radio station in Northern Nigeria to beam religious programs to the West African region.

To cultivate a receptive climate for its programs and to further Islamic causes and activities generally, the League contributes several million dollars annually to local Islamic organizations. It also enlists the assistance of the Saudi Arabian and other member governments to encourage political support for its activities on the part of the local governments. Moreover, the League does not appear to shirk from using the resources at its disposal to pressure local governments into adopting measures it favors. These measures have included application of the *Shari'a* as the personal and social law of the Muslim community, equal treatment for Muslim minorities, changes in educational curricula to conform to Islamic principles in Islamic countries and granting time on public coummunications facilities for proselytization and religious programs.

C. Bilateral Assistance

1. Algeria

a. Foundations of Foreign Policy and Foreign Aid

On an emotional and ideological level, Algeria's foreign policy is a product of the nation's "revolutionary experience"; an identification with and a willingness to speak out and even act in support of other national liberation movements and "anti-Colonial" struggles against "Imperialism." As a result, for most of the period since independence in 1962, Algeria has been active in Third World and other international fora as a leading proponent of radical political and economic policies aimed at enhancing the power and status of the developing countries. Many of these policies find expression in the New International Economic Order which is supposed to bring about a more even distribution of the world's wealth, improve the terms of trade for primary producers and speed the transfer of wealth and technology from industrialized to non-industrialized countries. Citing its own experience, Algeria has advocated that other countries follow policies of nationalization of local economic resources and state socialism.

On a practical level, Algeria's foreign policy is founded on hard-headed calculations of national geo-political and economic interests.[1] There are indications that Algeria's revolutionary rhetoric has begun to moderate in recent years in recognition of the country's growing interdependence with the West. Algeria has become increasingly reliant on Western capital, technology and markets to develop its oil and gas potential. The Algerian leadership has also become aware of the substantial domestic political and economic problems which must be faced as a national priority. The election of Benjadid Chadli – who is thought to be more concerned with overcoming Algeria's domestic troubles than with foreign policy issues – after the death of President Houari Boumedienne, may be one indication of this trend.

The 1974 agreement to partition the Spanish Sahara between Mauritania and Algeria's arch-rival for Maghreb primacy, Morocco, may have done more to focus Algerian foreign policy than any issue since independence. Indeed, since 1974, Algeria has become absorbed with the issue of the "Western Sahara". This issue demonstrates the matrix of concerns which

---

1 In our analysis of Algerian foreign policy, we have benefitted greatly from Robert Mortimer's paper, "Trans-Saharan Ties and Tensions: Maghrebi Policy in Sahelian West Africa" (unpublished).

characterize Algerian foreign policy. While Algiers undoubtedly sympathizes with the desire of the inhabitants of that region for independence, its support for Polisario seems also to be motivated by practical concerns; to contain Moroccan expansion and check its growth as a regional political and economic power; to ensure the establishment of a new state sympathetic to Algeria; and to achieve stability and a regional balance of power which will allow Algeria to deal with internal political and economic issues unencumbered by fears of Moroccan or Libyan activities to upset the regional status quo.[2]

Although the Western Sahara issue currently dominates Algerian foreign policy, it is not the only issue which motivates it. Algeria has retained a strong identification with Arab issues. The geographic distribution of Algerian bilateral aid (Table 29) indicates the enduring importance of the Arab bond. Bilateral aid rose to an unprecedented level of $ 263.5 million in 1978, as Algeria joined other members of the Arab League in supporting Syria, Jordan and the P.L.O., as it had supported Egypt, Syria and Jordan after the war against Israel in 1973. Algeria pledged $ 229 million at the Baghdad conference in late 1978.

However, those Arab issues which Algeria has chosen to champion are those which conform to the broad ideological guidelines of its foreign policy. A case in point has been Palestine. Algeria's consistent and vocal support for Palestinian rights appears to stem from its identification with movements of national liberation generally, as well as from an Arab nationalist commitment to aid in the restoration of Arab rights in Palestine.

If Algeria's foreign policy has been broadly international in focus, its objectives have been thoroughly secular in character. Islam is an important facet of identity and belief for the individual Algerian, perhaps even more so now as societies throughout the Middle East grapple for a renewed sense of cultural identification and distinction in the face of steady secularist pressures. However, in the years since independence, Islam seems to have been overshadowed on the national level by Algeria's self-image as revolutionary and anti-colonial. In comparison to its seemingly paramount considerations of national interest and Third World solidarity, Islam does not appear to have had a major impact on the formulation of foreign policy to this point.

---

2 For example, it has been suggested that peace "on Algerian terms" would enable Algeria to exploit the potentially rich iron ore deposits at Tindouf near the extreme Southwestern border with Morocco and Mauritania (*Financial Times*, March 28, 1980).

b. Aid to Sub-Saharan Africa

Unlike the other Arab aid donors, Algeria has been active politically in Africa as far South as what is now Zambia since the late 1950's.[3] After independence, Algeria continued to cultivate ties with Sub-Saharan Africa. Algeria's African policy has reflected the same blend of emotional identification with the Third World's struggle for liberation and greater political and economic power and practical considerations of national interest as Algeria's foreign policy generally. Algiers has frequently provided verbal and material support to African national liberation movements and appears to still retain an instinctive fondness for radical governments. But, Algeria has been most prominent in employing its credentials and prestige as a champion of the Third World and its limited financial resources to cultivate political support among African radicals and other OAU members for policies which carefully further its own national interests. These interests are most seriously engaged in the Western Sahara dispute with Morocco. Accordingly, Algeria's relations with Africa have taken on new meaning and intensity since 1974.

In the past 7 years, Algiers has concentrated much political effort and most of its foreign aid program on Africa to win the support of Trans-Saharan states, stretching from Mauritania to Chad, for Algeria's position of independence for that territory and recognition of the Polisario guerrilla movement as the legitimate government of the Saharan Arab Democratic Republic (SADR). The preoccupation with the Western Sahara has been clearly demonstrated by the pattern of Algeria's bilateral aid to Sub-Saharan Africa and the disbursement of the resources of the Algerian Trust Fund administered by the African Development Bank. Almost 75% of Algeria's bilateral aid to Africa and 88% of the Algerian Trust Fund were directed toward West African countries (see Tables 30 and 18) which could be expected to take a position sympathetic to Algiers on this issue of regional importance.

While the sums involved appear modest, several examples illustrate clearly Algeria's efforts to further its foreign policy objectives in the Western Sahara through its African aid program. Sierra Leone, the second ranking recipient, was granted $ 4 million in program aid in 1979 before it was to host the OAU summit in July 1980 at which Algeria and Libya exerted intense pressure on African delegations to recognize a Polisario government.[4] Mali, ranking third, has been particularly important to Algerian

---

3   Robert A. Mortimer, "The Algerian Revolution in Search of the African Revolution," *The Journal of Modern African Studies,* vol. 8, no. 3, 1970, cited by Mortimer, *op. cit.,* p. 3.
4   *Africa Confidential,* July 2, 1980.

policy.[5] Although it has been reluctant to recognize the SADR formally, Mali has cooperated closely with Algeria in other ways on the issue and its President is a member of the influential OAU Ad Hoc Committee on the Western Sahara. As a result, Mali has apparently been rewarded with considerably more aid than is recorded in Table 30. According to one source, it received $ 12.5 million between 1974—1977 for drought relief, balance of payments support and the purchase of communications equipment.[6] Mali was reportedly offered more aid in return for its continued "cooperation" at the "Sahara Summit" in March 1980.[7] Niger, which has recognized the SADR, ranks fourth as a recipient of Algerian aid. It received a telecommunications station in 1977 and by late 1978 had received Algerian finance for a small irrigation project, a local building program and $ 495,000 in food supports.[8]

While it has rewarded those states which support its policies, Algeria has been quick to freeze economic relations and stop foreign aid to states which obstruct its policy objectives. For example, Gabon, which by virtue of a $ 5 million trade credit for the purchase of Algerian railway cars in 1975 has received more recorded aid from Algeria than any other Sub-Saharan country, was one of only 4 African states to vote with Morocco at the United Nations in December 1979. Gabon has not drawn on its credit since 1976.[9] Senegal, which has consistently supported Morocco since 1974, last received Algerian financial assistance in that year.

c. Islam and Aid to Africa

Although at least 52 % of Algeria's bilateral aid to Sub-Saharan Africa has gone to members of the Islamic Conference (Table 30), this is the geographic coincidence of a policy calculated to win the support of key West African countries, such as Mali, Niger and Upper Volta, for a settlement in the Western Sahara on Algerian terms. As noted earlier, Islam is not a motive force in Algeria's foreign policy. Indeed, in both its aid program and in the development of economic relations, Algeria has exhibited a natural affinity for the more radical or revolutionary states in Africa, including Angola, Benin, Congo, Guinea, Guinea Bissau, Mozambique and the Seychelles — largely governments of non-Muslim states which profess secular, even anti-religious ideologies.[10] In fact, Algeria was apparently the

---

5 Mortimer, *op. cit.*, pp. 3—4.
6 *Marchés Tropicaux*, December 21, 1979.
7 *Mortimer*, op. cit., p. 4.
8 E.I.U., *Niger*, III 1978.
9 Mortimer, *op. cit.*, p. 6.
10 With the exception of Guinea and probably Guinea Bissau, these states all have small or negligible Muslim minorities.

only Arab donor which did not provide assistance to Uganda during the Amin regime. On the contrary, Algeria and Tanzania announced the establishment of a Joint Commission to seek "new areas of cooperation" between the two countries in the summer of 1979, immediately after Tanzanian forces successfully toppled Amin, and despite the fact that Arab countries, such as Libya and Saudi Arabia, and Amin tried to portray Nyerere's motives in terms of religious conflict.[11] Congenial ideological positions and years of cooperation with Tanzania on Third World issues appear to have been more influential in determining Algerian policy in this case than the dubious merits of an exhortation to Islamic solidarity.

d. Economic Relations with Sub-Saharan Africa

In the case of Algeria, analysis of its foreign aid program alone gives an incomplete picture of the extent and importance of economic relations and foreign policy interests in Sub-Saharan Africa. In comparison to other Arab donors, Algeria has had a limited financial surplus to share with others. Its ambitious program of domestic economic development has resulted in sizeable trade deficits financed by massive foreign borrowings. As a result, Algeria's foreign debt had risen to $ 23.4 billion by year end 1979.[12] Servicing that debt has consumed an increasing proportion of total export earnings and reached a level of 25.6 % in 1979.[13] Additionally, its financial support for Polisario undoubtedly has drained resources from other programs.

Consequently, while other Arab donors with less at stake in Africa have contributed far more money, Algeria has had to employ relatively low-cost measures aimed at developing mutual interests with which to bind countries closer to it and build political support for its policies. This effort has emphasized the development of mutually beneficial trade and economic relations. Where Afro-Arab trade exists in any significant amount, Algeria is one of the major Arab trading partners.[14] Following the traditional trade routes across the Sahara into West Africa, Algeria is an important buyer of agricultural exports from Angola, Benin, Cameroon, CAR, Congo, Gabon, Ghana, Guinea, Guinea Bissau, Ivory Coast, Madagascar, Mali, Mauritius, Niger and Zambia; supplying Algerian oil, petrochemicals, fertilizers, textiles and agricultural products in return.[15] To cite

---

11 *Africa Research Bulletin*, vol. 16, no. 7 (July 1979), cited by Kühlein, *op. cit.*, p. 66.
12 World Bank, *World Debt Tables*, Volume II, October 31, 1980, p. 4.
13 *op. cit.*, Volume I, p. xxiii.
14 Table 23 provides comparative data on Afro-Arab trade.
15 Various issues of the Economist Intelligence Unit, *Quarterly Surveys* provide details.

one prominent example, by the end of 1979 bilateral trade with Ivory Coast was expected to reach an annual level of $ 60 million.[16] Algerian exports are often supported by trade credits.

Although it has not been as active in this field as Libya, Algeria has also established joint venture companies in areas where it can employ its technical expertise to help exploit local natural resources or provide necessary services. While not without their problems, joint venture companies in marine transport in Benin, timber in Congo, fishing in Guinea Bissau and road transport in Mali are examples of this type of activity.[17] Furthermore, drawing on its own experience with a nationalized oil industry, Algeria has encouraged other African countries to follow suit and has provided technical assistance to implement such policies in Angola, CAR and Congo.[18] Algeria also has reportedly assisted Gabon with the establishment of a national airline, shipping company and railroad.[19]

In addition to economic relations, Algeria has endeavored to forge closer transport, cultural and military links with Africa, primarily with radical governments. Emphasizing Algier's role as a headquarters for radical and revolutionary movements, Air Algérie rapidly expanded its route network in Sub-Saharan Africa between 1973 and 1975. Simultaneously, Algeria opened its universities to Africans, providing scholarships to students from the Comoros and Seychelles islands, among other countries, whose interests may have been only partially educational.[20] Additionally, through the work of several Joint Commissions established with African countries — for example, Niger — and programs of youth exchange, Algeria has sought to expound its particular philosophy of revolutionary socialism while benefitting the countries in a tangible manner as well. These programs appear to be relatively small if the example of the Seychelles is indicative. Algeria reportedly provided 15 scholarships for Seychellian students and sent a team of 12 advisers to help that new island nation expand its educational program.[21]

Very little is reported publicly about Algeria's political and military support to African guerrilla movements and indigenous political opposition elements. The few items which have appeared suggest that such activity has been limited generally to radical groups and guerrillas opposed to the white minority governments in Southern Africa.[22] Algerian support for Senegalese leftists can be attributed primarily to Senegal's firm support of

---

16 E.I.U., *Ivory Coast*, I 1979.
17 *Marchés Tropicaux*, December 12, 1979; E.I.U., *Guinea Bissau*, IV, 1979.
18 E.I.U., *Angola*, II 1976; *CAR*, III 1974; *Congo*, IV 1976.
19 E.I.U., *Gabon*, IV 1974.
20 E.I.U., *Comoros*, III 1979; *Seychelles*, III 1979; *Algeria*, II 1980.
21 E.I.U., *Niger*, IV 1977.
22 Algeria reportedly helped arm FRELIMO guerrillas in Mozambique as early as 1969.

Morocco in the Western Sahara.[23] Algeria reportedly agreed to provide military training for Seychelles army personnel, in addition to educational assistance and a $ 1.1 million grant in 1979, after President René spoke "forcefully" in several Third World conferences in support of issues championed by Algeria.[24]

On balance, however, the amount of aid for ideological purposes alone to radical regimes which profess to style themselves after the Algerian "model", such as those in Congo and the Seychelles, does not appear to be substantial. While Algeria may still wish to cultivate such governments and finds shared ideological perceptions a useful point of departure, the pattern of aid commitments and economic relations strongly suggests that a country's stand on the Western Sahara — and not its professed radicalism — has been the key determinant of its bilateral financial and economic relations with Algeria.

2. Iraq

The aid program of Iraq has undergone dramatic changes in the past few years. From a very low level in 1977, Iraq suddenly became the third largest source of Arab aid in 1979 (Tables 1 and 31), ahead even of Kuwait. Preliminary information published by the OECD indicates that commitments in 1980 dropped slightly to $ 1,124 million. However, the outbreak of war with Iran in September 1980 brought Iraq's ad program to a precipitous halt. The enormous sums required to prosecute the war and for reconstruction will probably cause Baghdad to defer further foreign assistance for some time to come and may even cause Iraq to renege on its previous aid commitments. However, the past record of that aid program is particularly note-worthy because of the close link between the government's foreign policy objectives and the commitment of the financial resources at its disposal to achieve them.

a. Foundations of Foreign Policy and Foreign Aid

The progress of the Iraqi aid program has followed closely the course of internal political and economic changes which took place as a result of the oil price increases of 1973–1974 and Iraq's enhanced international stature — as it began to project the impact of those domestic developments abroad — beginning in 1978. The outline of these developments can be traced in the sums allocated over the years since 1973. Iraq's foreign aid

---

23 *Africa Confidential*, May 7, 1980.
24 E.I.U., *Algeria*, II 1980 and *Seychelles*, IV 1979.

fell rapidly and steadily from a peak of $ 545 million in 1974 to $ 229 million in 1977, a decline of 58 %, as the country focused on internal development (see Tables 1, 2 and 3). The change was most noticeable in bilateral aid which dropped from $ 472 million to $ 124 million, a decline of 74 % during the same period. However, total aid rose rapidly after 1977 to nearly $ 600 million in 1978 and more than doubled to $ 1.2 billion in 1979, with sudden shifts in the pattern of geographic distribution (see Table 31).[1] Commitments through the second quarter in 1980 were running at almost double the rate of the preceding year before the outbreak of war turned government's attention elsewhere.

Internal and external factors explain these startling changes and reveal the motives behind Iraq's aid program. Domestically, the 1975 Agreement with Iran quickly brought to an end the long-standing and costly Kurdish insurgency against the government. Drawing on its sharply increasing oil revenues, the regime extended a program of industrialization and agricultural improvement to the Kurdish North and the largely Shiite South in an effort to spread the benefits of the new wealth broadly in a manner which would pacify dissident elements and consolidate effective minority control in the hands of the ruling Ba'th party. These developments could come only at the price of gradually opening the country to Western technology and the return of thousands of Iraqi emigrants who had sought refuge in Arab and Western countries during the turmoil of the preceding 17 years.

Abroad, these changes were accompanied by a gradual moderation in the stridency of the regime's revolutionary rhetoric. Incidents of political subversion originating in Baghdad aimed at Saudi Arabia and the Gulf sheikdoms became less frequent as the Ba'thist regime began to sense that Iraq's national interests could be served by improved relations with the conservative Arab states in the Gulf. With Iraq's future prosperity dependent on the continuation of secure delivery of oil supplies to the West and further infusions of Western technology, there was a noticeable disengagement from the traditional reliance on the Soviet Union, spurred by further internal tension with the Iraqi Communist Party. These developments prompted the Gulf states and particularly Saudi Arabia to begin a process of cautious accommodation aimed at seeking a *modus vivendi* with the new Iraqi reality. While remaining suspicious of Baghdad's ulterior motives, the Gulf states could not simply close their eyes to Iraq's growing economic, political and military power. Fear of a separate Egyptian-Israeli peace agreement following President Sadat's historic visit to Jerusalem in November 1977 and the fall of the Shah one year later accelerated this process of rapprochement and brought Iraq back into the center of Arab politics for the first time since 1958.

---

1   OECD, *Development Cooperation, 1980 Review,* pp. 130 & 136.

Events abroad and enhanced political stability at home in 1978 and 1979 combined to turn the attention of Iraq's leadership to new opportunities for Baghdad to play an unaccustomed but ambitious role as a regional and international power. Sparked by the Egyptian-Israeli agreement, Iraq moved first into a prominent position in the familiar arena of Arab politics. President Sadat's revolutionary signature of the Camp David Agreement with Israel provided Iraq with a rare opportunity to reassert its claim to Arab leadership. Opposition to the Sadat initiative forged a rare and — as it proved — temporary unity of purpose among Arab moderates and radicals which Iraq was quick to exploit. In order to line up support at the Arab Summit Conference (which it hosted in Baghdad) condemning the Camp David Agreement in November 1978, the Iraqi government committed hundreds of millions of dollars to the "front line" states and other Arab governments, of which $ 505.5 million was extended to Syria, Iordan and the P.L.O. Bilateral assistance rose to $ 569 million in 1978, 96 % of which was committed to Arab countries (see Table 31). However, these sums were directed not only against Israel but against Iraq's rivals in the Arab world as well. In addition to Egypt, these rivals include primarily Algeria and Libya, which compete with Baghdad for leadership of the Arab radical bloc and have supported the rival Ba'thist party in Syria, and South Yemen whose Marxist government has consistently oppressed local Ba'thists loyal to Iraq.

The fall of the Shah gave Iraq — as the second strongest power in the Gulf — an opportunity to try and assume the Shah's self-appointed role as "policeman" of the Gulf and arbiter of regional politics extending as far as the Indian Ocean.[2] But, it appears to have been the Summit Conference of the Non-Aligned Movement in Havana in July 1979 which first impressed the Iraqi leadership that Baghdad could emerge as an international power as well. The decision of the conference to hold the next meeting in Baghdad in 1982 seemed to confirm that the opportunity was there to be exploited.

Iraq would not have undertaken such initiatives however, were it not for the personality of President Saddam Hussein. By all accounts, a man of considerable hubris and ambition, Hussein assumed the leadership of both the ruling Ba'th party and the government in July 1979 when he took over the Presidency of the state and Chairmanship of the Revolutionary Command Council from Ahmed Hassan al-Bakr. The Summit Conference in Havana that same month may have been his first journey outside the

---

2 For example, Iraq is believed to wish to prevent superpower dominance of the Indian Ocean. Aware of this, President René of the Seychelles Islands has made frequent statements in favor of keeping the area free of superpower influence and bases and was reportedly rewarded by Iraqi promises of aid and technical cooperation.

insular and conspiratorial world of Baghdad and the Soviet bloc and his first opportunity to rub shoulders with prominent leaders of the Third World and be accepted as their equal. For Hussein, this occasion may have been as influential in forming his ideas about the future role he and Iraq could play internationally as the Bandung Conference in 1955 was in shaping Gamal Abdel Nasser's vision of Egypt's future. Within the space of less than 9 months, the Gulf and the Third World suddenly appeared to open as new horizons into which Hussein could project his personal stature and, inseparably, the national power of Iraq in a leading role. Reportedly, he intended to cap this bold enterprise by election as President of the Non-Aligned Movement at the Summit planned for Baghdad.

Iraq's oil riches provided the means. Having been previously the most secretive of the Arab states about its aid program, announcements about the scope and content of aid grants became more frequent. In December 1979, President Hussein suddenly revealed that Iraq had given aid amounting to $ 2,200 million since 1974, including $ 700 million through the Iraqi Fund for External Development (IFED).[3] By October 1980, IFED reportedly had committed $ 1,744 million to a total of 27 developing countries, including 11 in Africa (Table 32).[4] The capital of IFED was quadrupled during the course of 1979 in two tranches to 250 million Dinars (about $ 700 million). Iraq also became the first OPEC member to offer oil officially at subsidized prices. In July, Iraq announced that it would compensate the poorer developing countries importing Iraqi oil under long-term contracts by means of long-term, interest free loans. Perhaps Iraq was responding to criticism from oil importers at the Non-Aligned Summit. But most significant was the potential political importance to Iraq's policy objectives of the countries to which this program applied.[5]

b. Foreign Policy and Aid to Sub-Saharan Africa

Following the Havana Summit, a reallocation of Iraq's foreign aid took place, that was as startling for its suddenness as it was for the sharp change of geographic priorities that brought Africa squarely into the Iraqi aid program for the first time. In an obvious effort to cultivate key leaders of the Third World, Iraq made sizeable loans to many developing countries, a part

---

3 Economist Intelligence Unit, *Iraq*, II 1980.
4 OECD, *op. cit.*, p. 136.
5 Economist Intelligence Unit, *Iraq*, IV 1979. Recipients of assistance under this program included Bangladesh, India, Madagascar, Morocco, Mozambique, Pakistan, the Philippines, Senegal, Somalia, Sri Lanka, Tanzania and Viet Nam. (OECD, *ibid.*, p. 130).

of which went to purchase Iraqi crude oil. Included in this program were Tanzania and Madagascar ($ 30 million each), Mozambique ($ 10 million) and Senegal, as well as two African members of the Arab league, Mauritania and Somalia (see Table 33). Zambia received $ 39 million of "project" aid, primarily for oil purchases and Guinea received a "project" loan for $ 6.5 million. India ($ 104 million), Cuba, Vietnam and other influential Third World countries also benefitted. As a result of this retargeting, $ 116 million, or 9.7 %, of total bilateral aid was directed to Africa in 1979. Other non-Arab countries (see Table 31) received an additional $ 369 million, 31 % of total bilateral aid.[6]

c. Islam and Foreign Aid to Africa

It is particularly noteworthy that, in contrast to the Gulf states and especially to Saudi Arabia, Islam appears not to have played a role in the selection of the African recipients of Iraqi aid. Prior to 1979, Iraq's aid to Africa was extended primarily to 3 member countries of the Islamic Conference – Chad, Guinea and Uganda – but political rather than religious factors can be called to account. In 1979, 94 % ($ 109 million) of the $ 116 million in bilateral aid to Africa went to non-Muslim countries. Indeed, Tanzania was a primary beneficiary because of President Nyerere's stature as a leader in Africa and the Third World, and despite his role in overthrowing Idi Amin.[7]

In addition to the aid provided by the government and the Iraqi Fund for Development, the Ministry of Religious Endowments (Awqaf) has reportedly provided minor amounts to African countries. These sums have included $ 5000 to the Higher Muslim Council in Kenya for the construction of a religious institute, a collection of books for a Muslim school in Ghana and an Islamic institute in Dakar, Senegal.[8]

Whether religion will become more important as a determinant of Iraqi foreign aid in the future than at present is difficult to predict. The Ba'th party's ideology is staunchly secular and this has proved to be a wise

---

6 Indicative of this redirection of priorites and in order to score a political point off Syria – whose Minister of Finance and National Economy was appointed to be its new Chairman – Iraq reportedly withdrew its capital from the Arab Fund for Economic and Social Development in 1978 and transferred it to the rejuvenated Iraqi Fund for External Development.

7 Reports suggest that Iraq specifically rejected Amin's urgent appeal for arms and troops to combat the Tanzanian-led invasion in early 1979. That Iraq may have been reluctant to join with Libya to support Amin after Qaddafi openly sided with Kurdish secessionists against Baghdad only adds another element to Iraqi calculations. (Economist Intelligence Unit, *Iraq*, I 1979)

8 Economist Intelligence Unit, *ibid.*

policy in a society as highly fragmented as Iraq. The impact of religion on future policy is likely to depend on the outcome of the present war with Iran and the extent to which that settlement affects the relative credibility and power of the militant Islamic conservative movement led by Ayatollah Khomeini and the secular Ba'thist regime led by President Saddam Hussein.

3. Kuwait

a. Foundations of Foreign Policy and Foreign Aid

Virtually defenseless, since independence Kuwait has relied for protection on quick and effective international diplomatic and military intervention by Arab and Western governments. To encourage the friendship and interest of governments, the state of Kuwait has followed a policy of enlightened self-interest, distributing almost $ 14 billion in foreign aid since 1973, and at least several billion more in preceding years.

In addition to national security, Kuwait's foreign policy has been motivated strongly by a desire to find a solution to the Palestinian problem and to support those Arab states bearing the burden of direct confrontation with Israel. This concern has been heightened by the presence of one of the largest resident Palestinian communities in the Arab world. Since 1973, the government has also been concerned to offset the anger and frustration of the developing countries over rising oil prices, while seeking to ensure "Third World solidarity" in support of the Arab position on Palestine.

Unlike Saudi Arabia, Kuwait's foreign policy and its aid program do not seem to be motivated to any great degree by concerns of Islamic revival or anti-Communism. This is not, however, to dismiss sentiments of Islamic fraternity or an aversion to Communism on the part of both individuals and the Government. Several factors account for this difference. First, Kuwait is a small nation with largely regional political interests. Geographically and figuratively, it is wedged between Saudi Arabia, Iraq and Iran. Kuwait has rarely been able to influence the policies of its larger neighbors. Rather, it has been deferential to their interests and primarily concerned with the preservation of its own territorial integrity and prosperity. It has also frequently mediated successfully behind the scenes and applied its financial wealth to support the inter-Arab and oil-related policy initiatives of others, though has seldom been an innovator.

Second, Kuwaiti society is fairly flexible and pragmatic, as befits an outward looking merchant state. It has also experienced a tendency toward secularization since the Second World War. Moreover, it is rich and self-indulgent. Finally, with its large Shiite Arab and Persian communities, it is religiously fragmented. In this environment, Islam and Communism are considered more matters of individual belief and internal state security than of foreign policy.

Finally, one cannot separate the role of Kuwait's foreign aid in its foreign policy from the manner in which that aid is extended. Kuwait aspires to become an important financial center. The government has facilitated this development through the creation of a number of institutions with diversified responsibilities for deploying the state's surplus in a productive and remunerative manner. Although most financial assistance is provided by the Ministry of Finance, a significant portion (perhaps as much as $ 3.6 billion) has been extended through institutional channels.

The most prominent of these institutions, and the one dedicated solely to foreign aid, is the Kuwait Fund for Arab Economic Development (KFAED), established in 1961 and for 10 years the only Arab development institution. Though Kuwait's foreign aid program was initiated to serve the state's national interests, an additional objective has been to ensure that a significant portion of that program furthers the economic and social development of recipient countries. This aspect of the foreign aid program is exemplified by the Kuwait Fund. The Fund is highly regarded for the independence of its policies and practices from governmental direction and, equally, for its hard-nosed attention to project analysis, documentation and implementation. Although it provides concessional assistance, the Fund reportedly is a stickler for correct financial practices and full repayment on agreed terms. Since its establishment, the Fund has served as a model for the establishment of other national and international funds throughout the Arab world.

In addition to KFAED, there are two state-owned investment companies, the Kuwait Investment Company (KIC) and the Kuwait Foreign Trading, Contracting and Investment Company (KFTCIC) (80% state-owned) which are responsible for developing and administering opportunities for the investment of state funds in commercially viable projects overseas. The funds committed by these institutions are considered investments of the state's financial surplus which are to provide secure, long-term income, not aid in the manner of the Kuwait Fund.

While the motives of these 3 institutions differ, their operations are all characterized by independence and a businesslike approach which helps, in turn, shape the policy and content of Kuwait's foreign aid program to a greater extent than is the case elsewhere among Arab aid donors.

b. Geographic Distribution of Foreign Aid

Kuwait's foreign policy interests lie predominately in the Arab world. In support of those interests and due to its considerable financial reserves, Kuwait has been the second largest Arab aid donor, committing almost

$ 14 billion between 1973–1980 (see Table 1). Fully three-quarters of all Kuwaiti aid, and 81 % of bilateral aid, has been extended to Arab countries (Tables 8 and 34). Most of this assistance has been provided through the Ministry of Finance. Details of this aid are secret, but the majority of it has probably been given in the form of grants to the "Confrontation" States.[1] In addition to bilateral grants, the government has contributed over $ 1.1 billion to the capital of Arab regional organizations (Table 6). Finally, the Kuwait Fund has provided almost $ 1.6 billion in project assistance to Arab countries. However, since the Fund began lending outside the Arab world in 1974, only 53 % of its loans have been to Arab countries (Table 35).

c. Aid to Sub-Saharan Africa

By comparison, Sub-Saharan Africa has received only 4 % of Kuwaiti bilateral and total assistance since 1973. And, both the relative and absolute amounts of bilateral aid declined steadily from 1976 to 1979, before rising sharply to $ 99 million in 1980 (see Table 34). Contributions to Arab-sponsored African multilateral institutions ceased in 1977 (Table 6), though Kuwaiti aid to African regional institutions has continued at a moderate level since, amounting to $ 146 million. The amounts extended to Sub-Saharan Africa seem modest compared to the $ 878 million provided to Arab League Africa (Table 11) and the $ 613 million given to Sudan alone.[2] Nevertheless, the $ 515 million in bilateral aid through 1980 and the $ 660 million provided overall are substantial sums and rank Kuwait second, behind Saudi Arabia, as a donor of assistance to Sub-Saharan Africa.

Prior to 1973, Kuwait's aid was directed almost exclusively to Arab countries and rarely to non-Arab African nations. Beginning in 1973 and particularly in 1974, Kuwait extended financial assistance to several Sub-Saharan countries. According to the data presented in Table 36, about $ 115 million of program assistance was committed in those two years, largely in the form of central bank deposits and balance of payments support. These payments included disbursements to Chad, Guinea, Equatorial Guinea, Madagascar and Senegal. It seems probable that these transfers were awarded at the time of state visits to Kuwait following the rupture of diplomatic relations with Israel.

---

1 The only official account of Kuwaiti aid is a study published by the Economic Research Department of the Ministry of Finance, "Kuwait Aid to Developing Countries, 1962–1978", March 24, 1979.
2 According to Kuwaiti officials, Sudan has been a particular favorite because of its "Arab" nature, relative poverty and favorable long-term agricultural prospects.

Since the Charter of the Kuwait Fund was amended in 1974 extending its operations to as many as 50 countries in Africa and Asia, the Fund has handled almost all of Kuwait's bilateral aid to Sub-Saharan countries (compare the figures in Tables 35 and 36). This aid has invariably been committed to development projects. As a result, there have been few direct grants or loans from the Kuwait government since 1974, with the exception of small gifts on the occasion of state visits.[3]

d. The Kuwait Fund for Arab Economic Development (KFAED)

As the Kuwait Fund has dominated the state's aid to Africa since 1974 — and monopolized it since 1976 — an analysis of the Fund's operating principles and procedures will, more than anything else, illustrate the motives and objectives of Kuwait's bilateral aid to the Sub-Saharan area.

According to a Fund official, the Fund is responsible for all of Kuwait's aid which is not motivated by political considerations.[4] Others have observed that the Fund's selection of recipients is not influenced by political or religious considerations, or a country's social system.[5] This contention appears to be confirmed by the statistics in Tables 35 and 36. The Fund has assisted radical states such as Angola, Benin, Guinea and Mozambique, as well as Lesotho which maintains diplomatic relations with Israel. Moreover, only about 40 % of the $ 300 million committed to Sub-Saharan Africa since 1976 has gone to members of the Islamic Conference.

Rather than subjective considerations, the Fund reportedly focuses on objective economic and social criteria, particularly a project's economic rate of return, selecting projects on the basis of the extent to which they further a recipient's social and economic development. Accordingly, the Fund has concentrated its resources on infrastructural projects, particularly alternative energy sources, transport and communications which benefit the country generally and create conditions for further indigenous development. According to the Fund, its annual budget of 100 million Kuwaiti Dinars (about $ 370 million) is awarded to the first 20 or 25

---

3 The only prominent recorded example was a grant of $ 2 million to the Comoros Islands approved during the visit of that nation's Prime Minister in 1978 (*MEES,* August 15, 1978).

4 Interview with Dr. Faisal al-Khaled, Deputy General Manager (Operations), (now General Manager) Kuwait Fund, Kuwait, October 15, 1980.

5 See, for example, the excellent description of Arab bilateral and multilateral funds in the survey by John Law, *Arab Aid: Who Gets It, For What and How,* Chase World Information Corp., New York, 1978. See also Aziz Alkazaz, *op. cit., passim; Financial Times,* February 26, 1979; and OECD, *Development Cooperation,* 1978, Paris, 1978, p. 151.

84

projects presented to the Fund with complete documentation. At present, there is no allocation of resources among the 60 countries which qualify for Fund assistance. While this might appear to favor well-organized countries such as Senegal — which has received twice as much Kuwaiti aid and investment as the next African country, Ghana — the Fund provides technical assistance grants to countries without the qualified manpower to prepare and present sensibly conceived projects. During the 1980 fiscal year, Comoros, Gambia, Mozambique, Seychelles and Sierra Leone received grants for this purpose.

In fact, the data in Table 36 suggest that the Fund is careful in practice to spread its resources fairly evenly, apparently selecting a large, important project, and possibly no more than 1 or 2 smaller projects, to finance in each country. It appears to have no hesitation in halting disbursements abruptly should circumstances change or a country misappropriate the resources placed at its disposal. Uganda appears to be a case in point where the Fund, and other Kuwaiti institutions, apparently disbursed only $ 2.5 million of the $ 28 million originally committed, and terminated virtually all financial relations with the Amin government as early as 1975.

In addition to the Kuwait Fund, the General Authority for the Gulf and South Arabia has provided aid to Arab countries since 1953. Attached to the Ministry of Foreign Affairs, the Authority builds educational and medical facilities for the states of the Arabian Gulf and Peninsula. In 1973, its operations were extended to the Southern Sudan in order to aid in the "rehabilitation of refugees".[6] The Authority has so far financed the construction of 2 schools, a dispensary and a residential compound for teachers from Northern Sudan in Juba, at an apparent cost of $ 4.2 million. The Authority's annual budget was raised in 1973 from 7 to 12 million KD (about $ 45 million). It expects to retain its exclusive Arab focus for the foreseeable future.

e. Aid to Islam in Africa

Aid recorded for Islamic or Arab educational purposes has amounted to no more than $ 27,000, provided to schools in Eritrea, Ghana and Kenya. Kuwait ceased contributing to the Islamic Solidarity Fund in 1977 and appears intent on concentrating its support for Muslim countries on projects which promote the general national welfare and development.

---

6   State of Kuwait, General Board for the South and Arabian Gulf, "Services Extended by the State of Kuwait to the South and Arabian Gulf", July 1979, pp. 13–14.

f. Investments in Africa

Like other oil producers, Kuwait has endeavoured to convert its surplus oil revenues into an internationally diversified portfolio of financial assets to provide long-term financial security against the day when oil reserves run dry. However, unlike other donor countries with the exception of Libya, Kuwait has tried to apply this policy in Africa as well. Of the $ 1,260 million in bilateral aid provided to Africa as a whole from 1973 through 1979, almost half ($ 614 million) was extended in the form of non-concessional assistance, divided equally between central bank deposits and the purchase of government debt instruments, on the one hand, and joint venture equity investments, on the other. However, the vast majority of this assistance — over $ 506 million — was provided to the Sudan ($ 414 million) and Mauritania ($ 92 million), where more than $ 209 million has been invested in agricultural and mineral projects. By comparison, only $ 88 million of non-concessional aid has been extended to all other Sub-Saharan countries. Of this amount, only $ 23.5 million has been in the form of equity investment, of which 95 % ($ 22.2 million) was concentrated in Senegal and Uganda. Non-concessional aid ceased in 1976, with the minor exception of further capital subscriptions in ongoing projects in Senegal and Mauritania in 1979.

The record of Kuwaiti investment in Africa has not been successful. The reasons are instructive and suggest that significant future investment is unlikely. In retrospect, the principal reason for disappointment with the results of Kuwait's African investments may be that unjustifiably high expectations attended the initiation of those investments. Investors in Africa must generally accept higher risk, frequently a longer pay-back period, and a far more difficult operating environment than is common in many other areas. For essentially conservative, risk averse investors such as the Kuwaitis, the differences of language and culture, shifts of political direction and comparable but culturally alien business practices in Africa have undoubtedly compounded the problems encountered and increased the level of frustration over unsatisfactory results.

Even if such results were acceptable by African standards, they may not have seemed so in comparison with the relatively easy and spectacular earnings from trade and real estate investment in the Middle East during the past seven years or the secure but lower returns offered by investment in the more mature economies of Europe and the United States. Consequently, the initial enthusiasm for African investment, which led a company such as KFTCIC and its affiliate, the Afro-Arab Company for Investment and International Trade (AFARCO) into the Sudan, Mauritania, Senegal, Uganda, Cameroon and Gabon, was largely dissipated by 1976, replaced by a reduced emphasis on trade and on the management of existing joint venture investments. This enthusiasm seems unlikely to revive, with the possible exception of mineral exploitation in trilateral partnership with experienced foreign mining companies.

4. Libya

Of all the Arab donors, Libya is the most actively involved politically and economically in Sub-Saharan Africa, especially in the belt of states along the rim of the Sahara with dominant or large Muslim communities. In terms of aid alone, Libya has contributed at least $ 500 million through bilateral and multilateral channels since 1973 (see Tables 6 and 37) and, possibly, substantially more as the sensitive nature of much of Libya's assistance may mean that a considerable amount has gone unreported. The sums that have been recorded rank Libya second to Saudi Arabia as a donor of aid to Africa. Indeed, Africa is relatively a far more important region for Libya — 15 % of all bilateral assistance and 14 % of all aid — than for any other Arab donor. By comparison, Arab countries received 44 % of Libya's bilateral aid and 38 % of total assistance, but only because of an unusually generous $ 503 million pledged at the Baghdad summit to Syria, Jordan and Palestine in 1978 (see Table 37).

a. Foundations of Foreign Policy and Foreign Aid

Libya's extensive African involvement arises from a diverse set of political, economic, territorial, and religious interests which are both more complex and more numerous than the apparent interests of other Arab donor states in the region. Even more diverse is Libya's program to attain its ends; a program of economic, financial, commercial, political, religious, educational and military asssistance which rivals European aid programs in complexity, but has no peer in the Arab world. With ample financial resources and limited domestic requirements, Libya has had considerable reserves on which to draw. The result has been an active, multifaceted foreign aid program in the service of a foreign policy renowned for its opportunism, subject to intense suspicion about its ultimate motives, and often feared for its occasionally aggressive and provocative intervention in a recipient country's domestic affairs.

With such diversity in its interests and in its aid program, it is not surprising that the government is often inconsistent in pursuit of its objectives. This has pointedly been the case with the use of Islam as an end and a means of Libyan foreign policy. As one example, Libya first backed the Eritrean Liberation Front (ELF), which stresses the Arab and Islamic roots of the Eritrean population, against the Marxist Ethiopian central government. Tripoli switched sides in 1977 when Libya's conservative Arab rivals increased their commitment to the ELF.[1] Two years later, in Uganda Libya sought to exploit Islamic solidarity when Qaddafi called on Arab nations to support Idi Amin in order "to save Islam" and accused Tanzania of mounting a "crusade" against Ugandan Muslims.[2] A further example is Libya's long-standing intervention in the civil war in Chad. At one time or another, Libya has supported each faction in the war, Muslim, Christian and animist to the point that aside from pure "Realpolitik" and, perhaps, territorial aggrandizement, no other permanent motive of Libyan foreign policy can be identified. The inconsistency of Libyan foreign policy makes bilateral relations highly sensitive to political shifts which are then quickly reflected in the pattern of foreign aid.

Libya's foreign policy can only be properly understood in the context of the personality of its leader, Colonel Mu'ammar al-Qaddafi. Reportedly, Qaddafi considers himself to be the ideological successor of Gamal Abd al-Nasir and has adopted Nasir's "three circle theory" as the geographic perimeter of his own revolutionary, Islamic, socialist ideology.[3] According to his analysis, the Arab, Islamic and African worlds share an identity of interests which can be summarized as political, economic and cultural independence from the West. To achieve this independence and obtain the maximum degree of political and economic power possible, Third World countries should forge a union of purpose and action and assert control over their own economic resources through the establishment of a New International Economic Order. For Muslims, this transformation can only take place with a revival of Islamic belief and practice, coupled with a cultural revolution that reinvigorates Islam as a "progressive" and "socialistic" force. The importance of Africa in this scheme was made explicit by a joint statement of intention, issued by Qaddafi and President Houari Boumedienne of Algeria in 1973, to improve relations with Sub-Saharan Africa "in order to accelerate the political, economic and social liberation of the African continent."[4]

---

1 *Revue Française d'Etudes Politiques Africaines,* No. 146, February 1978 and No. 163, July-August 1979.

2 *Marchés Tropicaux,* June 26, 1979 and Kühlein, *op. cit.,* p. 62 quoting the *Deutsche Monitor Dienst* für Afrika, March 27, 1979.

3 For an understanding of Libyan foreign policy, the following sources have proven helpful: Ahmad Yousef Ahmad, "Arab-Afro Relations and Their Implications for the Red Sea Region", 1980 (unpublished); Conrad Kühlein and Oswald Baumgarten, *Die Afro-Arabischen Beziehungen – Zusammenarbeit und Probleme,* Stiftung Wissenschaft und Politik, Ebenhausen, 1980, especially pp. 60–65; Robert A. Mortimer, "Trans-Saharan Ties and Tensions: Maghrebi Policy in Sahelian West Africa", (unpublished paper presented to the US State Department Conference on African-Arab Relations, May 2–3, 1980); and Philippe Rondot, "Libyen unter Oberst Khadafi, ein Experiment mit ungewissem Ausgang", *Europa Archiv,* Vol. 34, No. 13, July 10, 1979, pp. 401–410.

4 *Africa Confidential,* March 2, 1973, p. 6.

In order to attain these fundamental objectives, the government seeks to project Libya as an "Arab", "Islamic", "Trans-Saharan", regional and international power. The purpose of such a policy is to enable Libya to obtain the maximum degree of power and influence possible, where possible, in order to shape the policies of "friendly" states in a manner conforming to Libyan policy objectives.

b. The Role of Islam in Foreign Policy

While Libya has reportedly pursued its foreign policy goals around the world, the best opportunities for success appear to be states nearer to home which share common interests and bonds of "Arab", "Islamic" and "African" identity. Accordingly, Libya has focused much of its activity and financial resources on African states with strong Arab and/or Islamic characteristics, particularly those West African states with dominant or important Muslim communities, stretching from Senegal along the Sahel to Chad and as far East as Somalia. Indeed, there are indications that some Central African leaders, including Bokassa of the CAR, Bongo of Gabon and Ahidjo of Cameroon may have accepted Qaddafi's views on Islam, perceiving it as indigenous to the Third World and Africa; both a sign of independence from the West and a mark of new solidarity with the Arab states.[5] This view was particularly evident in the period immediately after the Arab-Israeli war in 1973–1974. Without these shared affinities, non-Muslim central and southern Africa countries have been more difficult for Libya to penetrate, although Libya has employed its oil wealth to advantage in Zaire, Uganda and Gabon where Islam and other factors offered opportunity.

For Libya, as for Saudi Arabia, Islam is one of the most effective and important means by which to achieve its foreign policy objectives. Where the role of Islam in Libyan foreign policy differs from Saudi Arabia, however, is that the equation of Islamic revival and anti-Communism, which motivates Saudi policy, does not appear to influence Libya. Instead, the fraternal bond of Islam appears to be a crucial element in the government's efforts to establish bilateral relations. But this bond is then expanded through a far broader variety of economic, financial, commercial and even military measures than is the case with any other Arab donor.

5 *Revue Française d'Etudes Politiques Africaines*, No. 140–141, August-September 1977.

c. Aid to Islam in Africa

To further Islam and the development of Muslim communities as it simultaneously seeks its secular political and economic ends, Libya has developed a diverse program of multilateral and bilateral assistance. Libya has been a prominent supporter of multilateral Islamic institutions. It is the second largest shareholder in the Islamic Development Bank (see Table 14) and, until 1977–1978, was the second largest contributor to the Islamic Solidarity Fund (see Table 27), having subscribed about $ 175 million to the capital of both institutions since 1973. Perhaps related to its decision to cease supporting the Fund, Libya joined with the UAE in late 1977 to collaborate in financing the establishment of 8 Islamic cultural centers in Africa and Asia.[7] Libya reportedly doubled its contribution to the Joint Commission to $ 12 million in February 1979.[8]

It is difficult to draw statistical conclusions regarding Libyan aid for Islam in Africa as the data available are partial and unconfirmed. Many of Libya's commitments may go unreported altogether. Nevertheless, the amount spent annually for purely Islamic purposes does not appear to be large. On the one hand, it is certainly more than the $ 1.2 million recorded in Table 38 – since the OECD has chosen to disregard Islamic aid for other than purely educational purposes – as the $ 12 million capital committed to the Joint Commission for the Establishment of Islamic Cultural Centers suggests. On the other hand, it seems unlikely to have amounted to more than several million dollars annually and is surely modest in comparison to Libya's joint venture investments in Africa totalling over $ 140 million (see Table 38). Much of the aid appears to have been provided to build and equip Islamic cultural centers (Gambia and Togo), Arab and/or Islamic schools and institutes (Mali, Gambia, Guinea, Niger and Upper Volta) and mosques (Benin, CAR and Niger), and to provide several hundred Islamic missionaries and teachers of Islam and the Arabic language (Gambia, Niger, Togo and Uganda).[9] Additionally, Libya provides scholarships to as many as 800 African students, which may be primarily for secular education at Libyan institutes and universities in Benghazi and Tripoli.[10]

It is not, however, the amount of Islamic aid extended by Libya, but the manner in which Libya's religious assistance is linked to the development of economic relations, the provision of secular financial support and the

---

7 For a description of the Commission's program, see p. 214 below. This agreement was reported by the Economist Intelligence Unit, *Libya,* I 1977.

8 *op. cit.,* I 1979.

9 See, for example, *Revue Française d'Etudes Politiques Africaines,* No. 160, April 1979, *Marchés Tropicaux,* June 29, 1979, and February 29, 1980, and various issues of the Economist Intelligence Unit, *Quarterly Survey* of East and West African countries.

10 Rondot, *loc. cit.*

attainment of often aggressive political goals that is the most distinctive and controversial feature of the Libyan aid program in Africa. While incomplete, enough information is available to suggest a pattern by which offers of assistance in various economic fields have frequently been joined with requests to be permitted to undertake religious programs which are of interest to the Libyan government. These programs have included support for the foundation of Islamic cultural and religious institutions, the establishment of "Voice of Islam" radio stations and missionary activities.[11] The terms under which these programs are put into effect are usually agreed as part of a framework of cooperation contained in economic and cultural agreements negotiated between the two parties. While not always negotiated simultaneously, such agreements have been signed with largely Muslim countries, including Gambia, Niger and Mali, and countries with Muslim minorities, such as Burundi, the CAR, Gabon, Liberia, Togo and Uganda.[12]

Several examples illustrate this pattern. The case of Libyan-Burundi relations is among the best documented.[13] Libya and Burundi first discussed bilateral economic relations in 1973. An economic and technical cooperation agreement was signed in April 1974. In January 1975, the Burundi-Libyan Joint Commission first met and agreed to establish a joint holding company which would carry out several agricultural, industrial and mineral projects. At this meeting, participants held the first discussion of a Libyan proposal to finance an Arabic language program on Radio Burundi, establish a department of Arabic and Islamic Studies at Bujumbura University and provide scholarships for students from Burundi at Libyan institutes and universities. In the Spring of 1977, the two countries reportedly agreed that Libya would provide Burundi with a 100 kw radio transmitter. In return, the new radio would broadcast daily a one-hour program of Arab music and readings from the Qur'an. Libya also agreed to provide 15 scholarships annually at Libyan universities, to build an Islamic primary school in the capital and to supply Islamic and other texts to the university. During this period, Burundi received $ 3.4 million from Libya for projects and joint venture investments though nothing has reportedly been committed since 1973. Disbursements apparently ceased in 1975.

---

11 It has also been suggested that Libya has offered African leaders considerable financial incentives to convert to Islam, but evidence is circumstantial.

12 See, for example, *Marchés Tropicaux*, February 29, 1980, and *Revue Française d'Etudes Politiques Africaines*, No. 149, May 1978.

13 The information in this paragraph was pieced together from several issues of the E.I.U. *Quarterly Surveys* covering Burundi and Libya. Assistance extended under the auspices of such programs is rarely recorded by the OECD and is often not included in Tables 38.

A second example was the agreement between Libya and Togo to establish diplomatic relations and a joint venture bank when President Eyadema visited Tripoli in October 1973.[14] Within months, they had signed a cultural agreement by which Libya agreed to finance the increased teaching of Arabic and Islamic studies, and to provide 8 professors and 20 university scholarships, as well as an oil refinery and several factories. In 1977, it was announced that Libya would build an Islamic cultural center complete with mosque, school, clinic, cinema and other facilities. In late 1979, Ramadan was declared a public holiday. Libya apparently provided Togo with $ 2.8 million of aid through 1976, of which $ 1.2 million was for Islamic purposes (see Table 38).

As a final example, Mali signed an economic and cultural agreement with Libya in November 1973.[15] As part of this pact, Libya agreed to finance the establishment of an Arab-Islamic school and an Islamic cultural center. The two countries have since set up a joint venture bank and meat export company. Since then relations have flourished and Libya has committed a total of $ 9.6 million since 1973 to a variety of projects in Mali.

Despite these examples, it is not possible to determine to what extent a host country's permission for religious activities has been a *sine qua non* of Libyan economic or financial assistance; for religion is only one among several motives of Libyan foreign policy. It does, however, seem safe to conclude that Libya has considered such permission as at least one significant determinant of the closeness of bilateral relations and has pressed for permission where possible. Furthermore, it may be that the failure to develop closer economic or financial relations with countries such as Liberia or Burundi after the first experiences of the 1973–1975 period can be attributed in part to the reluctance of these governments to accede to Libya's entreaties. In Liberia, both Libya and Saudi Arabia reportedly offered the prospect of enhanced commercial and financial relations in return for the chance to foster indigenous Islamic institutions.[16] Liberia apparently refused. Libya has not extended any assistance since 1974, although Saudi Arabia committed $ 20.7 million in 1978.

This conclusion is strengthened by the sharply negative reaction of several African governments, particularly those of the CAR, Niger, Senegal and Uganda after the fall of Idi Amin, to Libyan efforts to use Islam for political purposes and as a means to interfere in their domestic affairs, as well as the recent firm denunciation by the OAU of Libya's involvement in the final coup d'état in Chad.[17] The President of Niger publicly voiced his

---

14 E.I.U., *Togo,* IV 1973; I 1974, II 1977; I 1979.
15 E.I.U., *Mali,* IV 1973.
16 E.I.U., *Liberia,* III 1974.
17 See, for example, the E.I.U., *Uganda,* I and II 1979, *Le Monde,* June 26, 1980 and Rondot, *op. cit.* The Governor of the Central Bank of Rwanda resigned in

concern as early as 1974 after internal political disturbances. While maintaining a wide variety of economic relations with Libya, he stated that Niger would "reorganize" and "restructure" Islam "without being dependent on the Arab states".[18]

Libya's use of religion to foment domestic opposition to a government it considers hostile to its interests can be observed in the case of Senegal. The *Hizb Allah* (Party of God), founded by Sheikh al Hajj Ahmad Khalifa Niassé, has been particularly attractive to Libya as a tool of its foreign policy for several specific reasons.[19] First, it openly advocates policies which are congenial to Libya including introduction of the *Shari'a* and a reduction of French influence in Senegal. Second, and most important, it had threatened to undo the close political alliance between former President Leopold Senghor and the rural Muslim religious brotherhoods which contributed significantly to Senghor's power and the stability of Senegalese politics since independence. It was expected that the dissolution of this alliance could bring down Senghor, a leader who personally exemplified many of the moderate policies which Libya has been trying to excoriate in Africa. Not only was Senghor a moderate on South Africa and a strong supporter of a continued French presence in Africa, but he also backed Mauritania and Morocco in the Western Sahara war with the Polisario guerrillas. As a moderate, he received considerable financial assistance from Libyan rivals in the Arab world, Saudi Arabia and Morocco. Finally, he successfully blocked previous Libyan efforts to exploit Islam for political purposes in Senegal and denied Libya permission to open an Islamic cultural center in Dakar in 1979. As these factors accumulated, relations between the two countries reached such a state in June 1980 that Senegal severed diplomatic relations, charging Libya with trying to establish by force a radical Islamic Republic incorporating Mauritania, Niger, Chad, Mali and Senegal under Libyan control.[20]

d. Secular Foreign Policy Interests

Despite the importance of Islam in shaping the ideological context of Libyan foreign policy and serving as a fundamental means of that policy, Islam remains only one of Libya's foreign policy objectives. On occasion,

---

1978 after charging undue "Libyan influence in the economy". E.I.U., *Rwanda*, II 1978.

18 *Revue Française d'Etudes Politiques Africaines*, No. 149, May 1978.

19 According to reports in *Africa Confidential*, May 7, 1980 and E.I.U., *Senegal*, II and III 1979, the party has received Saudi, Iranian and Libyan financial support.

20 *Africa Confidential*, June 18, 1980. Simultaneously, a government official in Chad accused Qaddafi of trying to turn that country into an "Islamic-Arab" state. *Le Monde*, June 26, 1980.

it has been clearly subordinate to political considerations. This was demonstrated in 1979, for example, when Libya switched its support in Chad from its Muslim proteges in Frolinat to the Christian-dominated government of Colonel Abdul Qadir Kamougue after France withdrew its support for the government of General Felix Malloum.[21] Although frequently interwoven closely with Islamic objectives and furthered occasionally through Islamic measures, Libya's secular foreign policy interests require separate analysis. Largely political and economic in nature, these interests have been pursued no less vigorously or directly through Libya's foreign aid program.

Politically, Libya's foremost goal in Africa has been to eliminate Israeli influence wherever present and win African support for the Arab position on Palestine. Shortly after the Revolution which brought Colonel Qaddafi and his colleagues to power in 1969, Qaddafi began making personal overtures to African leaders to induce them to break diplomatic relations and other forms of cooperation with Israel. Reportedly, his promises of financial assistance amounting to $98 million and $2.4 million for "drought relief" were instrumental in the decision of Chad and Niger, respectively, to break with Israel in late 1972 and early 1973.[22] Equally, President Mobutu's meeting with Qaddafi following the Algiers Summit of the Non-Aligned Movement in late September 1973 resulted in an agreement to establish diplomatic relations and transport links, as well as the promised dispatch of a Libyan delegation to review prospects for financial and economic cooperation. These promises of aid and new diplomatic and economic links may have contributed to Zaire's dramatic announcement to sever close ties with Israel on the eve of the October 1973 war. Certainly, the cases of Mobutu and Amin suggest that Libya has been willing to reward handsomely prominent African leaders for outspoken support of the Arab position on the Middle East conflict. As indicated by the data in Table 38, Zaire and Uganda have been the two largest beneficiaries of Libyan aid, receiving $101 and $78 million, respectively, during that period, and since 1973, 47% of total Libyan bilateral aid to Sub-Saharan Africa. By 1974—1975, Libya's goal of substantially reducing if not eliminating the Israeli presence in Africa has been largely achieved. Thus, Qaddafi turned to other objectives.

Primary among these has been the twin goals of reducing the post-colonial, Western political and economic presence in Africa, while enhancing African control over the continent's substantial natural resources. Economically and politically, Libya's policy has not met with success. Unable to offer technical assistance, Libya's ability to influence African mineral producers

---

21 *Marchés Tropicaux*, June 29, 1979 and *Revue Française d'Etudes Politiques Africaines*, No. 163—164, Juli-August, 1979.
22 *Africa Confidential*, January 5, 1973, p. 8.

has been limited primarily to providing an alternative source of capital. In the case of the $ 101.3 million long-term loan to finance cobalt and copper production in Zaire, Libya was successful in joining the World Bank and the European Investment Bank as a co-financier. But whether it has thereby achieved a significant degree of ownership or leverage over the disposal of these reserves is doubtful. In Gabon and Niger, Qaddafi's repeated attempts to buy into the rich uranium reserves on which France relies to reduce its dependence on imported petroleum were reportedly rebuffed.[23] After the reported sale of 500 tons of uranium from Niger to Libya in 1980 new sales were halted, undoubtedly with strong French pressure to do so.[24] The sale of Niger uranium to Libya has had a severe negative impact on Franco-Libyan relations. The French blocked further arms sales and refused to allow Libya to participate in the equity and financing of Niger's third uranium mine being developed with French finance and management.[25]

Libya's concentration on Africa's mineral wealth has not been entirely disinterested. Rather, it has involved both apparent imperial territorial ambitions of its own in mineral (and uranium) rich northern Chad and Niger and determined efforts to buy into reserves of strategic minerals — including cobalt, copper, bauxite, alternative energy sources, and particularly uranium — for its own account in Guinea, CAR, Mauritania, Rwanda, Upper Volta, Chad, Niger, Gabon and Zaire.[26] African governments have so far been reluctant to replace established mining companies in order to rely on a technically inexperienced, unpredictable Libyan partner. As long as these and other mineral developments in Africa remain dependent on Western technicians and Western marketing organizations, principally the large mining companies, it is unlikely that Libya will be able to replace Western control successfully.

In addition to its interests in African mineral resources, Libya initiated a program as early as 1972 to forge close economic relations with African countries in many fields. The goal of this program was as ambitious as it was imaginative and stood in sharp contrast to the desultory efforts of several Arab-African joint venture banks and finance companies located in Cairo and Kuwait to develop Afro-Arab trade and investment following the 1973 Arab-Israeli war. A prominent feature of this program was Libyan participation in the ownership and management of companies en-

---

23 *Washington Post*, October 12, 1979.
24 *Africa Research Bulletin* (vol. 18, No. 1), January 15 – February 14, 1981, pp. 57 & 99.
25 E.I.U., *Niger*, II 1980.
26 See *Africa Confidential*, June 18, 1980, *Marchés Tropicaux*, September 21, 1979 and E.I.U., *Rwanda*, I 1980. For Libyan territorial claims in Chad, see *Marchés Tropicaux*, June 29, 1979 and *Revue Française d'Etudes Politiques Africaines*, No. 146 July-August 1979.

gaged in trade and development throughout Africa. Beginning as early as 1972, Libya claims to have established no less than 50 joint venture companies, including 8 banks and holding companies, active in the following sectors: agriculture, livestock, fishing, forestry, minerals, industry, tourism, transport and commerce.[27] These companies have been established in Benin, Burundi, CAR, Chad, Gabon, Gambia, Mali, Niger, Sierra Leone, Togo, Uganda and Upper Volta, usually as part of broad ranging economic, financial and commercial agreements. Libyan ownership has usually been more than 51% so that effective management control has rested with the Libyan government; although the capital of each company has rarely exceeded several million dollars.[28] The stated objective of these companies is, in the words of the Charter of the government-owned Libyan Arab Foreign Bank (LAFB), "to encourage the development of the region as a whole and neighboring and friendly countries in particular".[29]

Whether or not these companies have been successful is hard to judge. The banks, for example, were to participate in the financing of local enterprises, but mostly they seem to have been limited to trade finance. Nevertheless, as one example, the Libyan Arab Foreign Bank (LAFB), with affiliates established or planned in as many as 8 African countries, reported a dividend of $ 1 million from its Uganda affiliate in 1978 alone.[30]

As a result of its broadly diversified business activities, an astonishing 69% of all Libyan bilateral aid to Sub-Saharan African since 1973 ($ 265 million) has been provided on a non-concessional basis, primarily in the form of equity investments in joint venture projects ($ 109 million) and long-term loans through the LAFB ($ 114 million) on a commercial basis. The $ 101.3 million 15-year loan to a cobalt and copper mining project in Zaire in 1975 provided the bulk of the latter amount.[31]

However, Libya has also provided $ 116 million of concessional bilateral financial assistance to Africa since 1973. Additionally, it has been the

---

27 Announcements concerning the establishment of these companies are scattered throughout issues of the appropriate E.I.U. *Quarterly Surveys* and *Middle East Economic Digest*.

28 In the fall of 1978, Libya reportedly invested $ 27.5 million to purchase 55% of the equity of 3 joint venture companies in Uganda to be active in cement production, transport and livestock development. The Ugandan government was to hold a 45% share. This may have been Libya's largest joint venture investment in Africa to date. Whether it was more than a propaganda gesture remains to be seen. E.I.U., *Uganda* III 1978.

29 Libyan Arab Foreign Bank, *Annual Report*, 1978.

30 Libyan Arab Foreign Bank, *Annual Report*, 1978. See also *Marchés Tropicaux*, September 21, 1979. At one time or another, LAFB had or proposed joint ventures in Chad, CAR, Niger, Togo, Uganda, Mali, Rwanda and Upper Volta. The Uganda bank, established in 1972, apparently paid a dividend each year since 1974.

31 E.I.U., *Zaire*, I 1976.

96

second largest subscriber to the capital of the African Development Bank and the Arab Bank for Economic Development in Africa (ABEDA), with $ 100 million contributed to the latter. Finally, Libya may on occasion have made oil available at concessional prices to Sierra Leone and to refineries in Cameroon and Togo.[32]

Collaterally with its diverse economic activities, Libya has acted on a political level to try and reduce Western influence and power in Africa wherever possible. The focus of Libyan policy has been the elimination of foreign military bases, the weakening of support for the West by undermining moderate African governments opposed to Libyan policies, opposition to the white minority regimes in southern Africa and support for both African liberation movements and radical, anti-Western states. These policies have brought Libya into direct confrontation with France and its allies throughout much of Western Africa. Perhaps frustrated by his lack of success, Qaddafi has lashed out angrily accusing France of attempting to stem the expansion of Islam and Islamic influence in Sub-Saharan Africa.[33] It has also brought Libya into direct rivalry with Arab conservatives, particularly Saudi Arabia.

Reports of Libyan political initiatives are sketchy and details are rare, with the possible exception of Chad. However, although substantiating statistical evidence is unavailable, an affinity for political interference seems well established. Libya has used its resources to support internal opposition to moderate African governments it considers aligned with the West or with its rivals for Arab and Islamic leadership, such as Saudi Arabia, or otherwise opposed to its policies. Of significance for what it reveals about Libya's style of foreign policy, Tripoli has often, but not always, supported groups which express their opposition to a government in religious terms. Examples of this policy include several of the factions in the Chad civil war the previously mentioned *Hizb Allah* in Senegal, even though such opposition has been fundamentally political. Libyan financial support for a 1976 coup attempt by leftists against Sudanese President Numeiri is an example of Libyan involvement with a non-religious opposition group.[34] As another example, President Bokassa was in Tripoli reportedly negotiating to turn over to Libya French military bases in the CAR at Ndélé near Chad and Bonar near Cameroon in return for expanded Libyan financial assistance, when he was overthrown by a French-inspired coup d'état.[35] Such bases could have been useful to Libya but more probably to the

32 E.I.U., *Cameroon*, I 1976; *Sierra Leone*, II 1976; and *Togo*, I 1978.
33 See the article by Rondot; *Africa Confidential*, June 18, 1980; *Marchés Tropicaux*, September 21, 1979; and various articles in the *Revue Française d'Etudes Politiques Africaines* on the Franco-Libyan conflict in Africa.
34 *International Herald Tribune*, June 26, 1981.
35 *Washington Post*, October 12, 1979.

Soviet Union and would have represented a tremendous practical and psychological hurdle into former French West Africa.

Libya has taken direct action against South Africa, for example closing Libyan air space to South African overflights in 1973 and has provided military assistance to guerrillas opposing white minority regimes in southern Africa. Libya reportedly offered military arms and supplies to the ZAPU forces of Joshua Nkomo of Rhodesia. Libya has also reportedly provided economic assistance to states, such as Madagascar and Mauritius, which seek to formulate an independent foreign policy or reduce their economic dependence on South Africa.[36]

Libya has also supported liberation movements and radical governments where it suited Libyan foreign policy objectives. In addition to unconfirmed reports of military supplies to guerrillas in Guinea Bissau and Mozambique fighting the Portuguese in 1973, Libya has been the largest supporter of Guinea among the Arab donor states (see Table 38) and has reportedly cultivated close economic ties with Benin.[37] It has also been prominent as the principal Arab backer (in addition to South Yemen) of the Ethiopian government fighting the Eritrean guerrillas, although details of Libyan financial and military support are few.[38] If military training and logistical support prove insufficient, Libya has also demonstrated its readiness to intervene directly with Libyan forces as was the case in Chad and Uganda.[39]

While not denying the economic and financial benefits which have accrued to a number of states through Libya's foreign aid program, on balance the net effect has probably been negative for Libya's relations with Sub-Saharan Africa as a whole. Awareness of the close relationship between religion, politics and foreign aid has made most African states suspicious of Libya's intentions. Direct intervention in the domestic affairs of Chad and Uganda and support for opposition elements elsewhere has won Libya the enmity of many ruling governments. Some, such as Senegal, have broken off relations altogether. Other governments, such as those in Mali and Niger, are only too aware of the degree to which religion has exacerbated sensitive national cleavages in other countries such as Eritrea and the southern Sudan or caused the complete breakdown of all authority and public order, as in Chad and Uganda. Consequently, most Sub-Saharan governments have been careful to balance Libyan overtures with financial and political support from other Arab and non-Arab donors in order to

---

36 E.I.U., *Madagascar*, II 1974, *Mauritius*, III 1977 and *Rhodesia*, II 1979.

37 *Africa Confidential*, March 2, 1973, p. 6.

38 Ahmad Yousef Ahmad, *op. cit.*, pp. 118—119.

39 See Rondot, *op. cit.*; E.I.U., *Uganda*, II and III 1979 and *Chad*, III, 1979 and II 1980; and *Marchés Tropicaux*, June 29, 1979.

avoid becoming dependent on Libya and being drawn too tightly into Tripoli's orbit.[40]

Historically, African states have been most reluctant to act as a group against other members of the OAU, preferring to leave direct action to the discretion of individual countries. Although direct Libyan participation in the final military victory of the Chad civil war and Qaddafi's announced merger of the two countries brought a sharp condemnation, led by Nigeria, of Libya's intervention by the OAU and a call for Libya's ouster from the organization, this effort was ultimately unsuccessful und there was no formal collective OAU resolution. Libya's actions have undoubtedly sharpened the resistance of Sub-Saharan Africa nations to Libyan penetration, as indicated by the fact that 14 of the 50 OAU members have broken off diplomatic relations with Tripoli. However, despite considerable opposition to Libyan policies, African leaders who gathered for the OAU Summit in Nairobi in June 1981 decided not to upset the normal system of rotation under which Colonel Qaddafi will become Chairman of the OAU next year and host of the Summit Conference in 1982.[41] Furthermore, the final resolutions of the conference contained no condemnation of Libyan military intervention in Chad and no demand for an immediate withdrawal of Libyan forces.

5. Qatar

a. Foreign Policy and Foreign Aid

Qatar is the smallest independent state in the Gulf, with a native population of perhaps 100,000. Its inhabitants are followers of the conservative Hanbali school of Sunni Islamic law. In this and other matters it is closely identified with Saudi Arabia. Qatar's foreign policy focuses on Arab issues to the exclusion of virtually all else. It has no direct African interests.

In financial matters it is the most secretive of the Gulf States and publishes few official statistics. Because it has no bilateral fund, all foreign aid is handled by the Ruler and the Ministry of Finance. Without professional staff to analyze and follow up requests for aid, Qatar confines its assistance largely to cash grants and occasional loans, often co-financed, to a limited number of countries. As a result, its aid is disbursed quickly (see

---

40 Mortimer, *op. cit.*, p. 9. See also the interview with a leader of the reputed Mali Liberation Movement supported by Libya and Iraq as quoted in *Jeune Afrique*, vol. 19, No. 975 (August 12, 1979), pp. 31–33, cited by Kühlein, *op. cit.*, p. 64.

41 *African Economic Digest*, vol. 2, No. 275, July 3–9, 1981, p. 4 and *International Herald Tribune*, June 27–28, 1981. Under somewhat similar circumstances, President Amin of Uganda was endorsed as Chairman of the OAU when Uganda's turn came in the normal rotation.

Table 1). Qatar boasts the highest ratio of disbursements to commitments of any donor. The lack of professional expertise has also encouraged Qatar to support multilateral institutions to a greater extent than is the case for states with their own bilateral funds (see Table 3).[1]

b. Geographic Distribution of Aid Flows

Too small to be directly engaged widely abroad, Qatar concentrates its aid close to home. Arab countries have received 95 % of all bilateral assistance and almost 70 % of multilateral aid has gone to Arab regional institutions (Tables 39 and 6), the highest ratio in each category. Most of this aid has been extended to Egypt and other "Confrontation States." For example, of $ 236 million committed to Arab states in 1978, $ 210 million was given to Syria, Jordan and the P. L. O.

With its minimal interests in Africa, it seems almost extraordinary that Qatar should have provided any aid to Sub-Saharan countries. Yet it has contributed $ 61 million to Arab multilateral institutions in Africa and another $ 47 million bilaterally. Qatar's bilateral African aid has, with few exceptions, gone exclusively to member states of the Islamic Conference, divided equally between project and program support. In addition to the aid recorded in Table 40, Qatar reportedly provided $ 1 million in 1975 to renovate the main mosque in Conakry, Guinea, in conjunction with Saudi Arabia, Kuwait, Libya and Egypt.[2]

The major African beneficiaries have been Uganda and Mali (see Table 40). Qatar helped co-finance a road in Amin's northwestern home district with the Abu Dhabi Fund in 1977 and provided budgetary support in 1975 and 1976, but payments ceased over 18 months before Amin's fall. Mali received regular support until 1976 and one further commitment in 1979. But, since 1976, Qatar's enthusiasm for Africa appears to have abated. In fact, despite its pledge of an additional $ 118 million in aid by 1982 at the Afro-Arab Summit Conference in March 1977, Qatar has committed only $ 9 million to Sub-Saharan Africa since 1977.[3]

---

1   *Financial Times,* February 22, 1979.
2   E.I.U., *Guinea,* II 1975.
3   *Middle East Economic Survey,* March 6, 1978 and Table 40.

6. Saudi Arabia

a. The Special Role of Islam in Saudi Arabia

To understand Saudi foreign policy and the aid it extends at a level beyond compare to any other Arab country, one must understand the central role Islam plays in shaping the attitudes of the Saudi leadership and the policies of the government. Muslims the world over feel a sense of identity and community. This belief in the *umma* (community of believers) partly accounts for the precedence of aid to Islamic countries in the foreign aid programs of all Arab countries. But the degree of emphasis on Islam as a pillar, an objective and a primary tool of Saudi foreign policy and foreign aid is unique among Arab aid donors.

More than a religion, Islam is an all-encompassing way of life. As such, it helps shape the world view of the individual Saudi citizen and the nation collectively. It is also indigenous: Arabia was the birthplace of Islam, its early crucible and, most recently, the justification for the unification of Arabia under King Abdul Aziz ibn Sa'ud in the early 20th century. Islam remains a major legitimizing component of the modern Saudi state, the basis of the law and, jointly with tribal tradition, the basis of the social and political systems. Saudi Arabia probably comes closer than any modern nation to the principles and practices of the ideal Islamic state.

Internationally, Islam traditionally divided the world into Islamic and non-Islamic spheres, the *Dar al-Islam* and the *Dar al-Harb*. While the militancy with which early Islam maintained that dichotomy has attenuated (Iran under Khomeini notwithstanding), the conviction that the world remains divided into two Manichean camps is deeply imbedded in the belief and outlook of many Saudis and has a profound effect, therefore, on their perceptions of the world around them. The sharp edge of this dichotomy has been dulled for many by education, communications and travel, among other factors, but the attitude persists that the world is bipolar, divided among Muslims and non-Muslims on one level, between believers (in monotheism) and non-believers on another level. While Christianity is viewed by religious traditionalists in this context as an aggressive, hostile force and the West as a secular materialistic society antithetical to Islam, the greater evil is atheism, personified by Communism. Therefore, a tactical alliance with the West, led by the United States, is considered useful and necessary to confront the Communist threat to Islam. This has led one specialist in Saudi affairs to suggest that the division of the world into "Free World" and "Communist" has become a recent Saudi variant of classical Islamic bipolarity.[1]

---

1   David Long, "King Faysal's World View" in Willard Beling (ed.), *King Faysal and*

The fundamentalist Islamic view of the world is more prevalent in Saudi Arabia than elsewhere in the Arab world. But within the country there are differences over the extent to which traditional beliefs are to be translated into policy, between what might, for analytical purposes, be called "fundamentalists" and "pragmatists." As the eventual falling out between King Ibn Sa'ud and the *Ikhwan* testifies, this conflict between religious radicals and moderates is as old as the Saudi state, even as old as Islam itself.

The fundamentalists represent a conservative, even reactionary, view of Islam. They are sympathetic to the ideal of a true Islamic state and society and would work for its realization, not just in Saudi Arabia, but abroad. Their views appears to be represented by organizations such as the Muslim World League and much of the local religious establishment, but are probably shared as well by many average citizens and even by a number of the so-called "technocrats". However, there are no convenient, precise, socio-religious cleavages in Saudi society. On balance these groups probably have more influence on domestic than on foreign policy.

The pragmatists may include many of the individuals (technocrats and others) who have been educated outside the religious schools and institutes, whose work deals with essentially secular matters and who are, thereby, subject to a considerably broader range of "modern" influences and pressures. These individuals are more likely to shape foreign policy than the fundamentalists. They are also likely to be more sensitive to local realities in distributing foreign aid and more realistic about the extent to which Islamic orthodoxy can be exacted as a price for that aid.

b. *Islam in Foreign Policy*

It seems logical and natural that the Saudi domestic preoccupation with Islam should extend to foreign policy. As guardian of the two holiest places of Islam and as host to the *hajj* (pilgrimage) which brings over one million Muslims to the country annually, Saudi Arabia naturally assumes the mantle of Islamic leadership. It is a role in which it has no peer.

Islam's political employment abroad was initiated by King Sa'ud and seriously pursued with the financial and political commitment of the Saudi government by the late King Faisal due to his deep religious convictions and personal interest. From the late 1950s, Saudi Arabia promoted the doctrine of Islamic solidarity and unity as an antidote to Arab unity under the leadership of Egypt's inimical President Nasser. More broadly based than Arab unity, Islam embraced nations of Africa and Asia as well as the entire Arab world. Consistent with this policy, Saudi Arabia inspired, hosts

_____

the Modernisation of Saudi Arabia, Westview Press, Boulder, Colorado, 1980, pp. 173–183.

and has been the major contributor to all major Islamic organizations established since 1960, including the Islamic Conference, the Muslim World League and its affiliate, the Supreme World Council of Mosques, the Islamic Development Bank, and a host of lesser organizations including the Islamic Solidarity Fund, International Islamic News Agency and the Islamic Council of Europe.[2] (The aid programs of the first five organizations have been discussed in the appropriate section on multilateral institutions). So thoroughly does Saudi Arabia dominate these institutions — with the possible exception of the IDB — that they are widely viewed by outsiders as instruments of Saudi policy.

In its application to Saudi foreign policy, Islam has inter-related offensive and defensive characteristics and objectives. On the one hand, bilaterally and through its active support of the missionary and cultural programs of Islamic organizations such as the Muslim World League, the Supreme World Council of Mosques and the Islamic Solidarity Fund, the Kingdom seeks to spread a conservative version of Islamic belief and practice through support for Islamic proselytization.

However, it is the defensive role of Islam that has been the most prominent and distinctive hallmark of Saudi foreign policy. In Saudi Arabia, it is generally believed that as a complete system of universal moral values and legal precepts, Islam both fulfills individual requirements and strengthens and guards the family and society. Therefore, it is argued, Islam is the best philosophy to contain the stresses caused by rapid social change and modernization. It is thus capable of protecting Muslims from the evils of atheism and secular materialism, most dangerously manifested by the threat of Communist penetration and subversion.[3] This belief in the prophylactic power of Islam was given rare public expression in the introduction to the Second Five Year Plan (1975—1980). The first goal of the Plan was described as "maintaining the religious and moral values of Islam".[4] Closely related, but second, was "assuring the defense and internal security of the Kingdom". The third goal was to "foster social stability under circumstances of rapid social change".

---

2 While comprehensive figures are difficult to obtain, the level of Saudi assistance to these organizations can occasionally be gleaned from *Middle East Economic Survey* (for example, May 15 and July 24, 1978) and the *Journal of the Muslim World League*.

3 For further amplification of this argument, see Altaf Gauhar (ed.), *The Challenge of Islam*, Islamic Council of Europe, London, 1978, *passim* but especially pp. 285—310.

4 Adid Dawisha, "Saudi Arabia's Search for Security", *Adelphi Papers*, #158, International Institute of Strategic Studies, London, 1979, p. 6.

c. Saudi Foreign Policy Interests

Considering Saudi Arabia's resource endowment, political system, geo-political location, strategic importance and military vulnerability, it is no wonder that the government believes that the most severe threat to the nation stems from the radical left.[5] The seeds of radicalism, it is argued, have been sown by the unresolved Palestinian issue, Ba'athism and Communism. Which of these presents the greatest threat at any particular moment depends on circumstances. To protect the Kingdom, the government's policy has been to enlist its oil wealth to prevent the radicalization of states in the surrounding area by promoting regional stability and blocking Communist penetration and subversion. Furthermore, it has endeavoured to use its "special relationship" with the United States to encourage American pressure on Israel to accept a settlement sensitive to Palestinian interests.

To secure these vital foreign policy interests, Saudi Arabia has concentrated its financial resources in pursuit of five political objectives:
1. settlement of the Palestinian issue;
2. removal of Soviet influence and military power where implanted;
3. weaning pro-Soviet governments away from the East Bloc;
4. support for governments and non-governmental groups in countries threatened by Communist-inspired or Communist-led subversion or aggression;
5. support for anti-Communist, pro-Western governments.

Occasionally, the Saudis have ventured as far afield as non-Muslim states in Asia and central Africa, such as South Korea, Taiwan and Zaire, but typically they have concentrated on nearby countries which are both Islamic and Arab. These are the countries which they know best and with which they have historically had political and economic relationships. These are also the countries with whom the common bonds of Islam and, often, Arabism afford a basis of mutual identification and a point of access for Saudi Arabia's twin strategy of Islamic revival and anti-Communism.

d. Geographic Distribution of Saudi Aid

The decision to support a country and the level of aid to be extended is determined by an informal calculus which includes among its prominent components Islamic revivalism, anti-Communism, the Palestinian issue, Arab political "balance" and the strength of a recipient country's relations with potential Saudi rivals or opponents such as Algeria or Libya.

---

5 For a detailed analysis of Saudi foreign policy see the works of Adib Dawisha and David Long cited in the bibliography.

Cooperation between Riyadh and Washington to support anti-Communist governments, such as Zaire and Kenya, or anti-Soviet guerrillas in Afghanistan also plays an important role. The application of this calculus has been remarkably consistent and has resulted in the following apparent order of geographic priorities: (1) Arab "Confrontation States": Egypt (until 1979), Syria, Jordan, and the P.L.O.; (2) neighboring countries: North and South Yemen, Oman, Sudan, Somalia; Djibouti and the Eritrean Liberation Front in the Horn of Africa; (3) non-Arab Muslim countries: Pakistan, Turkey, and the Afghan rebels; (4) other countries threatened by Communism or radicalism: Zaire, Taiwan, South Korea and the Lebanese Christians.

These priorities are reflected clearly in the geographic distribution of Saudi bilateral aid. Of the $ 14,770 million committed from 1973 through 1979, $ 11,352 million (77 %) has gone to Arab countries and $ 2,325 million (16 %) to Asia. Sub-Saharan Africa has received only $ 437 million, a mere 3 % of Saudi assistance (see Table 41).

Not surprisingly, the principal recipients of this aid have been countries which rank high in the Saudi list of priorities, led by the "Confrontation States", countries in the Horn of Africa, Pakistan, Turkey and Mauritania.[6] Indeed, in one year (1976), Pakistan, which has received more aid than any other non-Arab, Islamic country, received more Saudi aid ($ 515 million) than was committed to all Sub-Saharan Africa in the seven-year period ending 1979.

In contrast to Sub-Saharan Africa, the Arab states in the Horn of Africa and Mauritania have been areas of acute concern and intense Saudi activity. In late 1977, Crown Prince Fahd stated that his foreign policy priorities — focused then on the Horn of Africa — included extracting the Russians from Somalia, assisting "moderate" forces in South Yemen, and helping the Sudan resist Communist subversion.[7] For these purposes, Saudi Arabia has committed at least $ 310 million to Somalia and over $ 946 million to the Sudan (see Table 42), excluding military assistance.[8] Even Djibouti, with less than one million inhabitants has received more Saudi aid than any single Sub-Saharan country, including such members of the Islamic Conference as Mali, Cameroon and Senegal (Table 42). Mauritania, which supported the Moroccan position in the Western Sahara in opposition to

---

6   According to Prince Fahad, Egypt alone received over $ 7 billion in economic and financial assistance between October 1973 and May 1979. (*Saudi Economic Survey*, May 9, 1979)

7   *New York Times*, December 23, 1977.

8   Estimates of aid to Somalia run as high as $ 400 million by 1977. (*Financial Times*, March 21, 1977, and Economic Intelligence Unit, *Saudi Arabia*, Fourth Quarter, 1977, p. 17) Additionally, Somalia reportedly received Saudi-financed arms shipments totalling at least $ 200 million. (Dawisha, *op. cit.*, p. 20)

Algeria until early 1980, has received at least $476 million in Saudi program and project assistance since 1973.[9]

The following table provides further confirmation of the political significance of these three countries for Saudi policy:

($ million)

Country	Project Aid	Program Aid	Total Aid
Mauritania	199.3	277.0	476.3
Somalia	100.0	197.7	297.7
Sudan	187.7	753.0	940.7
Total Aid	$487.0	$1227.7	$1714.7

Together they accounted for 12% of total Saudi bilateral commitments between 1973–1979; 300% more than the sum allocated to Sub-Saharan Africa.

e. Aid to Sub-Saharan Africa

The Saudis seek the same set of foreign policy objectives in Africa as elsewhere in non-Arab countries, but there is perceived to be considerably less danger to the kingdom from African radicalism outside the Horn of Africa. The modest amount of aid extended to Africa indicates that the Sub-Saharan area is of relatively low political importance to Saudi Arabia, both geographically remote and relatively unthreatened by Communist penetration. An added indication of this is the fact that over 90% of the aid extended is project related, largely for infrastructural projects.

Otherwise in Africa, as a review of Table 42 indicates, Saudi policy and Saudi aid follow the pattern already described. The Saudis shun radical or Marxist governments, such as Angola, Ethiopia, Mozambique and Tanzania; friends of Israel, such as Ivory Coast, Malawi, Sierra Leone and Swaziland; avoid rival spheres of influence, such as Chad, where Libya is actively involved; focus their support on Islamic states generally; support those which they are trying to wean from Marxism, such as Congo and Guinea; and support those threatened by Communist subversion, such as Zaire. A Saudi government official summarized the Kingdom's African policy one year ago as follows: "... (we) will increase financial aid to those countries ... (we) perceive as part of a *secondary* (emphasis added) defense line against Soviet subversion ... Somalia and the Eritrean rebels,

---

9 According to foreign diplomats in Jeddah, Saudi enthusiasm for and apparently aid to Mauritania has waned since late 1979 – early 1980 when that country declared its neutrality in the war against the Polisario guerrillas.

both fighting Marxist [and, unstated, Christian] Ethiopia . . ., the Sudan, Zaire and Morocco, which are viewed as stabilizing influences."[10] Zaire is a case in point. Although a non-Muslim state, Zaire was a substantial beneficiary of indirect Saudi military assistance in 1977. Riyadh reportedly spent tens of millions of dollars to pick up as much as one-half of the cost of the 1,500 man Moroccan expeditionary force sent to suppress the Angolan-inspired, Cuban-led Shaba rebellion.[11]

The Saudis also concentrate their aid to promote the social and economic development of certain moderate Islamic states, such as Cameroon, Mali and Senegal — the three largest recipients of Saudi aid to Sub-Saharan Africa through 1979 — as models for the rest of Africa to emulate. Senegal, for example, has followed a policy parallel to Riyadh backing Morocco on the Western Sahara and relations with Algeria and Libya have been cool. Though a Christian, former President Senghor staunchly backed the Arab position on Palestine. Mali too has been a pivotal state in the political manuvering over the Western Sahara issue and in Saudi efforts to counter the spread of Libyan influence in the Sahara. So clearly is aid tied to Saudi policy objectives that a country such as Uganda, and later Mauritania, experienced a sharp decline in the level of assistance once these objectives were achieved or local government policies run counter to Saudi interests.

Uganda has been a country of special importance in the development of Saudi financial assistance to Sub-Saharan Africa since 1972. As a sign of its importance to Saudi Arabia and, indeed to all Arab donors save Algeria, Uganda received more Arab bilateral aid ($ 183 million) than any other Sub-Saharan nation (see Table 15). In fact, the experience of Saudi Arabia and other Arab donor nations in Uganda may have had a major and largely negative impact on Saudi and Arab aid to Africa since.

For virtually all of the reasons he was derided in the West, Idi Amin focused Arab interest and financial assistance in Uganda during the years 1972–1979; a fascinating case of contradictory cultural perceptions. A member of the small Muslim minority of northwestern Uganda, Amin was the first African leader to break relations with Israel after 1967; an event appreciated all the more in the Arab world because of his extremely close Israeli connections until 1972.[12] Amin shrewdly pandered to King Faisal's well-known political syllogisms and religious faith and was rewarded with the King's special attention and a stream of Arab aid which

---

10 *International Herald Tribune,* October 8, 1979, p. 2 quoted by Kühlein and Baumgarten, *Die Afro-Arabischen Beziehungen — Zusammenarbeit und Probleme,* Stiftung Wissenschaft und Politik, Ebenhausen bei München, 1980, p. 67.

11 Dawisha, *op. cit.,* p. 26.

12 Only Guinea broke relations with Israel following the 1967 war. Uganda took that step in March 1972. On Amin's relations with Israel, see Ali Mazrui, "Religious Strangers in Uganda", *African Affairs,* vol. 76, no. 302, January 1977, pp. 21–38.

peaked at $ 100 million in 1975, the year in which recorded Saudi commitments began and virtually ceased.[13] By then, the Saudi government had committed over $ 35 million (and possibly a good deal more which went unreported) for economic and social development, and the King personally had made donations of at least several hundred thousand dollars to build mosques and Islamic cultural centers. Amin concentrated this aid in the undeveloped area of his native power base around Arua, seat of the proposed Islamic university.

Since 1972, the Arabs generally have viewed events in Uganda through the dual prism of Islam and the Palestinian issue. The Arabs, and particularly the Saudis, viewed Amin as a Muslim under attack by Tanzania's Roman Catholic President Nyerere, as a leader out to improve the fortunes of Uganda's impoverished Islamic minority at the expense of the largely Christian establishment, and as a staunch defender of the Arab position on Palestine in international councils.[14] Consequently, they were willing to dismiss his cruder excesses because of what were considered positive contributions from an Arab perspective.

Despite his apparent brutality, Amin's actions were never publicly disavowed by any Arab state. The rising scale of violence and the swelling death tolls in Uganda were even dismissed occasionally by Arabs as "exaggerations" conconcted by Western powers intent on denying control of the Nile headwaters to a Muslim power. Indeed, when he was overthrown the Saudi Foreign Minister and the Muslim World League publicly expressed fear that the new government would begin the repression of Uganda's Muslim community.[15] Privately expressed dissatisfaction with Amin focuses on his diversion of tens of millions of aid dollars for either personal gain or for purposes other than those intended. Less frequently he is criticized as an opportunist who exploited Islam for his own political ends. But the fact that he brought his country to the brink of disintegration and collapse through the injection of a volative religious ether into a violent tribal conflict is scarcely acknowledged.

f. Saudi Aid to Islam in Africa

The vast majority of Saudi aid to Africa is extended to Islamic countries. Of the $ 437 million in bilateral aid committed through 1979, $ 306 mil-

---

13 King Faisal stopped first in Kampala on his 4-state African visit in 1972. For an account of his praise of Amin, see *Financial Times,* November 17, 1972.

14 By early 1975, Uganda's entire cabinet was composed of Muslims, in a country where non-Muslims comprise an estimated 95 % of the population (70 % according to the Muslim World League) Economist Intelligence Unit, *Uganda,* I 1975.

15 *Deutsche Monitor Dienst,* May 14, 1979. To the best of our knowledge, there

lion (70%) went to member states of the Islamic Conference (see Table 42).[16] The balance ($131 million) was committed to one, rarely more, major infrastructural project in moderate countries such as Ghana, Kenya and Liberia, or Congo, usually to develop alternative energy sources, transport and communications facilities or public services. While these projects are top national priority for the recipients, multifaceted and sustained Saudi participation in a country's development seems to have been reserved exclusively for Islamic countries, such as Cameroon, Guinea, Mali, Niger and, under Amin, Uganda.

However, if Saudi aid goes primarily to Muslim states, it is given principally to further general social and economic development — as in "non-Muslim" nations — and, to a far lesser extent, for religious purposes. Of the aid to all Sub-Saharan nations recorded by the OECD between 1975—1978, fully 65% was extended through the Saudi Fund for Development. While the selection of recipients for Fund assistance is a political decision which remains with the government, the general developmental intentions of such aid is a matter of the public record (see Table 43).

As much as $22 million — or about 5% of total aid through 1979 recorded by OECD — seems to have been given to build Islamic educational and medical facilities in Mali, Niger, Comoros, Guinea and Uganda. Additionally, the government has a program to support Islamic cultural, educational and religious activities in Africa which are not recorded by the OECD. Details of this program are not published and it is, therefore, not possible to determine its scope or the resources committed to it. Piecing together various sources, it appears to amount to at least several million dollars annually.[17] Among the beneficiaries of Saudi government assistance have been mosques in Dakar and Accra, Islamic institutes and cultural centers in Liberia and Uganda, at least 16 Islamic schools and the proposed Islamic university in Niger. The amounts involved can occasionally be substantial. Saudi Arabia donated $12 million to build the King Faisal Mosque and Islamic Center in the capital of Chad, Ndjamena. Designed as a center for the propagation of Islam in Chad and the whole

---

were never any public Arab denunciations of the reported massacres by Amin and his subordinates during the long years of his rule.

16 Information concerning Saudi aid to Africa in 1980 is preliminary and covers only the commitments of the Saudi Fund for Development. The Fund extended $172 million of aid to Africa in that year, of which only 30% went to Muslim countries (see Table 42). More detailed statistics will probably increase the amount to Arab League members and possibly Islamic countries substantially. The figures in Table 42 for 1979 (far below trend) may underestimate Saudi commitments to Sub-Saharan countries by as much as $75 million and would increase the percentage to non-Islamic countries, according to figures provided recently by ABEDA.

17 *JMWL*, September 1974, p. 28 and October 1978, p. 62, and the Economist Intelligence Unit, *Quarterly Survey: Saudi Arabia*, III 1974.

of central Africa, the mosque includes schools for boys and girls, a library and a lecture hall.[18] The Grand Mosque in Bamako, Mali cost $ 4.2 million.[19]

Several government ministries include programs to assist Islam in Africa. The Ministry of Education has provided scholarships to students from Chad and Uganda to attend the Islamic universities at Medina and Riyadh and has sent a reported 995 Arabic teachers to African countries, including the Comoros, Ivory Coast, Niger and Nigeria.[20] The Ministry of Awqaf and Islamic Affairs also reportedly has a program to aid Africa. No details are available but it probably supports the building of mosques, Islamic institutions and cultural centers. Finally, a Saudi government Islamic educational organization, Dar al-Ifta in Riyadh, has dispatched Muslim teachers and missionaries to countries including Nigeria.[21]

Saudi Arabia also cooperates with other Muslim donors to fund Islamic organizations such as the Islamic Solidarity Fund and Muslim World League (their African interests are described separately) and has been the major financial supporter of the Islamic Conference. In conjunction with the Muslim World League, Saudi Arabia disburses several million dollars annually to Islamic societies and organizations in Africa. Much of this assistance is used to repair, complete or renovate existing mosques and Islamic centers. Additionally, Kuwait and Saudi Arabia jointly finance the Center for Islam in Africa located in Khartoum. Staffed largely by Egyptians, the Center trains Arab and African missionaries for service in Africa.

Despite the diversity of its program of assistance for Islamic purposes, it is not possible to identify precisely the amount of financial resources committed to Islamic organizations by Saudi Arabia on an annual basis. Nor is it possible to ascertain the sums ultimately disbursed in Africa. The level of overall Saudi support for Islamic ends is, however, considerable, probably on the order of $ 85−100 million annually. Moreover, although it may have been fairly constant after 1973, indications are that it has increased in recent years. For example, the Saudi contribution to the Islamic Solidarity Fund, which remained level at $ 5.5 million for each of the three years from 1976 to 1978, rose to $ 10 million in 1980. In similar fashion, the Saudi contribution to the Islamic Conference has also been increased. In 1977, the Kingdom contributed $ 38.7 million, distributed as follows:

$ 15 million − Islamic Waqfs Fund
$ 5.5 million −- Islamic Solidarity Fund
$ 5 million − Jerusalem Fund
$ 5 million − Islamic University in Niger

---

18 E.I.U., *Chad,* II 1978.
19 *Marchés Tropicaux,* December 21, 1979.
20 *JMWL,* October 1978, p. 62.
21 *JMWL,* September 1974, p. 28.

$ 5 million – Islamic University in Uganda
$ 3.2 million – Islamic News Agency[22].

By 1980, that amount had almost doubled to $ 65 million, divided as follows:

$ 20 million – Trust of the Islamic Solidarity Fund
$ 20 million – various bodies of the Islamic Conference and other organizations
$ 10 million – Islamic Solidarity Fund
$ 10 million – Trust of the Jerusalem Fund
$ 5 million – Jerusalem Fund.[23]

In addition to government assistance, King Faisal and other leading members of the Royal Family, as far back as 1968, have donated personal funds for Islamic projects around the world. These projects have included schools in Ghana and Togo, mosques and Islamic cultural centers from Japan to Africa and London, and translations and printing of the Qur'an in African dialects.

Saudi government officials and private citizens and officials of the Islamic missionary organizations are reticent about discussing with foreign researchers the relative importance of Islamic objectives in Saudi foreign policy and foreign aid activities to assist Muslim communities and propagate Islam in Africa. In part, this reticence may be due to the fact that there is sometimes less a clear policy and set of objectives than a reaction to events underlying Saudi foreign aid; a characteristic by no means confined to Saudi Arabia. However, in part, it may also be due to a recognition that the subject of Islamic aid is highly controversial and sensitive, particularly in the view of many recipient governments in Africa and elsewhere.

In the absence of a clear exposition of Saudi policy objectives, therefore, one must rely primarily on such circumstantial evidence as is available. This evidence may be found primarily in the political philosophy of Islam as explained in publications distributed by the Saudi-backed Islamic Council of Europe, in the objectives embodied in the programs of the Islamic organizations which aid Africa and are supported by Saudi Arabia, such as the Islamic Development Bank, the Islamic Solidarity Fund and the Muslim World League, and in the expressions of state policy objectives and priorities included in the public record, largely in the form of joint communiques issued to cap the state visits of most African leaders.

In sum, the evidence suggests that abroad as well as at home, Saudi Arabia enlists its moral and financial power in order to push for an Islamic revival and stricter, more conservative observance of Islamic principles and

---

22 *Middle East Economic Survey*, July 24, 1978.
23 *Deutsche Monitor Dienst*, May 21, 1980.

practice.[24] In return for the largesse of its aid program, the government expects reciprocity. According to individuals knowledgeable about Saudi governmental style, the explicit terms of reciprocity are rarely enunciated. But, as a review of ten joint communiques marking ten separate African state visits between July 1977 and September 1979 confirms, a recipient is left in no doubt how the Saudis feel about Palestine, Communism and the value of measures such as the introduction (or reintroduction) of the *Shari'a* and Islamic education or equality of treatment for the local Muslim community. A state's subsequent actions on such issues determines its success at winning sustained Saudi financial assistance.

The contents of these communiques also suggests that the Saudi government recognizes that aid for Islamic purposes is a sensitive subject for most African states. The government appears to distinguish clearly between Islamic and non-Islamic nations. For example, the communiques issued following the visits of the leaders of Islamic states, including Cameroon, Comoros, Guinea, Guinea Bissau and Upper Volta — all members of the Islamic Conference — called for "Islamic solidarity", "support" for the local Muslim community and, often, cited a mutual determination to "propagate Islam".[25] However, the communiques issued following the visits of the leaders of Burundi, Gabon, Kenya, Togo and Zaire — states with small Muslim minorities — made no mention of Islam whatsoever.

Further evidence is supplied by the rare public statements of Saudi leaders and officials on religious matters. These statements indicate that the government's primary concern is to ensure tolerance and fair treatment for local Muslim communities rather than to facilitate proselytization. King Faisal took a personal interest in such matters and apparently received assurances from President Tombalbaye during his visit to Chad in 1972 that although Chad was a secular state, Muslims (and, indeed, Christians), enjoyed full religious freedom. Despite these assurances, the negative intent of his subsequent "authenticity" campaign cooled relations with Saudi Arabia.[26] Relations only began to improve in 1975 after General Malloum, also a Christian, overthrew Tombalbaye, quickly restored civil and religious freedoms and balanced his cabinet with an equal number of Muslim and Christian Ministers.

In similar fashion, Faisal made clear to Ethiopia's new rulers in 1975 that Saudi Arabia would "not refrain from giving assistance to Ethiopia in any field . . . (so long as) Ethiopian Muslims are able to practice their religion freely".[27] The decision to refrain from assistance to Mozambique was

---

24 On the Islamic objectives of Saudi Arabia's foreign policy, see Dawisha, *op. cit.*, pp. 20–26 and Detlev Khalid, "The Phenomenon of Re-Islamization", in *Außenpolitik*, vol. 29, April 1978, pp. 433–453.

25 *Deutsche Monitor Dienst*, various dates.

26 E.I.U., *Chad*, IV 1972 and III 1975.

27 *Africa Confidential*, January 24, 1975, p. 8.

heavily influenced by that government's repression of the Muslim community (and other religions as well) and the nationalization of all religious property.[28]

Saudi Arabia's power to withhold aid from those countries which offend its religious principles is also the power to reward those which act in a manner toward Islam which the Saudis view favorably. Saudi policy has met with notable successes, though less so in Africa than elsewhere. Pakistan and the Comoros Islands are the most prominent examples of states which have reinstated the *Shari'a*, although this is still incomplete in Pakistan. Egypt, Sudan, Abu Dhabi, Mauritania (for the second time in ten years) and Bangladesh have introduced some Islamic legislation and regulations recently in place of Western-derived laws.[29] Chad, Gabon, Niger, Senegal and Somalia have reportedly been urged to do the same.[30]

The case of the Comoros Islands is confirmation of the financial benefits from Saudi Arabia which can accrue to a state from the "proper" observance of Islam. A coup d'état in May 1978 replaced the reformist President Ali Soilih. His successor, Ahmad Abdullah, departed on a visit to the Gulf states and Saudi Arabia shortly thereafter where he denounced his predecessor for trying to turn the Comoros into a communist state. An astute judge of his audience, Abdullah stated that "... we have to put Islam back in its rightful position. We must protect Islam from Communism".[31]

On his return he reinstituted the *Shari'a* and several other conservative Islamic practices, renaming the country the "Federal and Islamic Republic of the Comoros". By October, Saudi Arabia, Kuwait and Oman had reportedly donated $ 7 million in emergency assistance. Since 1979, Saudi Arabia, Kuwait and the UAE have extended an additional $ 35.5 million to assist the Comoros.

Despite the increased level of support for Islamic programs and the importance of the Islamic component in Saudi foreign policy, the available evidence indicates, on balance, that the Saudis are reluctant to press hard to accomplish their more ambitious Islamic objectives. While no precise explanation for this phenomenon can be advanced, several reasons can be suggested. First, seven years of experience in Africa since the Arab-Israeli war of October 1973, has given the Saudis an opportunity to reflect on the differences of culture and the role of religion between Saudi Arab society and Sub-Saharan Africa. Accordingly, they may have concluded that they are unlikely to reform traditionally syncretistic African Muslims in their

28 *JMWL*, June 1976.
29 For an account of the Saudi role in Pakistan see Detlev Khalid, *op. cit.*, pp. 433–440 and "The Final Replacement of Parliamentary Democracy by the 'Islamic System' in Pakistan", *Orient*, vol. 20, no. 4, December 1979, p. 19.
30 Dawisha, *op. cit.*, p. 26.
31 E.I.U., *Comoros*, IV 1978.

image of Muslim orthodoxy. Consequently, they may realize that the equation of Islamic revivalism and anti-Communism at the heart of Saudi policy may not transplant well from the Arabian peninsula to Sub-Saharan Africa.

Second, the Saudis may have recognized the conflict potential inherent in pursuing an activist Islamic policy and the reluctance of even Muslim African states to mix Islamic politics and aid.[32] Many of these nations may consider aid for Islamic purposes more a liability than a benefit. Even if the tragic impact of religion on the tribal-based conflicts in Chad, Nigeria, Uganda and the Ethiopian-Somali war is not publicly admitted, the Mecca incident and the impact of the Iranian Revolution may have convinced the Saudi leadership that militant Islam can be a two-edged sword. For example, awareness that the introduction of conservative Islamic measures in the Sudan could upset the fragile union of South and North which Saudi policy encouraged, may have convinced Riyadh not to press President Numeiri to honor his frequent promises to reintroduce certain aspects of the *Shari'a*.

Third, Islamic missionary activity has traditionally not been the responsibility of governments but an area of individual initiative and commitment. The Saudis may be reluctant to assume this task officially. Indeed, the failure of other governments to join in supporting Islamic organizations, such as the Islamic Solidarity Fund and the Muslim World League has left the Saudis in an uncomfortably exposed position which contradicts the fundamental community of purpose which should motivate such organizations.

Fourth, in view of the substantial financial incentives involved, the Saudis may question the sincerity of the motives of some prominent African converts to Islam, and, as a result, the wisdom of appearing to link piety and foreign aid.

Fifth, after the expenditure of at least $ 22 billion in foreign aid during the eight-year period from 1973 through 1980, the Saudi government may have had occasion to realize that foreign aid is not always a successful tool for securing national interests. Unlike an industrialized nation, reciprocity is the only tangible benefit to Saudi Arabia from its massive transfers. Despite aid of unprecedented proportions, Saudi foreign policy (and Islamic) objectives have not always been achieved, as events in Egypt, Pakistan or North and South Yemen confirm. In addition, untold sums have been diverted from their intended purposes or remain undisbursed pending project implementation.

In sum, the experience of the past seven years may have convinced the Saudi leadership that Islam is only one factor in an increasingly complex

---

32 On African fears of the introduction of Islamic fundamentalism in return for Arab aid, see Ahmad Yousef Ahmad, *op. cit.*, pp. 5—6.

and dangerous world and that its active employment may not always advance the country's paramount political interests in Africa. While maintaining support for Islamic missionary activities where they are welcomed, Saudi Arabia may feel it can secure those interests best by concentrating on the provision of financial assistance for projects which further the social and economic development of the recipient country and its inhabitants, both Muslim and non-Muslim. Preliminary information on Saudi commitments to Sub-Saharan Africa in 1980 may be an early confirmation of this observation. In that year, commitments amounted to $ 172 million spread over 11 Sub-Saharan nations. Aid to non-Islamic countries reached the unprecedented level of 70 % of total commitments, including $ 69 million for Zambia, $ 20 million for Kenya and $ 11 million each for Botswana and Togo. Moreover, the Saudis may now believe that their objectives can best be achieved through the auspices of the bilateral and multilateral institutions created expressly for the purpose of fostering social and economic development, including the Saudi Fund for Development, the Islamic Development Bank and the OPEC Fund for International Development. In comparison to the modest resources committed for Islamic assistance, which may amount to as much as $ 100 million in any one year, the capital committed annually to development institutions is substantial and rising. In 1980, the capital of the Saudi Fund was increased 50 % from $ 3 billion to $ 4.5 billion. In 1981, it was increased again to $ 7.5 billion (25 billion Saudi riyals). This trend can be expected to continue as long as the government continues to enjoy budgetary surpluses.[33]

7. United Arab Emirates

a. Foundations of Foreign Policy and Foreign Aid

The United Arab Emirates (UAE) are too small and disparate to undertake separate major foreign policy initiatives. However, the UAE has a distinct foreign policy, conducted almost exclusively by Abu Dhabi. This policy, while independent, follows closely the lead of Saudi Arabia and, in appearance, resembles the foreign policies of the other Arab Gulf states. As expressed by the former Foreign Minister, the UAE's foreign policy is based on the fact that the Federation is an Arab and Islamic state, a significant Gulf oil producer, and a member of both the Third World and the broader international community.[1] As such, the UAE is generally responsive to the issues which move those various interest groups but, primarily, those of concern to the Arab world. Sheikh Zayid, Ruler of the Abu Dhabi

33 *Middle East Economic Survey,* May 25, 1981.
1 *Financial Times,* June 26, 1978.

and President of the Federation stated the priority of Arab interests in the UAE's foreign policy: his twin goals are the restoration of "Arab solidarity" and the unification of word and action to "support Arab positions" and "confront Zionism".[2]

An important secondary interest is the maintenance of good relations with countries such as Pakistan and Bangladesh with which the UAE maintains close military and economic cooperation.

Anti-Communism and Islamic revival do not appear to be primary components of the UAE's foreign policy, as is the case in Saudi Arabia, but may be better characterized as important elements of the instinctive reaction of policy makers to the issues which confront them. Like their counterparts throughout the Gulf, some members of the political elite in Abu Dhabi may cherish privately, as an ideal, the reassertion of traditional Islamic values, including the reestablishment of an Islamic society and state. But their efforts on behalf of Islam are tempered by realism and pragmatism at home and abroad. UAE policy makers and, ultimately, Sheikh Zayid, are likely to respond positively to African leaders who appeal for assistance on the basis of need and Islamic fraternity and to take pride in the spread of Islam among the leaders and masses in Africa. However, insincerity or exploitation of Islam on the part of aid seekers would prompt a negative reaction which may explain the failure of President Bokassa to attract more than token Arab financial assistance for the Central African Republic after his well-publicized conversion to Islam in October 1976.

A further motive for the sizeable amounts of aid disbursed by Abu Dhabi in the name of the UAE is the personal generosity of Sheikh Zayid. In the view of many, this is probably the principal impulse for aid to Sub-Saharan Africa, an area where otherwise the UAE has no direct political interests.[3]

A final motive has undoubtedly been a sense of political obligation to African states for their support on the Palestinian issue. Abu Dhabi has discharged both this obligation and Sheikh Zayid's charitable impulses bilaterally and through the UAE's substantial contributions to multilateral institutions and the IMF Oil Facility.

b. Geographic Distribution of Aid

The geographic distribution of aid from the UAE reflects the overwhelming importance of the Arab world in the UAE's foreign policy. Arab countries received 82% ($ 5,512 million) of total bilateral commitments through 1979 (Table 44), 83% of the assistance provided by the Abu

---

2   *ibid.*
3   *ibid.*

Dhabi Fund for Arab Economic Development through 1980 (Table 46) and over 75% of all commitments. This ranks the UAE second only to Qatar in the relative share of assistance donated to the Arab world (see Tables 13 and 44). The share allocated to Arab countries has increased sharply from 1978 as a result of the UAE's commitment to the "Confrontation States" and to the Palestine Liberation Organization.[4] Abu Dhabi committed $365 million in support payments to Syria, Jordan and the P.L.O. at the Baghdad Summit and extended another $150 million as general support to Syria and Jordan. It also paid $150 million to Egypt in 1978 before signature of the Camp David Agreement.

Reflecting the importance of close economic relations with Pakistan and Bangladesh and the critical role of several thousand Pakistani soldiers and pilots in the UAE armed forces, Asian countries have received an additional $439 million in bilateral aid, 6.5% of total bilateral assistance through 1979.

c. Aid to Sub-Saharan Africa

Indicative of its relative lack of importance to the Federation's foreign policy interests, Sub-Saharan Africa has received a lower share (1.7%) of total bilateral aid from the UAE than from any other Arab donor. Indeed, Sub-Saharan states have received only an average of $10 million in bilateral aid annually, during the five-year period from 1976 through 1980. The total amount of $121 million extended bilaterally to Sub-Saharan states through 1980 compares unfavorably to the $609 million provided to Arab League African states during the same period. In addition to its bilateral assistance, through 1979 the UAE contributed $95 million to Arab institutions dealing with Africa. A close examination of the statistical evidence presented in Tables 44 and 45 confirms that the trend of aid from the UAE to Sub-Saharan Africa has been downward since 1974. In the case of the Abu Dhabi Fund commitments have declined since 1977.

Several reasons may account for the declining level of aid to Africa. Most important, according to local aid officials, was the lasting negative impression of Abu Dhabi's first efforts to aid Africa. In the early flush of burgeoning Afro-Arab relations, President Mobutu of Zaire visited Abu Dhabi in 1974. An outspoken recent convert to the Arab position on Palestine, he received a commitment of $50.3 million from Sheikh Zayid. As was frequently the case with aid from many Arab countries during that heady

---

4 Several estimates suggest that 75% of all assistance goes to these states and the P.L.O. With the cessation of aid to Egypt in 1979, the relative share may have declined recently. See, for example, *Middle East Economic Digest*, "United Arab Emirates — Special Supplement," July 1977 and *Financial Times*, June 26, 1978.

and chaotic period, the terms under which that assistance was extended may have been vague, if terms as such were even discussed. While the Zairean delegation may have requested financial support for specific purposes, there has been apparently no accounting for the employment of those funds nor any suggestion of repayment, and a strong suspicion exists in Abu Dhabi that they were diverted for "unproductive" purposes. The effect of this experience was two-fold; first, to instill a generally negative attitude toward subsequent aid to Sub-Saharan countries. Since 1974, bilateral assistance from Abu Dhabi to all of Sub-Saharan Africa has only marginally exceeded ($ 70.7 million) that one loan to Zaire (Table 45). The subsequent experience with two project loans to Uganda in 1977 and 1978, totalling $ 16.8 million, of which only a fraction was disbursed before Amin's overthrow, may have deepened the government's disenchantment with Sub-Saharan Africa.

A second result of these unfortunate experiences has been to sharply decrease the amount of program aid provided to non-Arab countries by Abu Dhabi's Ministry of Finance and to increase the country's reliance on institutional channels of assistance. Since 1977, an increasing share of the UAE's aid to Africa has been channelled through the Abu Dhabi Fund (Tables 45 and 46).

Modelling itself closely on its Kuwaiti counterpart, the Fund stresses social and economic criteria and local national development priorities in its selection of projects and favors co-financing with other institutional lenders. Whether or not this tendency will ultimately prove beneficial to Africa is doubtful. For the foreseeable future, it seems that lingering skepticism about Africa will lead to a continuation of the current low level of commitments at best. The fractional decline in the level of assistance from the Fund in 1980 to the lowest level since 1976 is one indiciation of this trend.

There are two principal reasons for such a pessimistic conclusion. First, despite good intentions, the operations and objectives of the Abu Dhabi Fund remain highly politicized and its lending policy conforms closely to the country's foreign policy objectives. Essentially, the Fund seeks to build a broad base of political support for the UAE and the Arab position on Palestine and to help soften the sting of rising oil prices. In pursuit of this dual objective, Abu Dhabi has spread its aid widely, committing $ 53 million to 16 African countries, an average of just over $ 3 million per project (Table 45). Such amounts are insignificant relative to Africa's financial requirements but comensurate with the UAE's limited political objectives in Africa. Unless the government's political considerations dictate a reordering of priorities, Africa is unlikely to receive more preferential treatment in the future. A second reason for this pessimistic forecast is the capital constraint confronting the Fund. According to the 1979 *Annual Report*, the Fund's resources have been nearly exhausted. By year-end 1979, it had made commitments of 2,962 million Dirham, far in excess of its paid-in capital and reserves of 1,798 million Dirham.[5] Moreover, it had already disbursed 1,546 million Dirham. The Fund's Board of Directors, which includes most of Sheikh Zayid's leading financial advisers, approved a doubling of its capital in March 1979. Although the sizeable increase in government revenues since would have justified such an increase, by mid-1981 the Ruler had still taken no action in more than 2 years to confirm this decision. The accession of Sheikh Rashid, Ruler of Dubai and a man with reportedly less charitable instincts than Sheikh Zayid, to the Prime Minister's office in mid-1979 may have delayed any decision, pending a review of the Federation's overall policy and aid priorities. But until a capital increase is approved, the Fund and the government's non-political aid can only mark time.[6]

d. Islam and Aid to Africa

While political factors appear to dominate the decision making process on aid to Africa, it seems clear that religion plays an important, if usually secondary, role. For example, the largest single loan (to Zaire in 1974) was made for political not religious reasons. However, with the exception of that loan, 70 % of the aid to Africa ($ 50 million) has gone to members of the Islamic Conference (Table 45). About 40 % of this amount ($ 21 million) was committed to Uganda under Idi Amin. Even as late as 1978, two projects located in Amin's home district around Arua were approved. But, according to an official of the Abu Dhabi Fund, even if the decision to support Uganda was motivated by political and religious considerations, these projects were approved because the Ugandan government placed them at the top of its lists of priorities. This explanation is consistent with the Fund's policy of reserving the ultimate decision on whether or not to aid a country, but allowing a recipient the right to request finance for projects in tune with its own development priorities. The application of this general maxim seems confirmed by the fact that the Fund disbursed almost $ 6 million of its previous loans in 1980, well after Amin had been overthrown. Since the Fund became fully operational in 1976, project assistance to other Sub-Saharan countries has been fairly evenly divided between member and non-member countries of the Islamic Conference.

---

5 Further commitments of 750 million Dirham were made in 1980.
6 In marked contrast, and confirmation of the continued primacy of "Arab" political interests in the UAE's aid program, is the $ 150 million reportedly extended to the Sudan in March 1980. Although $ 100 million has been allocated as a "project" loan for the new Khartoum International Airport, an additional $ 50 million was committed for balance of payments support.

In addition to its contributions to the Islamic Solidarity Fund and the Islamic Development Bank, the UAE has established a Joint Commission for the Establishment of Islamic Cultural Centers with Libya. Headquartered in Tripoli, the Commission has built a center in Rwanda which combines a mosque, school and dispensary, at a cost of $ 5 million. Eventually it is to be turned over to the control of the local Muslim community. According to an official of the Commission, the principal purpose of this center is to enable the local Muslim community to strengthen and protect its identity in the face of Christian evangelical activities aimed at conversion. A second cultural center was to have been located in Kampala, Uganda, but this plan was shelved after the fall of Idi Amin.

Finally, the UAE government, often in the person of one of the leading members of the ruling families, makes funds available for Islamic projects in response to specific requests. For example, the Crown Prince of Abu Dhabi, Sheikh Khalifa bin Zayid, son of the Ruler, reportedly donated $ 5 million for a technical secondary school in Mombasa, apparently aimed to further educational opportunities for the local Muslim community.[7]

---

7 *Marchés Tropicaux*, January 25, 1980.

D. Conclusion

We have argued throughout the course of this study that political interests dictate the distribution of Arab aid. For this reason, two thirds of the $ 5.5 billion in Arab bilateral aid to Africa between 1973—1980 has gone to Arab League members: Sudan, Mauritania, Somalia and Djibouti. Within Sub-Saharan Africa, the major recipients have been countries which are, by and large, politically important to the individual donor nations or the Arabs as a group. The principal beneficiaries have been Uganda (under President Amin), Guinea, Zaire, Mali and Senegal, states which were early and relatively effective supporters of the Arab position on Palestine. As a corollary, the Arabs have avoided assisting nations whose policies are deemed antithetical, including those nations which have maintained close diplomatic and/or non-diplomatic relations with Israel such as Ivory Coast and Malawi, or states which are considered aligned with one or more of their inter-Arab rivals. The more conservative donors have also shunned assistance to radical or Marxist states including Angola, Ethiopia, Equatorial Guinea and Sao Tome e Principe.

Non-political considerations and interests are also important. Foremost among these is Islam. As a group, the Sub-Saharan members of the Islamic Conference have received 57 % of all bilateral Arab assistance since 1973. Islam provides a common point of identity, a community of interest and a framework for cooperation between Arab and African Muslims. A recent example of the importance of this Islamic framework was the grant of $ 210 million to the seven states of the Sahel (Chad, Gambia, Mali, Mauritania, Niger, Senegal and Upper Volta: all members of the Islamic Conference) at the annual meeting of the Islamic Development Bank in January 1981 and the establishment of a Ministerial Commission for Islamic Solidarity with the Peoples of the Sahel Region.[1] With the exception of Zaire, the greatest concentrations of Arab aid have been in those countries where donor political interest and Islamic affinity coincide – Uganda, Guinea, Mali and Senegal (see also Table 15). However, without political motivation, Islam alone has generally not been sufficient to generate sustained financial assistance. This observation is not to minimize the importance of Islam in the selection of recipients or its latent social and political power in Africa; recent events in the Middle East and Northern Nigeria have demonstrated the potency of a revival of Islamic fundamentalism.

The evidence suggests that sustained donor interest in a country is reserved principally for Arab and Islamic African nations. But, with the exception

---

1   *Agence France Presse*, June 15, 1981.

of some relatively modest assistance from Saudi Arabia, Libya and the UAE for specifically Islamic purposes, the aid provided is concentrated in projects which further the economic and social development of the country — primarily its infrastructure — and has little distinguishable religious linkage and effect. Again, this is not to dismiss the critical role of Islam in Saudi Arabia's defensive strategy to strengthen Islamic faith, practice and institutions as an antidote to radical political movements or to minimize the danger of Libya's overt exploitation of Islam for political ends, but to place the forces behind Arab foreign policies and aid programs in Africa in their proper perspective.

Finally, the distribution of aid among sub-groups of Sub-Saharan African nations further demonstrates the importance of coincident political interests and common religious bonds in the selection of aid recipients. For example, the poorest Sub-Saharan nations, the 18 "Least Developed Countries" (LLDC's) received the smallest relative share of Arab assistance, 49 %.[2] Of the $ 900 million awarded to this group, $ 623 million (69 %) went to eight members of the Islamic Conference, but heavily concentrated (80 %) in just three politically significant states (Uganda, Guinea and Mali). Only $ 277 million went to the remaining 10 LLDC's.

In similar fashion, the aid extended to the 26 "Most Seriously Affected" (MSA's) Sub-Saharan nations was concentrated among a small group of Islamic countries of political importance to the donors.[3] Of the $ 1,272 million provided to MSA's, $ 970 million (76 %) went to the 10 members of the Islamic Conference, but almost two-thirds ($ 610 million) went to just 4: Uganda, Guinea, Mali and Senegal. The remaining $ 302 million was shared among the 16 non-Islamic nations in this group.

---

2 The Sub-Saharan nations designated as "LLDC's" include: Benin, Botswana, Burundi, Cape Verde, Central African Republic, Chad*, Comoros*, Ethiopia, Gambia*, Guinea*, Lesotho, Malawi, Mali*, Niger*, Rwanda, Tanzania, Uganda*, and Upper Volta*. Members of the Islamic Conference are designated by an asterisk. Somalia and Sudan are also included in this category.

3 Sub-Saharan "MSA's" include: Benin, Botswana, Burundi, Cameroon*, Cape Verde, Central African Republic, Chad*, Ethiopia, Gambia*, Guinea*, Guinea-Bissau*, Ghana, Ivory Coast, Kenya, Lesotho, Madagascar, Malawi, Mali*, Mozambique, Niger*, Rwanda, Senegal*, Sierra Leone, Tanzania, Uganda*, and Upper Volta*. Members of the Islamic Conference are designated by an asterisk. Mauritania, Somalia and Sudan are also included in this category.

Bibliography

Books

Mordechai Abir, *Oil, Power and Politics: Conflict in Arabia, the Red Sea and the Gulf*, Frank Cass, London, 1979.

Aziz Alkazaz, *Arabische Entwicklungshilfe-Institutionen*, Deutsches Orient-Institut, Hamburg, 1977.

Shimeon Amir, *Israel's Development Cooperation with Africa, Asia and Latin America*, Praeger, New York, 1974.

Bechtold and Tetsch, *Christian and Islamic Contributions towards Establishing Independent States in Africa South of the Sahara*, Institute for Foreign Cultural Relations, Stuttgart, 1979.

E. C. Chibwe, *Afro-Arab Relations in the New World Order*, Julien Friedmann, London, 1977.

Moshe Decter, *To Serve, to Teach, to Leave*, American Jewish Congress, New York, 1977.

Mohamed Diab, *Inter-Arab Economic Cooperation, 1951–1960*, A. U. B., Beirut, 1963.

Altaf Gauhar (ed.), *The Challenge of Islam*, Islamic Council of Europe, London, 1978.

Islamic Council of Europe, *Concept of Islamic State*, London, 1979.

—, *Universal Islamic Declaration*, London, 1980.

Conrad Kühlein and Oswald Baumgarten, *Die Afro-Arabischen Beziehungen, Zusammenarbeit und Probleme*, Stiftung Wissenschaft und Politik, Ebenhausen bei München, 1980.

John Law, *Arab Aid: Who Gets It, For What, and How*, Chase World Information Corporation, New York, 1978.

Victor T. LeVine and Timothy W. Luke, *The Arab-African Connection: Political and Economic Realities*, Westview Press, Boulder, Colorado, 1979.

Ali A. Mazrui, *Africa's International Relations*, Westview Press, Boulder, Colorado, 1977.

Hartmut Neitzel and Renate Nötzel, *Afrika und die arabischen Staaten*, Institut für Afrikakunde, Hamburg, 1979.

O. E. C. D., *Development Cooperation, 1979 Review*, Paris, 1979.

—, *Development Cooperation, 1980 Review*, Paris, 1980.

Dr. Said Ramadan, *Islamic Law, Its Scope and Equity*, no publisher, 1970.

J. Spencer Trimingham, *Islam in East Africa*, Clarendon Press, Oxford, 1961.

—, *Islam in West Africa*, Clarendon Press, Oxford, 1959.

—, *The Influence of Islam Upon Africa*, Praeger, New York, 1968.

UNCTAD, *Financial Solidarity for Development*, 2 volumes, U. N., New York, 1979.

World Bank, *Annual Report, 1980*, Washington, D. C.

—, *Debt Service Tables, 1980*, Washington, D. C.

—, *1980 World Bank Atlas*, Washington, D. C.

Articles and Papers

ABEDA, *"Afro-Arab Cooperation:* Main Landmarks of Progress", Khartoum, no date

—, *"Fifth Meeting of the Coordination Committee for Afro-Arab Cooperation"*, Khartoum, March 13, 1981.

Ahmad Yousef Ahmad, *Arab-African Relations and Their Implications for the Red Sea Region*, (unpublished), Al-Ahram Center for Political and Strategic Studies, Cairo, May 1980.

Adeed Dawisha, "Saudi Arabia's Search for Security", *Adelphi Papers* (No. 158), International Institute of Strategic Surveys, London, 1979.

Economic Research Department, Kuwait Ministry of Finance, *"Kuwait Aid to Developing Countries, 1962–1978"*, Kuwait, May 24, 1979.

Boguslaw Kacynski, "African-Arab Cooperation and the Evolution in the Position of the O.A.U. on the Middle East Conflict", *Studies on the Developing Countries*, Polish Institute of International Affairs, Warsaw, No. 9, 1978, pp. 29–47.

Detlev Khalid, "The Final Replacement of Parliamentary Democracy by the 'Islamic System' in Pakistan", *Orient*, vol. 20, No. 4 (December 1979), pp. 16–38.

–, "The Phenomenon of Re-Islamization", *Aussenpolitik* (English Edition), vol. 1, 29, 4/78, pp. 433–453.

David Long, "King Faysal's World View" in Willard Beling (ed.), *King Faysal and the Modernization of Saudi Arabia*, Westview Press, Boulder, Colorado, 1980.

Michael R. Lyall, "Arab/African/OECD Cooperation in Black Africa; Reality vs. Myth" (unpublished), March 1980.

Ali A. Mazrui, "Religious Strangers in Uganda", *African Affairs*, (vol. 76, No. 302), January 1977, pp. 21–38.

Robert A. Mortimer, "Trans-Saharan Ties and Tensions: Maghrebi Policy in Sahelian West Africa", (unpublished paper), Haverford College, May 1980.

O.E.C.D., "Flows of Resources from OPEC Members to Developing Countries: Statistical Tables – 1974–1978", Paris 1979.

–, "The Co-Financing of Development Projects by DAC and OPEC Members and International Financial Institutions: 1973–1979", Paris, May 1980.

Philippe Rondot, "Libyen unter Oberst Khadafi, ein Experiment mit ungewissem Ausgang", *Europe Archiv*, vol. 34, No. 13, July 10, 1979.

State of Kuwait, General Board for the South and Arabian Gulf, "Services Extended by the State of Kuwait to the South and Arabian Gulf", July 1979.

Statistical Economic and Social Research and Training Center for Islamic Countries, *Foreign Trade of Islamic Countries: The Present State and Problems*, Ankara, August 1980.

Periodicals

African Business, London

Africa Confidential, London, fortnightly, 1972–1980.

African Economic Digest, London

Africa Research Bulletin, London

Afrique Contemporaire, Paris, monthly, 1973–1980.

Annual Reports of the Various Funds and Institutions Studied in this Report.

Coordination Secretariat, Arab Fund for Economic and Social Development, *Summary of Loans and Technical Assistance Extended to Developing Countries*, Quarterly.

Deutsche Monitor Dienst, Bonn

Economist Intelligence Unit Ltd., *Quarterly Economic Review*, London. All African countries and Arab donor nations, 1973–1980.

Financial Times, London

Foreign Broadcast Information Service, Washington, D.C.

International Herald Tribune, Paris

International Institute of Strategic Studies, *The Military Balance and Strategic Survey*, annual edition, London, 1972–1980.

International Monetary Fund, *IMF Survey*, Washington, D.C.
–, *Direction of Trade Yearbook*, Washington, D.C.
Journal of the Muslim World League, Jeddah, Saudi Arabia, monthly, 1974–1980.
Le Monde, Paris
Marchés Tropicaux, Paris, weekly, 1973–1980.
Middle East Economic Survey, Cyprus
Morgan Guaranty Trust, *World Financial Markets*, New York
The Muslim World, Hartford, quarterly, 1973–1980.
Organization of Arab Petroleum Exporting Countries, *Bulletin*, Kuwait
Revue Française d'Etudes Politique Africaines, Paris, monthly, 1970–1980.
Saudi Economic Survey, Jeddah
Washington Post, Washington, D.C.

Tables

TABLE 1
Total Flows of Official Aid by Donor Country: 1973–1980[1]
($ Million)

Commitments

	1973	1974	1975	1976
Algeria	26.9	65.3	83.7	80.9
Iraq	115.2	545.0	434.9	301.3
Kuwait	815.3	1,473.8	2,865.7	2,833.4
Libya	507.3	563.9	684.6	406.9
Qatar	113.4	266.7	456.6	343.9
Saudi Arabia	673.1	2,438.1	2,964.8	4,159.1
UAE	425.3	951.7	1,297.8	1,518.4
Total	2,676.5	6,304.5	8,788.1	9,643.9

Disbursements

	1973	1974	1975	1976
Algeria	29.8	51.5	42.2	66.6
Iraq	10.6	440.2	254.4	254.7
Kuwait	566.0	1,191.8	1,682.5	1,875.7
Libya	403.8	263.4	362.7	363.2
Qatar	93.7	217.9	366.7	240.3
Saudi Arabia	334.9	1,622.1	2,466.5	2,817.2
UAE	288.6	749.4	1,206.5	1,143.3
Total	1,727.4	4,536.3	6,381.5	6,761.0

TABLE 1 (continued)

Commitments

	1977	1978	1979[2]	1980[2/P]	Total
Algeria	83.9	263.5	79.5	98.7	782.4
Iraq	228.9	602.3	1,227.4	1,124.0	4,579.0
Kuwait	2,118.8	1,413.0	942.4	1,263.8	13,726.2
Libya	372.8	953.9	139.0	744.4	4,372.8
Qatar	203.4	253.9	73.4	327.3	2,038.6
Saudi Arabia	3,694.2	3,767.0	1,678.0	2,543.0	21,917.3
UAE	1,395.5	1,047.9	1,238.6	1,229.3	9,104.5
Total	8,097.5	8,301.5	5,378.3	7,330.5	$ 56,520.8

Disbursements

	1977	1978	1979[2]	1980[2/P]	Total
Algeria	71.0	56.2	271.8	83.2	672.3
Iraq	114.2	239.0	846.9	828.6	2,988.6
Kuwait	1,905.0	1,562.8	1,054.7	1,192.0	11,030.5
Libya	266.1	576.7	104.8	280.9	2,621.6
Qatar	255.4	138.5	277.2	298.7	1,888.4
Saudi Arabia	2.678.4	1,761.4	2,297.5	3,033.0	17,011.0
UAE	1,329.5	829.3	1,114.0	1,174.3	7,834.9
Total	6,619.6	5,163.9	5,969.9	6,890.7	44,047.3

1 Does not include contributions to the IMF Oil Facility but includes contributions to the World Bank.
2 For 1979 contains only sketchy information on non-concessional flows. For 1980 includes only concessional assistance.
P = Preliminary

Source: OECD

TABLE 2
Total Flows of Bilateral Aid by Donor Country: 1973–1980[1]
($ Million)

Commitments

	1973	1974	1975	1976	1977
Algeria	23.3	5.7	35.8	44.6	10.0
Iraq	112.5	472.0	344.1	217.2	123.6
Kuwait	631.0	1,299.5	2,687.0	1,745.2	1,743.5
Libya	378.7	417.8	465.5	242.7	96.8
Qatar	112.6	211.3	387.0	104.0	104.6
Saudi Arabia	642.5	1,265.2	2,614.2	2,573.3	2,928.1
UAE	420.9	727.4	1,166.6	1,102.7	1,171.7
Total	$ 2,321.5	4,398.9	7,700.2	6,029.7	6,178.3
As % of total commitments	86.7%	69.8%	87.6%	62.5%	76.3%

Disbursements

	1973	1974	1975	1976	1977
Algeria	23.9	7.7	31.3	46.1	10.0
Iraq	3.0	388.9	225.4	187.3	37.6
Kuwait	365.7	1,104.4	1,624.5	1,453.1	1,159.4
Libya	269.4	219.4	238.4	245.9	71.9
Qatar	92.6	193.3	330.5	166.5	193.4
Saudi Arabia	319.4	948.2	1,828.1	2,114.2	1,748.4
UAE	283.7	601.0	1,124.1	997.6	994.6
Total	$ 1,357.7	3,462.9	5,402.3	5,210.7	4,215.3
As % of total commitments	78.5%	76.3%	84.6%	77.0%	63.6%

TABLE 2 (continued)

Commitments

	1978	1979	1980[P]	Total	As % of Total Commitments
Algeria	234.1	62.6	50.1	466.2	59.5
Iraq	568.7	1,194.4	1,036.7	4,069.2	88.9
Kuwait	1,270.4	817.7	1,061.8	11,256.1	82.0
Libya	794.0	110.9	662.5	3,168.9	72.3
Qatar	238.6	58.8	292.5	1,509.4	74.0
Saudi Arabia	3,275.9	1,471.3	2,201.6	16,972.1	77.4
UAE	975.0	1,191.2	1,162.1	7,917.6	86.9
Total	7,356.7	4,906.9	6,467.3	45,359.5	
As % of total commitments	88.6%	91.1%	88.2%		80.2%

Disbursements

	1978	1979	1980[P]	Total	As % of Total Disbursements
Algeria	5.5	233.7	40.6	398.8	59.3
Iraq	135.1	803.4	774.8	2,555.5	85.5
Kuwait	1,211.7	884.0	1,035.1	8,837.9	80.1
Libya	335.6	18.2	217.9	1,616.7	61.6
Qatar	48.0	258.6	265.7	1,548.6	82.0
Saudi Arabia	1,182.1	1,698.9	2,766.3	12,605.6	74.1
UAE	634.1	1,035.3	1,117.2	6,787.6	86.6
Total	3,552.1	4,932.1	6,217.6	34,350.7	
As % of total commitments	68.7%	82.5%	90.2%	77.9%	

P = Preliminary
1   Includes concessional + non-concessional commitments + disbursements until 1980.
    For 1980, includes only concessional flows.

Source: OECD

TABLE 3
Total Flows of Multilateral Aid by Donor Country: 1973–1980[1]
($ Million)

Commitments

	1973	1974	1975	1976	1977
Algeria	3.6	59.6	47.9	36.3	73.9
Iraq	2.7	73.0	90.8	84.1	105.3
Kuwait	184.3	174.3	178.7	1,088.2	375.3
Libya	128.6	146.1	219.1	164.2	276.0
Qatar	0.8	55.4	69.6	239.9	98.8
Saudi Arabia	30.6	1,172.9	350.6	1,585.8	766.1
UAE	4.4	224.3	131.2	415.7	223.8
Total	355.0	1,905.6	1,087.9	3,614.2	1,919.2
As % of total commitments	13.3%	30.2%	12.4%	37.5%	23.7%

Disbursements

	1973	1974	1975	1976	1977
Algeria	5.9	43.8	10.9	20.5	61.0
Iraq	7.6	51.3	29.0	67.4	76.6
Kuwait	200.3	87.4	58.0	422.6	745.6
Libya	134.4	44.0	124.3	117.3	194.2
Qatar	1.1	24.6	36.2	73.8	62.0
Saudi Arabia	15.5	673.9	638.4	703.0	930.0
UAE	4.9	148.4	82.4	145.7	334.9
Total	369.7	1,073.4	979.2	1,550.3	2,404.3
As % of total disbursements	21.5%	23.7%	15.3%	22.9%	36.3%

TABLE 3 (continued)

Commitments

	1978	1979	1980^P	Total	As % of Total Commit- ments
Algeria	29.4	16.9	48.6	316.2	40.4%
Iraq	33.6	33.0	87.3	509.8	11.1%
Kuwait	142.6	124.7	202.0	2,470.1	18.0%
Libya	159.9	28.1	81.9	1,203.9	27.5%
Qatar	15.3	14.6	34.8	529.2	25.9%
Saudi Arabia	491.1	206.7	341.4	4,945.2	22.5%
UAE	72.9	47.4	67.2	1,186.9	13.0%
Total	944.8	471.4	863.2	11,161.3	
As % of total commitments	11.3%	8.8%	11.7%		19.7%

Disbursements

	1978	1979	1980^P	Total	As % of Total Disburse- ments
Algeria	50.7	38.1	42.6	273.5	40.6%
Iraq	103.9	43.5	53.8	433.1	14.4%
Kuwait	351.1	170.7	156.9	2,192.6	19.8%
Libya	241.1	86.6	63.0	1,004.9	38.3%
Qatar	90.5	18.6	33.0	339.8	17.9%
Saudi Arabia	579.3	598.6	266.7	4,405.4	25.8%
UAE	195.2	78.7	57.1	1,047.3	13.3%
Total	1,611.8	1,034.8	673.1	$ 9,696.6	
As % of total disbursements	31.2%	17.3%	9.7%		22.0%

1 Includes concessional and non-concessional commitments and disbursements until 1980 but excludes contributions to the IMF Oil Facility and Trust Fund. For 1980, includes only concessional flows.
P = Preliminary

Source: OECD

TABLE 4
Arab-Sponsored Bilateral and Multilateral Financial Institutions

Name of Fund	Location	Year Established[1]	Original Authorized Capital ($ Million)	Current Capital ($ Million)	Geographic Focus and Purpose
A. *Bilateral Funds*					
Abu Dhabi Fund for Arab Economic Development	Abu Dhabi	1971	128.2	512.8	Arab countries only until 1974. Now Africa, Asia and Islamic countries anywhere.
Iraqi Fund for External Development	Baghdad	1974	169.3	677.0	All developing countries.
Kuwait Fund for Arab Economic Development	Kuwait	1961	172.5	7,400.0	Arab countries only until 1974. Now all developing countries.
Saudi Fund for Development	Riyadh	1974	2,900.0	8,000.0	All developing countries.
			$ 3,370.0	$ 16,589.8	
B. *Multilateral Institutions*					
1. *Arab Regional Institutions*					
Arab Fund for Economic and Social Development	Kuwait	1971	350.0	1,300.0	Members of the Arab League

134

TABLE 4 (continued)

Name of Fund	Location	Year Established[1]	Original Authorized Capital ($ Million)	Current Capital ($ Million)	Geographic Focus and Purpose
Arab Authority for Agricultural Investment and Development	Khartoum	1977	517.0	517.0	Members of the Arab League
Arab Monetary Fund	Abu Dhabi	1975	910.6	988.0	Members of the Arab League
OAPEC Special Account to Ease the Burden of Arab Petroleum Importing Countries	Kuwait	1974–76	36.9	fully disbursed	Arab petroleum importing countries
Gulf Organization for the Development of Egypt	Riyadh	1976–79	2,000.0	fully disbursed	Further Egypt economic development
			$ 3,814.5	$ 4,841.9	
2. *African Regional Institutions*					
Special Arab Aid Fund for Africa	Cairo	1974–76	200.0	360.0	Non-Arab African countries
Arab Bank for Economic Development in Africa	Khartoum	1974	231.0	378.25	Non-Arab African countries

TABLE 4 (continued)

Name of Fund	Location	Year Established[1]	Original Authorized Capital ($ Million)	Current Capital ($ Million)	Geographic Focus and Purpose
Arab Fund for Technical Assistance to African and Arab Countries	Cairo	1976	28.5	28.5	Least developed Arab and African countries
			$ 459.5	$ 766.75	
3. *Islamic Institutions*					
Islamic Development Bank	Jeddah	1975	859.6	2,550.0	Aid Muslim countries and communities.
Islamic Solidarity Fund	Jeddah	1974	not applicable	62.8[2]	Aid Muslim countries and communities.
Muslim World League	Mecca	1962	budget not available		Aid Muslim communities
			$ 861.1	$ 2,612.8	
4. *Other Multilateral Institutions*					
OPEC Fund for International Development	Vienna	1976	800.0	4,000.0	Program and project lending to "most seriously affected" developing countries
			$ 800.0	$ 4,000.0	

1 Years of operation if no longer in existence.
2 Sum of annual donations: 1974/75 – 1979/80.

Source: Reports of various funds and institutions.

TABLE 5
Aggregate Commitments to Arab-Sponsored and International
Institutions: 1973–1979
($ Million)

Year	Arab-Sponsored Institutions[1]		International Organizations[2]	
	$	As % of Total	$	As % of Total
1973	$ 16.2	4.6%	$ 338.8	95.4%
1974	750.1	39.4	1,155.5	60.6
1975	754.8	69.4	333.1	30.6
1976	2,657.5	73.5	956.7	26.5
1977	1,463.7	76.3	455.5	23.7
1978	310.9	32.9	633.9	67.1
1979	197.9	42.0	273.5	58.0
Total	$ 6,151.1	59.7%	$ 4,147.0	40.3%

1 Includes ABEDA, SAAFA, AFTAAC, Islamic Development Bank, Islamic Solidarity Fund and the OPEC Fund for International Development as well as Arab regional institutions.
2 Includes the African Development Bank and Fund as well as the other International Organizations listed in Table 5.

Source: OECD

TABLE 6
Commitments of Official Assistance to Multilateral Institutions:
1973—1979*
($ Million)

	1973	1974	1975	1976
Algeria:				
African Regional Institutions[1]	0	33.0	15.0	0
Geographically Unspecialized Institutions[2]	0	6.0	6.1	15.8
Arab Regional Institutions	1.1	6.6	24.3	6.6
International Organizations[3]	2.5	14.0	2.5	13.9
Total Multilateral Commitments	3.6	59.6	47.9	36.3
Iraq:				
African Regional Institutions[1]	0	52.0	16.0	30.0
Geographically Unspecialized Institutions[2]	0	0	0	21.0
Arab Regional Institutions	2.0	20.4	68.2	12.3
International Organizations[3]	0.7	0.6	6.6	20.8
Total Multilateral Commitments	2.7	73.0	90.8	84.1
Kuwait:				
African Regional Institutions[1]	0	50.0	10.0	30.0
Geographically Unspecialized Institutions[2]	0	25.6	24.3	61.1
Arab Regional Institutions	8.1	65.0	106.6	749.3
International Organizations[3]	176.2	33.7	37.8	247.8
Total Multilateral Commitments	184.3	174.3	178.7	1,088.2
Libya:				
African Regional Institutions[1]	0	52.4	27.8	34.8
Geographically Unspecialized Institutions[2]	0	34.6	30.4	48.9
Arab Regional Institutions	3.3	41.5	87.8	23.0
International Organizations[3]	125.3	17.6	73.1	57.5
Total Multilateral Commitments	128.6	146.1	219.1	164.2

TABLE 6 (continued)

	1973		1974	
Qatar:				
African Regional Institutions[1]	0		20.0	
Geographically Unspecialized Institutions[2]	0		4.8	
Arab Regional Institutions	0.3		30.1	
International Organizations[3]	0.5		0.5	
Total Multilateral Commitments	0.8		55.4	
Saudi Arabia:				
African Regional Institutions[1]	0		78.0	
Geographically Unspecialized Institutions[2]	0		52.6	
Arab Regional Institutions	0		68.1	
International Organizations	30.6		974.2	
Total Multilateral Commitments	30.6		1,172.9	
United Arab Emirates:				
African Regional Institutions[1]	0		42.0	
Geographically Unspecialized Institutions[2]	0		28.0	
Arab Regional Institutions	1.4		64.8	
International Organizations[3]	3.0		89.5	
Total Multilateral Commitments	4.4		224.3	
Total:				
African Regional Institutions[1]	0	0	327.4	17.1%
Geographically Unspecialized Institutions[2]	0	0	151.6	8.0
Arab Regional Institutions	16.2	4.6%	296.5	15.6
International Organizations[3]	338.8	95.4	1,130.1	59.3
Total Multilateral Commitments	$ 355.0	100.0%	$ 1,905.6	100.0%

TABLE 6 (continued)

	1975		1976	
Qatar:				
African Regional Institutions[1]	10.4		10.0	
Geographically Unspecialized Institutions[2]	8.8		14.8	
Arab Regional Institutions	45.4		202.1	
International Organizations[3]	5.0		13.0	
Total Mulitlateral Commitments	69.6		239.9	
Saudi Arabia:				
African Regional Institutions[1]	35.0		40.0	
Geographically Unspecialized Institutions[2]	49.6		151.7	
Arab Regional Institutions	98.4		830.9	
International Organizations	167.6		563.2	
Total Multilateral Commitments	350.6		1,585.8	
United Arab Emirates:				
African Regional Institutions[1]	11.0		20.0	
Geographically Unspecialized Institutions[2]	26.7		44.9	
Arab Regional Institutions	70.8		315.1	
International Organizations[3]	22.7		35.7	
Total Multilateral Commitments	131.2		415.7	
Total:				
African Regional Institutions[1]	125.2	11.5%	164.8	4.6%
Geographically Unspecialized Institutions[2]	145.9	13.4	358.2	9.9
Arab Regional Institutions	501.5	46.1	2,139.3	59.2
International Organizations[3]	315.3	29.0	951.9	26.3
Total Multilateral Commitments	$ 1,087.9	100.0%	$ 3,614.2	100%

TABLE 6 (continued)

	1977	1978	1979	Total $	Total %
Algeria:					
African Regional Institutions[1]	15.9	6.3	3.3	73.5	27.5
Geographically Unspecialized Institutions[2]	25.8	6.3	0	60.0	22.4
Arab Regional Institutions	29.3	10.5	12.8	91.2	34.1
International Organizations[3]	2.9	6.3	0.8	42.9	16.0
Total Multilateral Commitments	73.9	29.4	16.9	$ 267.6	100.0 %
Iraq:					
African Regional Institutions[1]	13.0	0	6.7	117.7	27.9
Geographically Unspecialized Institutions[2]	0	12.5	0	33.5	7.9
Arab Regional Institutions	87.9	19.8	19.7	230.3	54.5
International Organizations[3]	4.4	1.3	6.6	41.0	9.7
Total Multilateral Commitments	105.3	33.6	33.0	$ 422.5	100.0
Kuwait:					
African Regional Institutions[1]	27.5	10.8	17.6	145.9	6.4
Geographically Unspecialized Institutions[2]	95.4	25.0	0	231.4	10.2
Arab Regional Institutions	176.7	33.2	33.1	1,172.0	51.7
International Organizations[3]	75.7	73.6	74.0	718.8	31.7
Total Multilateral Commitments	375.3	142.6	124.7	2,268.1	100.0
Libya:					
African Regional Institutions[1]	24.9	0	6.7	146.6	13.1
Geographically Unspecialized Institutions[2]	69.2	31.3	0	214.4	19.1
Arab Regional Institutions	101.9	26.1	16.2	299.8	26.7
International Organizations[3]	80.0	102.5	5.2	461.2	41.1
Total Multilateral Commitments	276.0	159.9	28.1	1,122.0	100.0

TABLE 6 (continued)

	1977		1978	
Qatar:				
African Regional Institutions[1]	21.0		0	
Gegraphically Unspecialized Institutions[2]	23.8		6.3	
Arab Regional Institutions	52.2		6.3	
International Organizations[3]	1.8		2.7	
Total Multilateral Commitments	98.8		15.3	
Saudi Arabia:				
African Regional Institutions[1]	54.0		10.8	
Geographically Unspecialized Institutions[2]	251.7		50.1	
Arab Regional Institutions	211.6		39.8	
International Organizations	248.8		390.4	
Total Multilateral Commitments	766.1		491.1	
United Arab Emirates:				
African Regional Institutions[1]	22.0		0	
Geographically Unspecialized Institutions[2]	58.7		27.5	
Arab Regional Institutions	118.0		16.2	
International Organizations[3]	25.1		29.2	
Total Multilateral Commitments	223.8		72.9	
Total:				
African Regional Institutions[1]	178.3	9.3 %	27.9	3.0 %
Geographically Unspecialized Institutions[2]	524.6	27.3	159.0	16.8
Arab Regional Institutions	777.6	40.5	151.9	16.1
International Organizations[3]	438.7	22.9	606.0	64.1
Total Multilateral Commitments	$ 1,919.2	100.0 %	$ 944.8	100.0 %

TABLE 6 (continued)

	1979		Total $	Total %
Qatar:				
African Regional Institutions[1]	6.7		68.1	13.8
Geographically Unspecialized Institutions[2]	0		58.5	11.8
Arab Regional Institutions	6.3		342.7	69.3
International Organizations[3]	1.6		25.1	5.1
Total Multilateral Commitments	14.6		494.4	100.0
Saudi Arabia:				
African Regional Institutions[1]	38.5		256.3	5.5
Geographically Unspecialized Institutions[2]	0		555.7	12.1
Arab Regional Institutions	39.7		1,288.5	28.0
International Organizations	128.5		2,503.3	54.4
Total Multilateral Commitments	206.7		4,603.8	100.0
United Arab Emirates:				
African Regional Institutions[1]	12.2		107.2	9.6
Geographically Unspecialized Institutions[2]	0		185.8	16.6
Arab Regional Institutions	16.6		602.9	53.8
International Organizations[3]	18.6		223.8	20.0
Total Multilateral Commitments	47.4		1,119.7	100.0
Total:				
African Regional Institutions[1]	91.7	19.5%	915.3	8.9%
Geographically Unspecialized Institutions[2]	0	0	1,339.3	13.0%
Arab Regional Institutions	144.4	30.6	4,027.4	39.1%
International Organizations[3]	235.3	49.9	4,016.1	39.0%
Total Multilateral Commitments	$ 471.4	100.0%	$ 10,298.1	100.0%

* May not add due to the exclusion of minor commitments to "other" institutions and rounding.

1 ABEDA, AFTAAC, SAAFA and includes $ 130.9 million donated to the African Development Bank and Fund between 1974 and 1979.

2 Includes the Islamic Development Bank, Islamic Solidarity Fund and OPEC Fund for International Development.

3 Includes the IMF, UN, World Bank and regional development banks excluding Africa, but not the IMF Oil Facility or Trust Fund.

Source: OECD

TABLE 7

Non-Concessional Commitments by Donor Country: 1973–1979

($ Million)

	1973	1974	1975	1976	1977	1978	1979[1]	Total	As % of Total Flows
Algeria	3.7	1.9	19.1	3.0	22.4	5.0	0	$ 55.1	8.1%
Iraq	0	47.3	64.1	4.0	93.3	9.8	22.2	240.7	7.0
Kuwait	412.8	503.7	1,738.8	1,376.2	512.0	199.4	197.6	4,940.5	39.6
Libya	268.9	284.6	372.1	189.7	236.4	323.8	25.0	1,700.5	46.9
Qatar	20.3	126.5	87.6	8.0	51.2	0.1	0	293.7	17.2
Saudi Arabia	105.0	1,567.5	299.6	584.0	591.9	234.9	32.3	3,415.2	17.6
United Arab Emirates	108.4	257.8	385.5	72.9	145.4	193.2	85.4	1,248.6	15.9
Total	$ 919.1	$ 2,789.3	$ 2,966.8	$ 2,237.8	$ 1,652.6	$ 966.2	$ 362.5	$ 11,894.3	24.2%
As % of Total Flows	34.3%	44.2%	33.8%	23.2%	20.4%	11.6%	6.7%		

1 Includes only non-concessional bilateral commitments in 1979. Statistics concerning non-concessional assistance are considered very incomplete in 1979 and of lesser accuracy than in previous years.

Source: OECD

TABLE 8
Geographic Distribution of Total Arab Aid Commitment: 1973–1979[1]
($ Million)

	Arab Countries[1]		Sub-Saharan[1] Africa		Asia[1]	
	$	%	$	%	$	%
1973	2,087.0	78.0	64.7	2.4	184.1	6.9
1974	3,467.6	56.4	571.1	9.3	511.9	8.3
1975	6,911.0	80.0	467.8	5.4	632.7	7.3
1976	6,472.4	69.2	392.7	4.2	1,343.3	14.4
1977	4,943.8	61.8	499.7	6.2	965.8	12.1
1978	6,310.8	73.4	453.0	5.3	825.2	9.6
1979	4,021.6	66.9	402.4	6.7	454.7	7.6
Total	$ 34,214.2	69.2%	$ 2,851.4	5.8%	$ 4,917.7	9.9%

TABLE 8 (continued)

	Other[1] Countries		International Organizations[2]		Total
	$	%	$	%	$
1973	1.9	0.1	338.8	12.7	2,676.5
1974	472.3	7.7	1,130.1	18.4	6,153.0
1975	315.4	3.6	315.3	3.6	8,642.2
1976	196.4	2.1	951.9	10.2	9,356.7
1977	1,148.2	14.4	438.7	5.5	7,996.2
1978	399.4	4.6	606.0	7.1	8,594.4
1979	896.2	14.9	235.3	3.9	6,010.2
Total	$ 3,429.8	6.9%	$ 4,016.1	8.1%	$ 49,429.2

1 Includes bilateral commitments and capital commitments to multilateral institutions focused exclusively on a geographic area under the appropriate regional headings. The commitments of the Islamic Development Bank, OPEC Fund and Islamic Solidarity Fund which benefit countries in the Arab world, Sub-Saharan Africa, Asia and, in the case of the OPEC Fund, Latin America, have been included in the appropriate regional category.
2 Includes the IMF, UN, World Bank and regional development banks excluding Africa, but not the IMF Oil Facility or Trust Fund.

Source: OECD and various funds and institutions

TABLE 9
Consolidated Annual Geographic Distribution of Bilateral Official Aid Commitments by Region: 1973–1979
($ Million)

	Arab Countries		Sub-Saharan Africa		Asia		Other Countries*		Total
	$	As % of Total	$	As % of Total	$	As % of Total	$	As % of Total	$
1973	2,070.8	89.2	64.7	2.8	184.1	7.9	1.9	0.1	2,321.5
1974	3,171.1	72.1	243.7	5.5	511.9	11.6	472.3	10.7	4,399.0
1975	6,409.5	83.2	342.6	4.4	632.7	8.2	315.4	4.1	7,700.2
1976	4,313.7	71.5	210.8	3.5	1,309.8	21.7	195.4	3.2	6,029.7
1977	4,047.4	65.5	208.3	3.4	816.7	13.2	1,105.9	17.9	6,178.3
1978	5,996.9	81.5	325.1	4.4	694.8	9.4	399.9	4.6	7,356.7
1979	3,639.4	74.2	197.8	4.0	277.0	5.6	792.7	16.2	4,906.9
Total	$ 29,648.8	76.2 %	$ 1,593.0	4.1 %	$ 4,427.0	11.4 %	$ 3,223.5	8.3 %	$ 38,892.3

* Includes amounts unallocated or unspecified.

Source: OECD

146

TABLE 10
Geographic Distribution of Disbursements of Bilateral Concessional
Assistance Ranked by Recipient Countries: 1976–1980
($ Million)

		1		2	
Algeria	1976	Benin	1	Niger	1
	1977	*	10	—	—
	1978	Niger	0.5	Africa Unspecif	5
	1979	Syria	132.2	Jordan	89.3
	1980	Lebanon	28.6	PDRY	10
Iraq	1976	India	100	Sudan	29
	1977	Jordan	9	Afghanistan	8
	1978	Jordan	38	India	35
	1979	Syria	274.9	LDC's	220
	1980	Jordan	278.7	Syria	183.3
Kuwait	1976	Egypt	107.16	Jordan	57.4
	1977	Egypt	315.2	Syria	180.7
	1978	Egypt	135.0	Jordan	107.5
	1979	Syria	291.3	Jordan	224.4
	1980	Syria	294.5	Jordan	227.8
Libya	1976	N. Vietnam	5.6	Guinea-Bissau	3.0
	1977	Pakistan	15.0	Malaysia	5.0
	1978	Pakistan	20.0	Niger	10.4
	1979	Greece	11	Malta	8.5
	1980	Syria	200	Lebanon	10
Qatar	1976	Egypt	75.6	Jordan	13.9
	1977	Egypt	95.0	Uganda	2.5
	1978	Iran	3.0	Jordan	1.0
	1979	Syria	121.5	Jordan	82.8
	1980	Syria	121.5	Jordan	82.5
Saudi Arabia	1976	Pakistan	514.8	Egypt	491.2
	1977	Egypt	299.6	Syria	250.9
	1978	Egypt	211.2	Syria	177.9
	1979	Syria	367.2	Morocco	318.6
	1980	Syria	541.5	Jordan	392
UAE	1976	Egypt	348.6	Syria	251.8
	1977	Egypt	171.9	Syria	117.9
	1978	Egypt	162.1	Syria	103.0
	1979	Syria	269.6	Jordan	155.3
	1980	Syria	214	Jordan	148.1

TABLE 10 (continued)

		3		4	
Algeria	1976	Upper Volta	1	–	
	1977	–		–	
	1978	–		–	
	1979	Arab	7.2	Sierra Leone	2
	1980	Mauritania	2	–	
Iraq	1976	Jordan	23	Sri Lanka	10
	1977	Yemen	7.6	PDRY	3
	1978	Somalia	15	PDRY	13.3
	1979	Jordan	185.7	Arab	59.4
	1980	India	79.4	Lebanon	60.9
Kuwait	1976	Yemen	23.6	Mauritania	20.6
	1977	Jordan	90.1	Yemen	26.2
	1978	Syria	58.2	Morocco	24.7
	1979	LDC's	58.9	Bahrain	56.6
	1980	Bahrain	82.9	Arab	62.9
Libya	1976	Pakistan	3.0	Yemen	2.2
	1977	Madagascar	1.0	Rwanda	0.1
	1978	Malaysia	5.0	Madagascar	1.0
	1979	Jordan	1.7	–	
	1980	PDRY	7.2	Niger	0.7
Qatar	1976	Syria	7.1	Oman	5.0
	1977	Gambia	1.1	Yemen	0.9
	1978	–		–	
	1979	Arab	26	Morocco	17.2
	1980	Arab	26	Sudan	10
Saudi Arabia	1976	Syria	189.8	Sudan	167.0
	1977	Jordan	171.1	Somalia	161.2
	1978	Lebanon	121.5	Yemen	100.5
	1979	Jordan	246.2	Sudan	243.3
	1980	Morocco	328.1	Turkey	260.9
UAE	1976	Jordan	87.8	Oman	39.7
	1977	Jordan	51.5	Oman	29.7
	1978	Jordan	50.6	Pakistan	15.0
	1979	Egypt	122.3	Oman	78.2
	1980	Lebanon	95.8	Pakistan	78

TABLE 10 (continued)

		5		6	
Algeria	1976	—			
	1977	—			
	1978	—			
	1979	Seychelles	1		
	1980	—			
Iraq	1976	Somalia	7.5	Bangladesh	2
	1977	—		—	
	1978	Tunisia	8	CAR	6
	1979	Mauritania	30	Lebanon	15
	1980	Arab	39.6	Somalia	21.5
Kuwait	1976	Bahrain	20.1	India	17.9
	1977	PDRY	17.8	Mauritania	16.0
	1978	Bahrain	21.6	Yemen	19.4
	1979	Arab	48.5	Sudan	28.4
	1980	Lebanon	37.6	Bangladesh	33.4
Libya	1976	Cameroon	2.0	PDRY	1.8
	1977	Seychelles	0.1	—	
	1978	PDRY	1.0	—	
	1979	—		—	
	1980	—		—	
Qatar	1976	Tunisia	5.0	Yemen	4.7
	1977	Cape Verde	0.5	—	
	1978	—		—	
	1979	Zaire	4.8	Lebanon	2.2
	1980	Somalia	8.4	Afghanistan	5
Saudi Arabia	1976	Jordan	165.0	Yemen	122.0
	1977	Bangladesh	150.0	Yemen	132.8
	1978	Mauritania	100.0	Djibouti	60.0
	1979	Yemen	93.2	Oman	85.5
	1980	Pakistan	248.8	Yemen	228.4
UAE	1976	Morocco	35.5	Yemen	35.5
	1977	Bahrain	21.5	PDRY	17.4
	1978	India	7.1	Oman	6.1
	1979	Morocco	61.6	Somalia	53.7
	1980	Sudan	69.8	Morocco	60.6

TABLE 10 (continued)

		7		8	
Algeria	1976				
	1977				
	1978				
	1979				
	1980				
Iraq	1976	Uganda	3	PDRY	3
	1977	–		–	
	1978	Afghanistan	3	Sudan	2
	1979	Mozambique	10	Tunisia	10
	1980	Pakistan	19.5	Mozambique	10.3
Kuwait	1976	Sri Lanka	10	PDRY	8.9
	1977	India	13.7	Bahrain	13.0
	1978	India	18.2	PDRY	12.1
	1979	Yemen	23.8	Tunisia	14
	1980	Tunisia	24.2	Yemen	24.4
Libya	1976	Bangladesh	1.8	Malta	1.7
	1977	–		–	
	1978	–		–	
	1979	–		–	
	1980	–		–	
Qatar	1976	Mali	2.0	Uganda	2.0
	1977	–		–	
	1978	–		–	
	1979	Mauritania	1.8	Somalia	1.5
	1980	Mauritania	3.3	Cameroon	3
Saudi Arabia	1976	Bahrain	100.0	PDRY	100
	1977	Sudan	86.2	Mauritania	80
	1978	Jordan	43.0	Sudan	37.3
	1979	Arab	76.3	India	36.8
	1980	Sudan	125.2	Arab	115.2
UAE	1976	India	31.6	Bahrain	27.1
	1977	Morocco	15.9	Tunisia	11.1
	1978	Iran	6.0	Bahrain	5.7
	1979	Africa	45.9	Bahrain	32.3
	1980	Bahrain	50.7	Oman	49.6

TABLE 10 (continued)

		9		10	
Algeria	1976				
	1977				
	1978				
	1979				
	1980				
Iraq	1976	Yemen	2.7		
	1977	–			
	1978	–			
	1979	Cuba	10	Zambia	9
	1980	Madagascar	9.4	Vietnam	6.4
Kuwait	1976	Somalia	3	Sudan	2.7
	1977	Bangladesh	12.5	Morocco	10.9
	1978	Sudan	11.4	Oman	10.6
	1979	Bangladesh	12.5	Mauritania	10.2
	1980	Mauritania	22.1	Pakistan	19.6
Libya	1976	Malaysia	1.5	Turkey	1.3
	1977	–		–	
	1978	–		–	
	1979	–		–	
	1980	–		–	
Qatar	1976	PDRY	2.0	Mauritania[1]	1.5
	1977	–			
	1978	–			
	1979	Sudan	0.6	Domincan Rep.	0.1
	1980	Djibouti	2	Sierra Leone	2
Saudi Arabia	1976	Mauritania	94.1	Thailand	75.6
	1977	Morocco	50.0	Pakistan	42.1
	1978	Pakistan	32.5	Indonesia	27.4
	1979	Somalia	29.7	Tunisia	25.1
	1980	Oman	111	Djibouti	99.9
UAE	1976	Sudan	25.4	PDRY	18.4
	1977	Mauritania	10.0	Somalia	9.4
	1978	Bangladesh	3.1	Malaysia	2.9
	1979	Lebanon	28.5	Yemen	19.2
	1980	Somalia	48.6	Arab	45.7

1 Gabon 1.5   Senegal 1.5   * Indicates "unspecified developing countries"

"PDRY" = Peoples' Democratic Republic of Yemen

Source: OECD "Flows of Resources from OPEC Members to Developing Countries",
1979 + 1980, Paris.

TABLE 11
Geographic Distribution of Bilateral Aid Commitments by Region
Within Africa: 1973–1980
($ Million)

	1973		1974	
	$	%	$	%
Algeria:				
Arab League Africa[2]	0.4	26.7	0.3	5.4
Sub-Saharan Africa	1.1	73.3	5.3	94.6
Total Africa	$ 1.5		5.6	
Iraq:				
Arab League Africa	0	0	59.0	100.0
Sub-Saharan Africa	12.0	100.0	0	0
Total Africa	12.0		59.0	
Kuwait:				
Arab League Africa	75.9	82.0	196.0	64.7
Sub-Saharan Africa	16.7	18.0	106.9	35.3
Total Africa	$ 92.6		302.9	
Libya:				
Arab League Africa	35.0	56.5	26.2	31.6
Sub-Saharan Africa	27.0	43.5	56.8	68.4
Total Africa	$ 62.0		83.0	
Qatar:				
Arab League Africa	1.0	100.0	42.0	92.3
Sub-Saharan Africa	0	0	3.5	7.7
Total Africa	$ 1.0		45.5	
Saudi Arabia:				
Arab League Africa	17.0	70.8	55.9	77.1
Sub-Saharan Africa	7.0	29.2	16.6	22.9
Total Africa	$ 24.0		72.5	
United Arab Emirates:				
Arab League Africa	6.0	62.5	23.1	30.2
Sub-Saharan Africa	3.6	37.5	53.4	69.8
Total Africa	$ 9.6		76.5	
Total Arab League Africa	$ 135.3	66.7%	402.5	62.4%
Total Sub-Saharan Africa	67.4	33.3%	242.5	37.6%
Total Africa	§ 202.7		$ 645.0	

TABLE 11 (continued)

	1975		1976	
	$	%	$	%
Algeria:				
Arab League Africa	0	0	0	0
Sub-Saharan Africa	7.6	100.0	3.9	100.0
Total Africa	7.6		3.9	
Iraq:				
Arab League Africa	11.1	47.2	29.0	59.2
Sub-Saharan Africa	12.4	52.8	20.0	40.8
Total Africa	23.5		49.0	
Kuwait:				
Arab League Africa	143.5	75.8	278.5	76.0
Sub-Saharan Africa	45.8	24.2	88.1	24.0
Total Africa	189.3		366.6	
Libya:				
Arab League Africa	0.3	0.2	0	0
Sub-Saharan Africa	147.7	99.8	37.3	100.0
Total Africa	148.0		37.3	
Qatar:				
Arab League Africa	6.3	31.0	2.1	14.3
Sub-Saharan Africa	12.0	69.0	12.6	85.7
Total Africa	18.3		14.7	
Saudi Arabia:				
Arab League Africa	157.7	60.4	287.3	87.2
Sub-Saharan Africa	103.0	39.6	42.3	12.8
Total Africa	260.7		329.6	
United Arab Emirates:				
Arab League Africa	90.0	88.7	75.9	92.0
Sub-Saharan Africa	11.5	11.3	6.6	8.0
Total Africa	101.5		82.5	
Total Arab League Africa	408.9	54.6 %	672.8	76.1 %
Total Sub-Saharan Africa	340.0	45.4 %	210.8	23.9 %
Total Africa	$ 748.9		$ 883.6	

TABLE 11 (continued)

| | 1977 | | 1978 | |
	$	%	$	%
Algeria:				
Arab League Africa	0	0	0	0
Sub-Saharan Africa	0	0	5.5	100.0
Total Africa	0		5.5	
Iraq:				
Arab League Africa	0	0	26.8	69.1
Sub-Saharan Africa	0	0	12.0	30.9
Total Africa	0		38.8	
Kuwait:				
Arab League Africa	39.7	32.7	37.1	43.1
Sub-Saharan Africa	81.7	67.3	49.0	56.9
Total Africa	121.4		86.1	
Libya:				
Arab League Africa	0	0	0	0
Sub-Saharan Africa	6.2	100.0	106.9	100.0
Total Africa	6.2		106.9	
Qatar:				
Arab League Africa	0	0	1.0	100.0
Sub-Saharan Africa	9.6	100.0	0	0
Total Africa	9.6		1.0	
Saudi Arabia:				
Arab League Africa	451.2	83.2	542.7	79.1
Sub-Saharan Africa	91.0	16.8	143.6	20.9
Total Africa	542.2		686.3	
United Arab Emirates:				
Arab League Africa	229.7	91.3	2.5	23.6
Sub-Saharan Africa	21.9	8.7	8.1	76.4
Total Africa	251.6		10.6	
Total Arab League Africa	720.6	77.4%	610.1	65.2%
Total Sub-Saharan Africa	210.4	22.6%	325.1	34.8%
Total Africa	$ 931.0		$ 935.2	

TABLE 11 (continued)

| | 1979 | | 1980[1] | |
	$	%	$	%
Algeria:				
Arab League Africa	0	0	n.a.	
Sub-Saharan Africa	4.0	100.0	n.a.	
Total Africa	4.0			
Iraq:				
Arab League Africa	77.0	40.0	1.1	5.8
Sub-Saharan Africa	115.7	60.0	18.0	94.2
Total Africa	192.7		19.1	
Kuwait:				
Arab League Africa	96.8	78.0	10.3	
Sub-Saharan Africa	27.3	22.0	99.1	
Total Africa	124.1		109.4	
Libya:				
Arab League Africa	25.0	100.0	n.a.	
Sub-Saharan Africa	0	0	n.a.	
Total Africa	25.0			
Qatar:				
Arab League Africa	3.8	30.2	n.a.	
Sub-Saharan Africa	8.8	69.8	n.a.	
Total Africa	12.6	100.0%		
Saudi Arabia:				
Arab League Africa	272.4	89.0	17.7	9.3
Sub-Saharan Africa	33.7	11.0	172.0	90.7
Total Africa	306.1		189.7	
United Arab Emirates:				
Arab League Africa	73.6	89.9	107.8	93.4
Sub-Saharan Africa	8.3	10.1	7.6	6.6
Total Africa	81.9		115.4	
Total Arab League Africa	548.6	73.5%	136.9	31.6%
Total Sub-Saharan Africa	197.8	26.5%	296.7	68.4%
Total Africa	$ 746.4		$ 433.6	

TABLE 11 (continued)

	Total	
	$	%
Algeria:		
Arab League Africa	0.7	2.5
Sub-Saharan Africa	27.4	97.5
Total Africa	$ 28.1	100.0 %
Iraq:		
Arab League Africa	204.0	51.8
Sub-Saharan Africa	190.1	48.2
Total Africa	$ 394.1	100.0 %
Kuwait:		
Arab League Africa	877.8	63.0
Sub-Saharan Africa	514.6	37.0
Total Africa	$ 1,392.4	100.0 %
Libya:		
Arab League Africa	86.5	18.5
Sub-Saharan Africa	381.9	81.5
Total Africa	$ 468.4	100.0 %
Qatar:		
Arab League Africa	56.2	54.7
Sub-Saharan Africa	46.5	45.3
Total Africa	$ 102.7	100.0 %
Saudi Arabia:		
Arab League Africa	$ 1,801.9	74.7
Sub-Saharan Africa	609.2	25.3
Total Africa	$ 2,411.1	100.0 %
United Arab Emirates:		
Arab League Africa	608.6	83.4
Sub-Saharan Africa	121.0	16.6
Total Africa	$ 729.6	100.0
Total Arab League Africa	$ 3,635.7	65.8 %
Total Sub-Saharan Africa	1,890.7	34.2 %
Total Africa	$ 5,526.4	

1   For 1980, preliminary data only where available. For Iraq, Kuwait, Saudi Arabia
    and the United Arab Emirates refers primarily to commitments of the respective
    national funds. Final statistics are likely to show a far higher level of commit-
    ments to ALA countries in 1980.
2   Djibouti, Mauritania, Somalia and Sudan.

Source: OECD

TABLE 12
Project and Program Aid Committed to Africa
by Donor Country: 1973–1979*

Type of Aid	Algeria		Iraq	
A. *"Project" Aid:*				
Project finance	$ 5.7		73.5	
Emergency Assistance	5.6		17.3	
Health + Education	—		10.0	
Cultural	—		5.0	
Islamic	—		—	
Joint Venture Investments	1.3		76.8	
Total Project Aid	$ 12.6		182.6	
As % of Total Identifiable Aid		54.5 %		48.7
B. *"Program" Aid:*				
General Support Payments	$ 4.6		29.0	
Budgetary Support	—		10.0	
Balance of Payments	0.9		22.0	
Financial Support	—		1.1	
Central Bank Deposits	—		—	
Oil Credits	—		118.0	
Line of Credit	5.0		—	
Supply of Goods + Trade Credits			12.0	
Total Program Aid	$ 10.5		192.1	
As % of Total Identifiable Aid		45.5 %		51.3
C. Not Available	$ 5.0		0.3	
Grand Total	$ 28.1		375.0	

TABLE 12 (continued)

Type of Aid	Kuwait		Libya	
A. *"Project" Aid:*				
Project finance	733.5		129.8	
Emergency Assistance	3.7		15.3	
Health + Education	1.2		3.3	
Cultural	—		1.6	
Islamic	0.01		—	
Joint Venture Investments	97.9		143.4	
Total Project Aid	836.31		293.4	
As % of Total Identifiable Aid		74.1		65.5
B. *"Program" Aid:*				
General Support Payments	16.4		12.0	
Budgetary Support	—		2.1	
Balance of Payments	5.0		2.0	
Financial Support	184.9		137.8	
Central Bank Deposits	72.6		—	
Oil Credits	10.0		—	
Line of Credit	—		—	
Supply of Goods + Trade Credits	2.8		0.8	
Total Program Aid	291.7		154.7	
As % of Total Identifiable Aid		25.9		34.5
C. Not Available	120.2		20.0	
Grand Total	1248.21		468.1	

TABLE 12 (continued)

Type of Aid	Qatar		Saudi Arabia	
A. *"Project" Aid:*				
Project finance	48.1		870.3	
Emergency Assistance	20.9		21.6	
Health + Education	0.003		16.6	
Cultural	—		0.02	
Islamic	—		5.7	
Joint Venture Investments	—		—	
Total Project Aid	69.003		914.22	
As % of Total Identifiable Aid		74.9		44.8
B. *"Program" Aid:*				
General Support Payments	23.1		390.7	
Budgetary Support	—		184.4	
Balance of Payments	—		100.0	
Financial Support	—		—	
Central Bank Deposits	—		250.0	
Oil Credits	—		200.0	
Line of Credit	—		—	
Supply of Goods + Trade Credits	—		—	
Total Program Aid	23.1		1125.1	
As % of Total Identifiable Aid		25.1		55.2
C. Not Available	0		172.8	
Grand Total	92.1		2212.1	

TABLE 12 (continued)

Type of Aid	UAE		Total
A. *"Project" Aid:*			
Project finance	443.4		$ 2304.3
Emergency Assistance	9.5		93.9
Health + Education	5.6		36.7
Cultural	—		6.6
Islamic	0.01		5.7
Joint Venture Investments	—		319.4
Total Project Aid	458.51		$ 2766.6
As % of Total Identifiable Aid		81.8	59.3 %
B. *"Program" Aid:*			
General Support Payments	96.3		$ 572.1
Budgetary Support	5.5		202.0
Balance of Payments	—		129.9
Financial Support	—		323.8
Central Bank Deposits	0.1		322.7
Oil Credits	—		328.0
Line of Credit	—		5.0
Supply of Goods + Trade Credits	—		15.6
Total Program Aid	101.9		$ 1899.1
As % of Total Identifiable Aid		18.2	40.7 %
C. Not Available	11.7		$ 330.0
Grand Total	572.1		$ 4995.7

* Includes Djibouti, Mauritania, Somalia and Sudan.

Source: OECD

TABLE 13

Consolidated Geographic Distribution of Official Bilateral Aid
Commitments by Region and Donor Country: 1973–1979

($ Million)

| | Arab Countries | | Sub-Saharan Africa | | Asia | | Other Countries* | | Total |
	$	%	$	%	$	%	$	%	$
Algeria	310.8	74.7	27.4	6.6	1.0	0.2	76.9	18.5	416.1
Iraq	2,015.3	66.4	172.0	5.7	476.3	15.7	368.9	12.2	3,032.5
Kuwait	8,210.9	80.5	419.4	4.1	686.1	6.7	877.9	8.6	10,194.3
Libya	1,092.3	43.6	377.3	15.1	484.1	19.3	552.8	22.1	2,506.5
Qatar	1,154.7	94.9	46.5	3.8	15.5	1.3	0.2	0	1,216.9
Saudi Arabia	11,352.4	76.9	437.1	3.0	2,325.4	15.7	655.6	4.4	14,770.5
United Arab Emirates	5,512.4	81.6	113.3	1.7	438.6	6.5	691.2	10.2	6,755.5
Total	$ 29,648.8	76.2 %	$ 1,593.0	4.1 %	$ 4,427.0	11.4 %	$ 3,223.5	8.3 %	$ 38,892.3

* Includes unallocated or unspecified amounts.

Source: OECD

161

TABLE 14
Arab Sponsored Multilateral Institutions Dealing with Africa:
1973−1978[1]

| Country | Arab Institutions Specialized in Africa | | | | | |
| | AFTAAAC | | ABEDA | | SAAFA[2] | |
	$	%	$	%	$	%
Algeria	2	7.5	30	7.9	14.5[5]	−
Iraq	6	22.6	40	10.6	65	18.1
Kuwait	1.5	5.7	40	10.6	70	19.4
Libya	3	11.3	60	15.9	81	16.7
Qatar	1.4	5.3	40	10.6	20	5.6
Saudi Arabia	9	26.4	90	23.8	90	25.0
United Arab Emirates	5	18.9	40	10.6	50	13.9
Other Arab Countries and Institutions	0.6	2.3	38.25	10.1	5	1.4
Non-Arab Countries and Institutions	0	0	0	0	0	0
Total Capital	28.5		378.25		360	
Seven Donor Countries	27.9		340		355	
As % of Capital		97.9		88.9		98.6
Arab Capital as % of Institutional Total		100		100		100

TABLE 14 (continued)

| Country | Institutions with an Afro-Arab Focus | | | | | |
| | OPEC Fund | | Islamic Development Bank | | Islamic Solidarity[3] Fund | |
	$	%	$	%	$	%
Algeria	40	2.4	32.5	3.2	0	0
Iraq	50.2	3.1	13.0	1.3	3.5	5.6
Kuwait	150.1	9.2	129.9	12.8	3.5	5.6
Libya	81.0	4.9	162.4	16.0	10.5	16.7
Qatar	37.9	2.3	32.5	3.2	1.5	2.4
Saudi Arabia	418	25.5	259.8	25.6	26.5	42.2
United Arab Emirates	67.4	4.1	142.9	14.1	13.5	21.5
Other Arab Countries and Institutions	0	0	96.1	9.5	0.02	0.03
Non-Arab Countries and Institutions	797.8	48.6	144.2	14.2	3.8	6.1
Total Capital	1642.4		1013.2		62.8	
Seven Donor Countries	844.6		772.9		59.0	
As % of Capital		51.4		76.3		93.9
Arab Capital as % of Institutional Total		51.4		85.8		94.0

TABLE 14 (continued)

| Country | Private Banks with African Interests | | | | | |
| | Arab-African Bank[4] | | Arab International[4] Bank | | Arab Bank for Inv. and Foreign Trade | |
	$	%	$	%	$	%
Algeria	1.1	2.0	0	0	5	33.3
Iraq	5.6	10.0	0	0	0	0
Kuwait	23.7	42.4	0	0	0	0
Libya	0		38.6	28.8	5	33.3
Qatar	0.3	0.5	6.4	4.7	0	0
Saudi Arabia	0	0	0	0	0	0
United Arab Emirates	0	0	38.6	28.8	5	33.3
Other Arab Countries and Institutions	25.3	45.1	50.8	37.8	0	0
Non-Arab Countries and Institutions	0	0	0	0	0	0
Total Capital	56.0		134.4		15.0	
Seven Donor Countries	30.7		83.6		15	
As % of Capital		54.8		62.2		100
Arab Capital as % of Institutional Total		100		100		100

1 Does not include capital subscriptions subsequent to 1978; as % of total capital.
2 Amalgamated with ABEDA in 1977.
3 Contributions, not capital.
4 Capital converted at $ 2.80 = 1 £ Sterling.
5 Algerian Trust Fund.

Source: OECD and UNCTAD

TABLE 15
African Countries Ranked by Amount of Consolidated Bilateral Aid
Commitments: 1973–1980[1]
($ Million)

Country	Amount	Country	Amount
1. Sudan (a) (b)	$ 1966.4	24. Togo	22.9
2. Mauritania (a) (b)	887.3	25. Mozambique	21.7
3. Somalia (a) (b)	704.8	26. Rwanda	18.5
4. Uganda (b)	183.3	27. Botswana	18.3
5. Guinea (b)	171.9	28. Burundi	18.1
6. Zaire	166.4	29. Equatorial Guinea	16.2
7. Mali (b)	136.3	30. Lesotho	10.6
8. Senegal (b)	117.8	31. Benin	10.5
9. Zambia	109.8	32. Upper Volta (b)	7.4
10. Madagascar	84.0	33. Mauritius	5.8
11. Cameroon (b)	78.3	34. Cape Verde	4.7
12. Djibouti (a) (b)	77.2	34. Sierra Leone	4.7
13. Gabon (b)	75.8	36. Central African	
14. Chad (b)	75.1	Republic	4.0
15. Tanzania	70.0	37. Ethiopia	2.2
16. Ghana	63.8	37. Seychelles	2.2
17. Niger (b)	62.8	39. Zimbabwe	0.1
18. Congo	58.2	40. Angola	0
19. Gambia (b)	55.4	40. Ivory Coast	0
20. Comoros (b)	50.8	40. Malawi	0
21. Kenya	45.4	40. Sao Tome e Principe	0
22. Liberia	30.7	40. Swaziland	0
23. Guinea-Bissau (b)	26.1		

(a) = Member of the Arab League   (b) = Member of the Islamic Conference
1 = Preliminary data for 1980 only.

TABLE 16
Apparent Consumption of Crude Oil and Refined Products
In Sub-Saharan Countries: 1973–1979[1]
(X'000 BBL/D)

Country	1973	1974	1975	1976
Angola	13.8	14.4	6.7	3.6
Benin	2.9	2.9	3.3	2.3
Botswana	0.6	0.6	0.2	0.3
Burundi	0.4	0.4	0.4	0.6
Cameroon	6.1	5.6	7.3	6.4
Cape Verde	0.1	0.0	1.1	0.5
Central African Republic	1.3	1.3	0.9	1.0
Chad	1.2	1.4	1.2	1.4
Comoros	0.2	0.2	0.2	0.3
Congo	3.9	3.6	4.9	5.2
Equatorial Guinea	0.2	0.2	0.5	0.5
Ethiopia	14.6	14.5	9.9	8.5
Gambia	0.4	0.4	0.7	0.6
Ghana	15.1	18.7	18.6	18.7
Guinea	5.9	6.0	6.0	6.2
Guinea-Bissau	0.7	0.6	0.6	0.5
Ivory Coast	25.4	25.2	24.9	27.5
Kenya	37.7	40.5	37.4	31.9
Lesotho	0.2	0.1	0.2	0.2
Liberia	10.2	9.8	8.9	8.5
Madagascar	10.6	9.0	9.1	10.2
Malawi	2.5	2.4	2.3	2.9
Mali	1.9	2.2	2.4	2.3
Mauritius	2.7	3.1	4.4	5.2
Mozambique	6.2	3.3	8.9	8.6
Namibia	1.9	2.1	2.0	2.2
Niger	2.2	2.1	2.5	2.5
Rwanda	0.5	0.5	0.6	0.8
Sao Tome e Principe	0.1	0.1	0.1	0.1
Senegal	8.1	9.9	11.5	12.2
Seychelles	0.4	0.4	0.5	0.5
Sierra Leone	4.0	3.5	1.5	1.5
Swaziland	0.3	0.3	0.3	0.5
Tanzania	20.5	14.8	12.9	17.6
Togo	2.5	2.4	2.1	2.6
Uganda	8.3	8.1	7.9	7.3
Upper Volta	1.4	1.6	1.8	1.7
Zaire	15.9	15.2	14.9	13.1
Zambia	18.9	17.1	24.2	18.2
Zimbabwe	12.4	12.1	12.1	13.2
TOTAL	262.2	256.6	255.9	247.9

TABLE 16 (continued)

Country	1977	1978	1979[2]
Angola	7.4	3.0	3.5
Benin	2.6	2.7	2.9
Botswana	0.3	0.5	0.9
Burundi	0.5	0.6	1.4
Cameroon	7.3	9.7	11.0
Cape Verde	1.3	0.7	1.0
Central African Republic	1.2	1.2	1.7
Chad	1.5	1.5	1.7
Comoros	0.3	0.3	0.6
Congo	8.0	13.4	17.0
Equatorial Guinea	0.5	0.5	0.8
Ethiopia	10.1	8.7	10.2
Gambia	0.8	0.9	1.3
Ghana	19.8	20.1	20.6
Guinea	6.3	6.4	7.0
Guinea-Bissau	0.6	0.7	1.0
Ivory Coast	27.7	28.7	30.7
Kenya	31.1	29.4	30.7
Lesotho	0.3	0.2	0.6
Liberia	11.3	10.8	11.4
Madagascar	9.3	10.3	11.0
Malawi	2.9	2.7	3.6
Mali	2.6	2.7	3.2
Mauritius	5.5	5.4	5.9
Mozambique	10.4	12.3	12.7
Namibia	2.1	2.3	2.9
Niger	2.6	2.8	3.5
Rwanda	0.9	0.9	1.4
Sao Tome e Principe	0.2	0.2	0.5
Senegal	12.5	13.9	15.0
Seychelles	1.1	0.6	0.9
Sierra Leone	1.4	6.3	6.9
Swaziland	0.4	0.4	0.8
Tanzania	13.3	16.7	17.7
Togo	3.2	4.5	4.9
Uganda	6.4	8.4	9.3
Upper Volta	2.2	2.4	2.7
Zaire	16.0	12.0	16.4
Zambia	14.9	17.9	18.9
Zimbabwe	13.7	13.7	14.8
TOTAL	260.5	276.4	309.0

1 The data refer to "apparent inland" consumption and are derived from the formula P + M − X − B ± S. The symbols used are: P = production; M = imports; X = exports; B = bunkers; S = addition to stocks.
2 Estimates.

Source: U.N., *World Energy Supplies, 1973–1978*, New York, 1980

TABLE 17

Petroleum Imports of Reporting African Countries: 1973–1980

($ Million)

	1973	1974	1975	1976	1977	1978	1979	1980[1]
Burundi	1.63	2.62	3.30	4.25	5.56	6.67	12.60	15.25
Ethiopia	20.10	49.13	68.45	53.62	75.70	62.66	97.80	143.50
Ivory Coast	25.27	129.06	145.96	149.33	169.54	171.15	290.00	392.00
Kenya	46.71	190.96	236.40	223.37	242.01	238.96	321.30	547.50
Madagascar	14.91	44.79	68.22	52.17	44.16	52.80	41.00	121.00
Malawi	8.95	14.80	17.78	21.95	23.69	30.18	30.10	69.00
Mauritius	11.50	27.97	31.97	30.87	40.97	45.71	72.90	105.00
Niger	6.68	13.05	12.83	14.75	18.40	22.08	32.00*	50.00
Rwanda	2.25	4.89	8.03	9.64	12.23	14.80	21.50*	34.00
Senegal	21.15	58.25	60.15	71.13	85.01	102.00	133.50	234.00
Sierra Leone	9.23	25.23	22.37	11.21	25.47	33.33	48.30*	76.00
Tanzania	48.14	140.56	79.58	94.16	101.89	135.25	171.90	310.00
Togo	4.84	10.98	13.00	12.78	20.38	13.37	94.80	30.00
Upper Volta	n.a.	9.40	13.36	10.75	17.75	21.30	30.90*	49.00
Zambia	31.62	89.43	93.71	108.35	104.03	102.11	148.00*	234.00
TOTAL	253.00	811.10	875.10	868.30	986.80	1,052.40	1,546.60	2,410.30

* Estimated
1 Projected

Source: The Chase Manhattan Bank, N.A., Economics Department and IMF, *International Financial Statistics*, various issues.

TABLE 18
Geographic Distribution of Commitments by Multilateral Institutions
Special Arab Fund for Africa (SAAFA): 1974–1977
($ Million)

Country	1974	1975	1976
Angola	–	1.0[3]	–
Benin	2.4	–	–
Botswana	–	5.4	–
Burundi	2.0	–	–
Cameroon (b)	–	5.7[1]	–
Cape Verde Islands	–	0.5	10.0
Central African Republic	2.4	–	–
Chad (b)	8.8	–	–
Comoros Islands (b)	–	–	10.5
Congo	–	–	–
Djibouti (a)	ineligible as Arab League member		
Equatorial Guinea	0.5	–	–
Ethiopia	–	14.2	–
Gabon (b)	ineligible as oil exporter		
Gambia (b)	0.7	–	–
Ghana	–	8.8[1]	–
Guinea (b)	–	1.6[1]	–
Guinea-Bissau (b)	1.3[2]	–	–
Ivory Coast	–	7.2[1,5]	–
Kenya	–	3.6	–
Lesotho	2.8	–	–
Liberia	3.6	–	–
Madagascar	4.8	–	–
Malawi	7.5	–	–
Mali (b)	7.8	–	–
Mauritania (a)	ineligible as Arab League member		
Mauritius	–	2.7	–
Mozambique	–	1.0[3]	26.0
Niger (b)	–	5.4[1]	–
Rwanda	2.0	–	–
Sao Tome e Principe	–	0.5	10.0
Senegal (b)	–	7.5	–
Seychelles	–	–	–
Sierra Leone	3.6	–	–
Somalia (a)	–	7.5	–
Sudan (a)	ineligible as Arab League member		

169

TABLE 18 (continued)

Country	1974	1975	1976
Swaziland	–	4.2	–
Tanzania	14.2	–	–
Togo	–	1.8[1]	–
Uganda (b)	11.3	–	–
Upper Volta (b)	–	5.4[1]	–
Zaire	–	12.4	–
Zambia	12.7	–	–
Zimbabwe	–	–	–
Total Sub-Saharan Africa	$ 88.4	$ 96.1	$ 56.8

TABLE 18 (continued)

Country	1977	Total Commitments	Disbursements
Angola	13.2	13.2	13.2
Benin	–	2.4	2.4
Botswana	–	5.4	5.4
Burundi	–	2.0	2.0
Cameroon (b)	–	2.8	2.8
Cape Verde Islands	–	10.5	10.5
Central African Republic	–	2.4	2.4
Chad (b)	–	8.8	8.8
Comoros Islands (b)	–	10.5	10.5
Congo	–	0	0
Djibouti (a)	ineligible as Arab League Member		
Equatorial Guinea	–	0.5	0.5
Ethiopia	–	14.2	14.2
Gabon (b)	ineligible as oil exporter		
Gambia (b)	–	0.7	0.7
Ghana	–	4.4	4.4
Guinea (b)	–	0.8	0.8
Guinea-Bissau (b)	–	0.3	0.3
Ivory Coast	–	3.6	0
Kenya	–	3.6	3.6
Lesotho	–	2.8	2.8
Liberia	–	3.6	3.6
Madagascar	–	4.8	4.8
Malawi	–	7.5	0
Mali (b)	–	7.8	7.8
Mauritania (a)	Ineligible as Arab League Member		
Mauritius	–	2.7	2.7
Mozambique	–	27.0	26.0
Niger (b)	–	2.7	2.7
Rwanda	–	2.0	2.0
Sao Tome e Principe	–	10.5	10.5
Senegal (b)	–	7.5	7.5
Seychelles	–	0	0
Sierra Leone	–	3.6	3.6
Somalia (a)	–	7.5	7.5
Sudan (a)	ineligible as Arab League member		
Swaziland	–	4.2	4.2
Tanzania	–	14.2	14.2

TABLE 18 (continued)

Country	1977	Total Commitments	Disbursements
Togo	–	1.8	0.9[4]
Uganda (b)	–	11.3	11.3
Upper Volta (b)	–	2.7	2.7
Zaire	–	12.4	12.4
Zambia	–	12.7	12.7
Zimbabwe	–	0	0
Total Sub-Saharan Africa	$ 13.2	$ 254.50	$ 236.2[6]

a) Member of the Arab League
b) Member of the Islamic Conference
1 Shared evenly between SAAFA and the Algerian Trust Fund (ATF).
2 $ 1 million provided by the ATF.
3 Earmarked for Angola and Mozambique on independence by the ATF but unpaid.
4 Negotiated and disbursed bilaterally by Algeria.
5 Amounts earmarked for Ivory Coast and Togo by SAAFA were withdrawn.
6 Includes $ 14.45 million disbursed as part of the ATF administered by the African Development Bank.

Source: OECD, ABEDA, UNCTAD and Alkazaz, op. cit., pp. 114–121.

TABLE 19

Geographic Distribution of Aid from Multilateral Institutions
Arab Fund for Technical Assistance to African and Arab Countries
(AFTAAAC)
($ Million)

	1977	1978	1979	Total
Angola				0
Benin	0.13			0.13
Botswana				0
Burundi	0.26	0.12		0.38
Cameroon (b)		0.004		0.004
Cape Verde Islands		0.19		0.19
Central African Republic				0
Chad (b)				0
Comoros Islands (b)	0.61	0.66		1.27
Congo				0
Djibouti (a)	1.71	3.12		4.83
Equatorial Guinea				0
Ethiopia				0
Gabon (b)				0
Gambia (b)				0
Ghana		0.004		0.004
Guinea (b)	0.05	0.14		0.19
Guinea Bissau (b)	0.02	0.002		0.022
Ivory Coast				0
Kenya	0.05	0.08		0.13
Lesotho		0.03		0.03
Liberia		0.05		0.05
Madagascar				0
Malawi				0
Mali (b)		0.03		0.03
Mauritania (a)	0.16	0.25		0.41
Mauritius		0.07		0.07
Mozambique				0
Niger (b)		0.4		0.4
Rwanda		0.01		0.01
Sao Tome e Principe				0
Senegal (b)		0.3		0.3
Seychelles				0
Sierra Leone (b)	0.09	0.01		0.1
Somalia (a)	1.13	0.38		1.51

TABLE 19 (continued)

	1977	1978	1979	Total
Sudan (a)	0.03			0.03
Swaziland				0
Tanzania		0.07		0.07
Togo				0
Uganda (b)	0.51	0.25		0.76
Upper Volta (b)				0
Zaire				0
Zambia	0.26	0.13		0.39
Zimbabwe				0
Africa Unspecified	0.52	0.4		0.92
Arab Unspecified	0.02	0.41		0.43
Total Africa	5.55	7.11		12.66
Total Sub-Saharan Africa	2.5	2.95		5.45
As % of Total	45.0%	41.5%		43.0%
Total Arab League States (a)	3.05	4.16		7.21
As % of Total	55.0%	58.5%		57.0%
Total Sub-Saharan Members of the Islamic Conference (b)	1.28	1.8		3.08
As % of Total Sub-Saharan Africa	51.2%	60.9%		56.5%

Source: OECD and BADEA

TABLE 20
Geographic Distribution of Commitments by Multilateral Institutions
Arab Bank for Economic Development in Africa (ABEDA): 1975–1980
($ Million)

Country	1975	1976	1977	1978
Angola				
Benin	8			4.6
Botwana				2.2
Burundi		4		6
Cameroon (b)	10		10	
Cape Verde Islands				1
Central African Republic				
Chad (b)				9.7
Comoros Islands (b)				
Congo	10			
Dijbouti (a)			not eligible	
Equatorial Guinea				
Ethiopia				0.5
Gabon (b)				
Gambia (b)		3.3		0.6
Ghana (b)	5		10	
Guinea (b)			4.8	1
Guinea Bissau (b)				1.1
Ivory Coast				
Kenya		5		
Lesotho				6
Liberia			3.2	3.9
Madagascar	5		10	1.9
Malawi				
Mali (b)		15	5	1.9
Mauritania (a)			not eligible	
Mauritius		10		
Mozambique				
Niger (b)	7			8.9
Rwanda		5	6	
Sao Tome e Principe				
Senegal (b)	1.6		7.2	0.9
Seychelles				
Sierra Leone		5		
Somalia (a)			not eligible	
Sudan (a)			not eligible	

TABLE 20 (continued)

Country	1975	1976	1977	1978
Swaziland				
Tanzania	5		10	
Togo				
Uganda (b)				4.9
Upper Volta (b)		4.5		1.9
Zaire	10			4.4
Zambia		10		
Zimbabwe				
African Regional or Unallocated	10	0.1		6.5
Total	$ 71.6	61.9	66.2	67.9
Sub-Saharan Members of the Islamic Conference (b)	$ 23.6	27.8	37.0	30.9
As % of Total	33.0 %	44.9 %	55.9 %	45.5 %

TABLE 20 (continued)

Country	1979	1980	Total
Angola	10		10
Benin			12.6
Botswana		7.3	9.5
Burundi		10	20
Cameroon (b)		9	29
Cape Verde Islands	2.4		3.4
Central African Republic			0
Chad (b)			9.7
Comoros Islands (b)	1.6	8	9.6
Congo			10
Djibouti (a)		ineligible	
Equatorial Guinea			0
Ethiopia			0.5
Gabon (b)			0
Gambia (b)	5.2		9.1
Ghana (b)			15
Guinea (b)	6		11.8
Guinea Bissau (b)			1.1
Ivory Coast			0
Kenya	5		10
Lesotho	3.9		9.9
Liberia			7.1
Madagascar			16.9
Malawi			0
Mali (b)	10		31.9
Mauritania		ineligible	
Mauritius			10
Mozambique		10	10
Niger (b)			15.9
Rwanda			11
Sao Tome e Principe			0
Senegal (b)		10	19.7
Seychelles		1.2	1.2
Sierra Leone		8.5	13.5
Somalia (a)		ineligible	
Sudan (a)		ineligible	
Swaziland			0
Tanzania		8	23
Togo			0

TABLE 20 (continued)

Country	1979	1980	Total
Uganda (b)			4.9
Upper Volta (b)			6.4
Zaire			14.4
Zambia			10
Zimbabwe			0
African Regional or Unallocated			16.6
Total	44.1	72.0	$ 383.7
Sub-Saharan Members of the Islamic Conference (b)	22.8	27.0	$ 169.1
As % of Total	51.7 %	37.5 %	44.1 %

(a) Member of Arab League

Source: ABEDA

TABLE 21

OPEC Fund for International Development

Geographic Distribution of Aid Commitments: 1976–1980

($ Million)

| | Arab Countries | | Sub-Saharan Africa | | Asia | | Latin America | | Total |
	$	%	$	%	$	%	$	%	$
1976	7.5	17.5	4.2	9.6	31.2	72.9	0	0	42.8
1977	39.4	16.3	82.7	33.6	99.8	41.4	21.0	8.7	241.1
1978	39.6	22.3	49.5	31.2	61.5	34.7	20.8	11.7	177.3
1979	26.7	12.5	73.4	34.5	80.9	38.0	31.9	15.0	218.9
1980	30.2	12.0	101.0	40.3	85.3	34.0	34.3	13.7	250.8
Total	$143.4	15.6%	$310.8	33.7%	$358.7	39.0%	$108.0	11.7%	$920.9

Source: Fund Annual Reports and Coordination Secretariat at the Arab Fund for Economic and Social Development, "Summary of Loans and Technical Assistance Extended to Developing Countries" (Quarterly).

179

TABLE 22
Geographic Distribution of Commitments by Multilateral Institutions
OPEC Fund for International Development: 1976–1980
($ Million)

Country	1976	1977	1978
Angola	–	–	–
Benin	–	2.0	1.6
Botswana	–	1.0	–
Burundi	–	1.7	–
Cameroon (b)	–	5.0	–
Cape Verde Islands	–	1.6	1.0
Central African Republic	1.8	–	–
Chad (b)	–	2.4	2.5
Comoros Islands (b)	–	0.5	1.5
Congo	–	–	4.0
Djibouti (a)	–	–	–
Equatorial Guinea	–	0.5	–
Ethiopia	–	4.8	–
Gabon (b)	Not eligible as OPEC Member		
Gambia (b)	–	1.7	2.0
Ghana (b)	–	7.8	–
Guinea (b)	2.4	–	4.5
Guinea Bissau	–	1.7	1.0
Ivory Coast	–	–	–
Kenya	–	8.0	5.3
Lesotho	–	1.9	–
Liberia	–	–	3.0
Madagascar	–	3.1	–
Malawi	–	1.8	–
Mali (b)	–	3.6	3.5
Mauritania (a)	–	1.6	5.0
Mauritius	–	–	–
Mozambique	–	6.6	–
Niger (b)	–	2.9	–
Rwanda	–	4.1	–
Sao Tome e Principe	–	0.4	–
Senegal (b)	–	3.4	4.0
Seychelles	–	0.3	0.3
Sierra Leone	–	2.1	–
Somalia (a)	–	2.1	2.7
Sudan (a)	7.4	3.3	9.5

TABLE 22 (continued)

Country	1976	1977	1978
Swaziland	—	—	—
Tanzania	—	5.5	5.0
Togo	—	—	—
Uganda (b)	—	4.6	—
Upper Volta (b)	—	4.4	5.4
Zaire	—	—	5.0
Zambia	—	—	—
Zimbabwe	—	—	—
Total Africa[1]	11.6	89.7	71.7[2]
Sub-Saharan Africa	4.2	82.7	49.5
As Percentage of Africa	36.2%	92.2%	69.0%
Arab League States (a)	7.4	7.0	17.2
As Percentage of Africa	63.8%	7.8%	24.0%
Sub-Saharan Members of Islamic Conference (b)	2.4	36.3	23.4
As Percentage of Sub-Saharan Africa	57.1%	43.9%	47.3%

TABLE 22 (continued)

Country	1979	1980	Total
Angola	–	3.0	3.0
Benin	4.5	4.5	12.6
Botswana	2.0	1.0	4.0
Burundi	4.5	5.0	11.2
Cameroon (b)	4.5	–	9.5
Cape Verde Islands	1.0	1.5	5.1
Central African Republic	–	–	1.8
Chad (b)	–	–	4.9
Comoros Islands (b)	–	1.0	3.0
Congo	–	8.0	12.0
Djibouti (a)	–	1.5	1.5
Equatorial Guinea	1.0	–	1.5
Ethiopia	–	–	4.8
Gabon (b)	Not eligible as OPEC member		–
Gambia (b)	1.0	1.5	6.2
Ghana (b)	3.7	7.5	19.0
Guinea (b)	2.0	–	8.9
Guinea Bissau	1.0	2.0	5.7
Ivory Coast	–	–	–
Kenya	–	4.0	17.3
Lesotho	3.0	1.5	6.4
Liberia	–	5.0	8.0
Madagascar	6.5	5.0	14.6
Malawi	–	–	1.8
Mali (b)	7.0	6.0	20.1
Mauritania (a)	–	5.5	12.1
Mauritius	–	2.0	2.0
Mozambique	5.0	3.5	15.1
Niger (b)	3.9	4.0	10.8
Rwanda	4.5	3.0	11.6
Sao Tome e Principe	–	–	0.4
Senegal (b)	–	9.5	16.9
Seychelles	0.2	0.5	1.3
Sierra Leone	1.6	1.0	4.7
Somalia (a)	5.0	5.5	15.2
Sudan (a)	–	7.7	27.9
Swaziland	–	–	–
Tanzania	–	10.0	20.5
Togo	3.5	–	3.5

TABLE 22 (continued)

Country	1979	1980	Total
Uganda (b)	—	5.0	9.6
Upper Volta (b)	1.5	6.0	17.3
Zaire	7.0	—	12.0
Zambia	—	—	—
Zimbabwe	—	—	—
Total Africa[1]	78.4	121.2	372.2
Sub-Saharan Africa	73.4	101.0	310.8
As Percentage of Africa	93.6%	83.3%	83.4%
Arab League States (a)	5.0	20.2	56.7
As Percentage of Africa	6.4%	16.7%	15.2%
Sub-Saharan Members of Islamic Conference (b)	23.6	40.5	126.2
As Percentage of Sub-Saharan Africa	32.2%	40.1%	40.6%

1 Totals do not add due to rounding.
2 Includes $ 5.0 million for regional African programs.

Source: OPEC Fund for International Development

TABLE 23
Contributions of the 4 Arab States to African Development
Pledged at the Afro-Arab Summit Conference, March 1977
($ million)

Type of Aid	Saudi Arabia	Kuwait	UAE	Qatar	Total
Bilateral					
Development Assistance	850	200	100	50	1200
Feasibility Studies	16	10	5	0	31
Multilateral					
ABEDA	120	20	20	20	180
African Development Bank	12	10	10	5	37
OAU Liberation Committee	2	1	2	1	6
Totals	1000	241	137	76	1454

Source: ABEDA, *Features, Figures and Trends of Arab Aid to the Third World*, Khartoum, November 1978, p. 4. Cited by Ahmad Y. Ahmad, *op. cit.*, p. 4.

TABLE 24
Sub-Saharan Trade with Arab Donor Countries: 1975–1979
($ Million)

| | 1975 | | | |
| | Exports | | Imports | |
	$	%	$	%
Angola	0.5	0.1	0	—
Benin	0	—	18.4	8.9
Burundi	0	—	0	—
Cameroon	1.7	0.4	0.7	0.1
CAR	0	—	0.07	0.1
Chad	0.06	0.1	0	—
Congo	0.2	0.1	0.23	0.1
Equatorial Guinea	0	—	0.01	0.1
Ethiopia	31.0	12.9	38.6	12.4
Gabon	0.5	0.1	0.2	nmf
Gambia	0	—	0	—
Ghana	1.1	0.1	50.2	6.3
Guinea	3.0	2.1	3.6	3.1
Guinea Bissau	0.3	4.9	0	—
Ivory Coast	13.0	1.1	46.2	4.1
Kenya	5.7	0.9	80.1	8.5
Liberia	0	—	44.4	13.4
Madagascar	1.2	0.4	0.2	0.1
Malawi	0	—	0.02	nmf
Mali	1.1	2.0	1.0	0.4
Mauritius	0	—	0.21	0.1
Mozambique	0.7	0.4	29.0	7.1
Niger	0.2	0.2	7.9	7.8
Rwanda	0	—	2.0	2.1
Senegal	0	—	0	—
Sierra Leone	0.1	0.1	0.3	0.2
Tanzania	1.7	0.4	92.2	10.9
Togo	0.3	0.2	2.0	1.1
Uganda	4.7	1.7	0.7	0.4
Upper Volta	0	—	0	—
Zaire	0	—	79.0	6.2
Zambia	0	—	111.0	12.0
TOTAL	$ 67.1		$ 608.2	
As % of Total African Imports/Exports		0.61%		4.7%

TABLE 24 (continued)

| | 1976 | | | |
| | Exports | | Imports | |
	$	%	$	%
Angola	14.1	2.3	0	–
Benin	0	–	24.1	–
Burundi	0	–	0.01	nmf
Cameroon	3.4	0.7	0.01	nmf
CAR	0	–	0.01	nmf
Chad	4.5	4.6	0.2	0.2
Congo	0	–	0.64	0.4
Equatorial Guinea	0	–	0	–
Ethiopia	21.0	7.6	45.5	13.0
Gabon	0.2	nmf	0.1	nmf
Gambia	0	–	0	–
Ghana	2.4	0.3	71.9	7.0
Guinea	3.9	1.8	2.0	2.0
Guinea Bissau	0.1	1.9	0.5	1.3
Ivory Coast	13.0	0.8	16.3	1.3
Kenya	3.2	0.4	61.8	6.4
Liberia	0	–	53.0	13.3
Madagascar	1.1	0.4	48.7	17.1
Malawi	0	–	0	–
Mali	1.5	1.5	1.4	0.6
Mauritius	0.02	nmf	1.3	0.4
Mozambique	2.5	0.8	70.0	15.8
Niger	0.3	0.2	7.4	5.9
Rwanda	0	–	1.9	1.8
Senegal	0	–	0	–
Sierra Leone	0.1	0.1	0	–
Tanzania	1.0	0.2	31.4	4.8
Togo	0	–	0.6	0.3
Uganda	1.2	0.3	0.4	0.3
Upper Volta	0	–	0	–
Zaire	0	–	8.4	0.8
Zambia	0	–	88.0	13.4
TOTAL	$ 73.5		$ 535.6	
As % of Total African Imports/Exports		0.57%		4.5%

TABLE 24 (continued)

| | 1977 | | | |
| | Exports | | Imports | |
	$	%	$	%
Angola	31.5	3.2	0	—
Benin	0.11	0.2	29.8	9.0
Burundi	0	—	0.01	nmf
Cameroon	0.4	0.1	0.04	nmf
CAR	0	—	0.01	nmf
Chad	3.0	2.4	0.2	0.1
Congo	.4	0.2	.13	0.1
Equatorial Guinea	0	—	0	—
Ethiopia	16.0	5.3	41.1	8.4
Gabon	.2	nmf	.2	nmf
Gambia	.1	0.2	0	—
Ghana	4.8	0.4	26.5	2.0
Guinea	5.0	1.9	3.9	2.8
Guinea Bissau	.01	0.1	0.7	2.3
Ivory Coast	5.8	0.3	44.4	2.5
Kenya	5.9	0.5	94.1	7.3
Liberia	.2	nmf	0	—
Madagascar	2.4	0.7	20.1	6.7
Malawi	0	—	.03	nmf
Mali	2.2	1.6	1.8	0.6
Mauritius	.08	nmf	.01	nmf
Mozambique	1.5	0.4	74.2	14.1
Niger	1.8	1.5	17.0	7.0
Rwanda	0	—	1.5	1.3
Senegal	.3	0.1	11.7	1.6
Sierra Leone	.2	0.1	0	—
Tanzania	4.0	0.7	42.0	5.1
Togo	0	—	.4	0.1
Uganda	12.2	2.2	.2	0.1
Upper Volta	0	—	0	—
Zaire	.1	nmf	0	—
Zambia	.1	nmf	84.0	12.5
TOTAL	$ 98.3		$ 494.0	
As % of Total African Imports/Exports		0.62%		3.23%

TABLE 24 (continued)

| | 1978 | | | |
| | Exports | | Imports | |
	$	%	$	%
Angola	34.6	3.3	0	—
Benin	0.12	0.3	28.3	7.6
Burundi	0	—	.04	nmf
Cameroon	0.2	nmf	0.4	nmf
CAR	0	—	0.01	nmf
Chad	3.3	3.2	0.2	0.1
Congo	.4	0.1	.12	nmf
Equatorial Guinea	0	—	0	—
Ethiopia	17.5	5.7	39.0	7.5
Gabon	.2	nmf	.2	nmf
Gambia	.1	0.3	0	—
Ghana	5.3	0.4	25.2	2.0
Guinea	5.5	1.9	3.7	1.8
Guinea Bissau	.01	0.1	.01	nmf
Ivory Coast	6.3	0.2	42.2	2.0
Kenya	13.7	1.3	44.0	2.6
Liberia	.2	nmf	0	—
Madagascar	2.7	0.8	19.1	5.6
Malawi	0	—	.02	nmf
Mali	2.4	1.8	1.7	0.5
Mauritius	.09	nmf	.02	nmf
Mozambique	1.5	0.5	70.5	11.8
Niger	2.0	1.3	16.1	4.7
Rwanda	0	—	1.4	0.9
Senegal	.3	0.1	11.1	1.4
Sierra Leone	.2	0.1	0	—
Tanzania	4.8	0.9	40.0	3.3
Togo	0	—	.4	0.1
Uganda	13.4	3.6	.14	nmf
Upper Volta	0	—	0	—
Zaire	.1	nmf	0	—
Zambia	.1	nmf	80.0	12.5
TOTAL	$ 115.0		$ 423.9	
As % of Total African Imports/Exports		0.69 %		2.27 %

TABLE 24 (continued)

| | 1979 | | | |
| | Exports | | Imports | |
	$	%	$	%
Angola	64.6	4.1	0	—
Benin	.02	.04	12.2	2.9
Burundi	0	0	.06	.04
Cameroon	.3	.02	.9	.1
CAR	.03	.03	.01	.01
Chad	6.9	5.5	.42	.2
Congo	.2	.05	1.1	.3
Equatorial Guinea	.05	.5	0	—
Ethiopia	39.6	9.9	1.5	.3
Gabon	0	—	.9	.2
Gambia	.5	1.0	.3	.2
Ghana	3.9	.3	.1	.01
Guinea	6.1	1.9	9.2	4.0
Guinea Bissau	0	—	.03	.05
Ivory Coast	54.7	1.9	86.4	3.4
Kenya	22.4	2.0	70.4	4.3
Liberia	0.5	.04	7.6	0.4
Madagascar	1.8	0.5	80.9	12.2
Malawi	0	—	0	—
Mali	1.6	1.2	1.7	0.5
Mauritius	0	—	.07	.01
Mozambique	28.0	7.0	7.3	1.9
Niger	5.6	1.8	42.4	8.1
Rwanda	0	—	0.4	0.2
Senegal	0.1	.02	184.3	15.5
Sierra Leone	0.6	.2	.9	.2
Tanzania	10.0	1.6	13.0	1.1
Togo	0	—	.1	.02
Uganda	27.6	6.1	3.1	1.3
Upper Volta	0	—	0	—
Zaire	.4	.01	0	—
Zambia	0	—	134.1	17.7
TOTAL	$ 275.5		$ 659.4	
As % of Total African Imports/Exports		.62 %		1.62 %

nmf = no meaningful figure

Source: IMF, *Direction of Trade Yearbook, 1979 & 1980*

TABLE 25
Geographic Distribution of Commitments
by Multilateral Institutions:
Islamic Development Bank: 1976–1980
($ Million)

Country	1976	1977	1978
AFRICA:			
Cameroon	7.0	8.3	—
Chad	—	—	6.1
Comoros	—	—	—
Gambia	—	—	—
Guinea	—	5.3	10.8
Guinea Bissau	—	—	—
Mali	—	—	—
Niger	—	5.6	8.9
Senegal	—	6.3	15.0
Uganda	—	—	8.2
Upper Volta	—	—	—
Total Sub-Saharan Africa[1]	7.0	25.5	49.0
As % of Total	42.9%	15.3%	18.1%
ARAB:			
Djibouti	—	—	—
Mauritania	—	0.8	—
Somalia	—	7.5	3.3
Sudan	—	14.3	10.0
Total Arab League Africa	0	22.6	13.3
As % of Total	—	13.6%	5.0%

TABLE 25 (continued)

Country	1976	1977	1978
Algeria	—	20.2	35.0
Bahrain	—	—	—
Egypt[1]	—	12.0	6.0
Iraq	—	—	—
Jordan	9.3	—	17.2
Kuwait	—	—	—
Lebanon	—	—	—
Libya	—	—	—
Morocco	—	10.0	19.2
Oman	—	—	—
Palestine	—	—	—
Qatar	—	—	—
Saudi Arabia	—	—	—
Syria	—	—	6.4
Tunisia	—	7.0	15.0
United Arab Emirates	—	—	5.1
Yemen Arab Republic	—	0.4	—
People's Democratic Republic of Yemen	—	2.0	—
Total Arab	9.3	74.2	117.2
As % of Total	57.1 %	44.6 %	43.4 %
ASIA:			
Afghanistan[1]	—	—	8.0
Bangladesh	—	13.0	12.4
Indonesia	—	—	10.0
Maldives	—	—	—
Malaysia	—	12.5	—
Pakistan	—	21.4	36.2
Turkey	—	19.6	37.4
Total Asia	0	66.5	104.0
As % of Total	—	40.0 %	38.1 %
GRAND TOTAL	$ 16.3	$ 166.2	$ 270.2

TABLE 25 (continued)

Country	1979	1980	Total
AFRICA:			
Cameroon	–	3.5	18.8
Chad	–	–	6.1
Comoros	–	2.5	2.5
Gambia	–	4.4	4.4
Guinea	–	35.0	51.1
Guinea Bissau	10.0	8.5	18.5
Mali	8.0	7.0	15.0
Niger	21.0	17.6	53.1
Senegal	–	54.1	75.4
Uganda	0.4	–	8.6
Upper Volta	0.1	12.2	12.3
Total Sub-Saharan Africa[1]	39.5	144.8	$ 265.8
As % of Total	9.4%	21.7%	17.3%
ARAB:			
Djibouti	–	0.2	0.2
Mauritania	10.0	16.0	26.8
Somalia	32.8	34.1	77.7
Sudan	65.2	70.1	159.6
Total Arab League Africa	108.0	120.4	$ 264.3
As % of Total	25.8%	18.0%	17.2%

TABLE 25 (continued)

Country	1979	1980	Total
Algeria	10.0	47.0	112.2
Bahrain	3.9	–	3.9
Egypt[1]	–	–	18.0
Iraq	–	–	–
Jordan	6.5	19.5	52.5
Kuwait	–	–	–
Lebanon	–	9.8	9.8
Libya	–	11.0	11.0
Morocco	34.5	38.5	102.2
Oman	6.2	–	6.2
Palestine	0.2	6.2	6.4
Qatar	–	–	–
Saudi Arabia	–	–	–
Syria	–	24.9	31.3
Tunisia	11.1	11.0	44.1
United Arab Emirates	10.0	–	15.1
Yemen Arab Republic	2.2	31.3	33.9
People's Democratic Republic of Yemen	18.5	20.5	41.0
Total Arab	211.1	340.1	$ 751.9
As % of Total	50.4 %	50.9 %	48.8 %
ASIA:			
Afghanistan[1]	–	–	8.0
Bangladesh	46.3	50.0	121.7
Indonesia	–	9.0	19.0
Maldives	–	10.0	10.0
Malaysia	10.4	–	22.9
Pakistan	40.1	70.3	168.0
Turkey	71.6	43.9	172.5
Total Asia	168.4	183.2	$ 522.1
As % of Total	40.2 %	27.4 %	33.9 %
GRAND TOTAL	$ 419.0	$ 668.1	$ 1,539.8

1 Gabon was admitted to membership in March 1981. The memberships of Afghanistan and Egypt have been suspended.

Source: Islamic Development Bank

TABLE 26

Muslim Population as a Percentage of Total Population in African Countries

Country	Population Estimate (U.S. Dept. of State)	Population Estimate (Muslim World League)	Range of Other Estimates	Rank of Bilateral Aid Commitments
Djibouti*	90% +	99%	84–99 %	12
Gambia*	"	84	56–90	19
Mauritania*	"	99	95–99	2
Somalia*	"	99	74–99	3
Comoros*	75–89%	95	67–99	20
Guinea*	"	90	51–95	5
Niger*	"	85	78–97	17
Senegal*	"	95	77–83	8
Sudan*	"	83	68–75	1
Mali*	60–74%	90	60–70	7
Chad*	30–59%	90	45–90	14
Ethiopia*	"	65	20–42	37
Guinea Bissau*	"	75	27–56	23
Tanzania*	"	90	13–35	15

TABLE 26 (continued)

Country	Population Estimate (U.S. Dept. of State)	Population Estimate (Muslim World League)	Range of Other Estimates	Rank of Bilateral Aid Commitments
Benin*	10–24%	55	1.5–15	31
Cameroon*	"	55	14 –20	11
Ghana +	"	40–50	3.5–20	16
Ivory Coast*	"	60	19 –25	40
Liberia +	"	30	10 –26	22
Madagascar +	"	25	1.2– 8	10
Malawi +	"	23	9 –33	40
Mauritius	"	n.a.	16 –17	33
Mozambique	"	30	0 –33	25
Sierra Leone*	"	65	33 –69	34
Uganda +	"	30	5	4
Upper Volta*	"	55	15 –60	32
Equatorial Guinea +	Less than 10%	25	1% >	29
Gabon +	"	30	0 – 1.3	13
Kenya +	"	25	7 –11	21
Central African Republic*	"	60	3 – 6	36
Togo*	"	55	1.4– 6	24
Angola	"	insignificant	negligible	40
Botswana	"	Muslim minorities	"	27

TABLE 26 (continued)

Country	Population Estimate (U.S. Dept. of State)	Population Estimate (Muslim World League)	Range of Other Estimates	Rank of Bilateral Aid Commitments
Burundi	Less than 10%	Muslim minorities	1% >	28
Cape Verde	,,	,,	1% >	34
Congo	,,	,,	1% >	18
Lesotho	,,	,,	1% >	30
Rwanda	,,	,,	1% >	26
Sao Tome e Principe	,,	,,	none	40
Seychelles	,,	,,	0–2	37
Swaziland	,,	,,	none	40
Zaire	,,	,,	2% >	6
Zambia	,,	,,	0.5% >	9
Zimbabwe	,,	,,	negligible	39

* Indicates "Islamic" States according to the Muslim World League.
+ Indicates states with important Muslim minorities according to the League. All other states are "non-Muslim" states except Madagascar which is divided 50/50 between a Muslim minority in the North and a non-Muslim South.

TABLE 27

Contributions to the Islamic Solidarity Fund by Country: 1974/75–1979/80

($ Thousand)

Country	1974/5	1975/6	1976/7	1977/8	1978/9	1979/80	Total
Saudi Arabia	0	5,500	5,500	5,500	0	10,000	26,500
Libya	0	4,500	0	5,993	0	0	10,493
United Arab Emirates	1,500	0	3,000	3,000	3,000	3,000	13,500
Iraq	0	0	1,000	499	1,000	1,000	3,499
Kuwait	0	1,500	2,000	0	0	0	3,500
Qatar	0	1,500	0	0	0	0	1,500
Yemen	0	0	0	0	22	0	22
Pakistan*	0	0	250	0	20	20	290
Bangladesh*	0	0	0	0	248	0	248
Indonesia*	0	0	0	250	0	0	250
Cyprus*	0	0	0	1	2	0	3
Gabon*	0	0	42	0	0	0	42
Gambia*	0	0	0	5	0	0	5
Mali*	0	0	0	0	0	1,719	1,719
Unspecified	0	600	608	0	0	0	1,208
Total	1,500	13,600	12,400	15,248	4,292	15,739	62,779

* Amounts given in earlier years may include contributions from these countries.

Source: UNCTAD for years 1974/5 through 1976/77. For subsequent years, General Secretariat of the Organization of the Islamic Conference, Islamic Solidarity Fund

TABLE 28
Geographic Distribution of Assistance by Multilateral Institutions:
Islamic Solidarity Fund:
Commitments
($ Thousand)

Country	1976/77	1977/78	1978/79	Total
ARAB:				
Palestine	1500	1500	1775	4775
Saudi Arabia	550	630	475	1655
Somalia (a)	0	900	40	940
Sudan (a)	0	100	820	920
Lebanon	0	500	400	900
Egypt	30	500	320	850
Mauritania (a)	0	225	425	650
Syria	250	0	250	500
Djibouti (a)	0	0	350	350
Jordan	0	300	0	300
Yemen	0	300	0	300
Tunisia	250	0	0	250
PDRY	0	200	0	200
Bahrain	0	0	135	135
UAE	0	0	100	100
Morocco	0	0	90	90
Total Arab League	2580	5155	5180	12915
Total Arab League Africa (a)	0	1225	1635	2860
AFRICA:				
Uganda (b)	1500	1500	500	3500
Niger (b)	1500	1749	0	3249
Mali (b)	50	381	485	916
Senegal (b)	350	304	120	774
Gambia (b)	250	400	20	675
Guinea (b)	650	0	0	650
Gabon (b)	515	10	0	525
Guinea Bissau (b)	500	0	0	500
Ethiopia (Eritrea)*	150	0	250	400
Upper Volta (b)	50	220	55	325
Chad (b)	30	200	10	240
Nigeria*	90	5	0	95
Kenya*	30	43	20	93
South Africa*	40	0	20	60

TABLE 28 (continued)

Country/Year	1976/77	1977/78	1978/79	Total
Mauritius*	0	56	0	56
Cameroon (b)	50	0	0	50
Sierra Leone*	40	0	10	50
Liberia*	35	0	0	35
Ghana*	35	0	0	35
Tanzania*	30	0	0	30
Total Africa	5895	4868	1490	12253
Total Members of the Islamic Conference (b)	5445	4764	1230	11399
ASIA:				
Philippines*	1250	370	280	1900
Pakistan	500	100	500	1100
Bangladesh	0	750	310	1060
Indonesia	75	350	345	770
India*	100	235	140	475
Turkey	100	250	110	460
Malaysia	155	80	150	385
Maldives	0	50	0	50
Other Asia*	95	215	450	760
Total Asia	2275	2400	2285	6960
Cyprus*	250	50	80	380
Europe*	365	847	772	1984
US and Canada*	280	737	410	1427
Latin America*	60	20	5	85
Other*	10	19	0	22
Subtotal	965	1673	1267	3898
Grand Total	11715	14082	10222	36019
Member Countries of the Islamic Conference	8855	11499	7785	28139
As a % of Total	75.6%	81.7%	76.2%	78.1%
Non-Member Countries*	2860	2583	2437	7880
As a % of Total	24.4%	18.3%	23.8%	21.9%

* indicates non-member countries

Source: General Secretariat of the Organization of the Islamic Conference, Islamic Solidarity Fund

TABLE 29

Geographic Distribution of Commitments of Official Bilateral Aid: 1973–1979: Algeria
($ Million)

	Arab Countries		Sub-Saharan Africa		Asia		Other Countries*		Total
	$	%	$	%	$	%	$	%	$
1973	22.2	95.3	1.1	4.7	0	0	0	0	23.3
1974	0.4	7.0	5.3	93.0	0	0	0	0	5.7
1975	0	0	7.6	21.2	1.0	2.8	27.2	76.0	35.8
1976	1.0	2.2	3.9	8.7	0	0	39.7	89.0	44.6
1977	0	0	0	0	0	0	10.0	100.0	10.0
1978	228.6	97.7	5.5	2.3	0	0	0	0	234.1
1979	58.6	93.6	4.0	6.4	0	0	0	0	62.6
Total	$ 310.8	74.7%	$ 27.4	6.6%	$ 1.0	0.2%	$ 76.9	18.5%	$ 416.1

* Includes unallocated or unspecified amounts

Source: OECD

TABLE 30
Geographic Distribution of Bilateral Aid by Country: 1973–1980:
Algeria
($ Million)

| | 1973 | | 1974 | |
	Commit-ments	Disburse-ments	Commit-ments	Disburse-ments
Angola				
Benin			1.3	1.3
Botswana				
Burundi				
Cameroon (b)				
Cape Verde Islands				
Central African Republic				
Chad (b)	0.08	0.08	0.005	0.005
Comoros Islands (b)				
Congo				
Djibouti (a)				
Equatorial Guinea				
Ethiopia				
Gabon (b)				
Gambia (b)				
Ghana				
Guinea (b)			0.7	1.2
Guinea-Bissau (b)				
Ivory Coast				
Kenya				
Lesotho				
Liberia				
Madagascar				
Malawi				
Mali (b)	0.4	0.4	1.7	1.7
Mauritania (a)	0.4	0.4	0.3	0.3
Mauritius				
Mozambique				
Niger (b)	0.4	0.4	0.5	0.5
Rwanda				
Sao Tome e Principe				
Senegal (b)	0.1	0.1	0.3	0.3
Seychelles				
Sierra Leone				

TABLE 30 (continued)

| | 1973 | | 1974 | |
	Commit- ments	Disburse- ments	Commit- ments	Disburse- ments
Somalia (a)				
Sudan (a)				
Swaziland				
Tanzania				
Togo				
Uganda (b)				
Upper Volta (b)	0.08	0.08	0.005	0.005
Zaire				
Zambia			0.8	0.8
Zimbabwe				
Africa Unallocated or Unspecified				
Total Africa	1.5	1.5	5.6	6.1
Total Sub-Saharan Africa (SSA)	1.1	1.1	5.3	5.8
SSA as % of Total Africa	73.3 %	73.3 %	94.6 %	95.1 %
Total Arab League Africa (a) (ALA)	0.4	0.4	0.3	0.3
ALA as % of Total Africa	26.7 %	26.7 %	5.4 %	4.9 %
Total Sub-Saharan Members of the Islamic Conference (b)	1.1	1.1	3.2	3.7
As % of Total SSA	100.0 %	100.0 %	60.4 %	63.8 %

TABLE 30 (continued)

	1975		1976	
	Commit-ments	Disburse-ments	Commit-ments	Disburse-ments
Angola				
Benin			1.0	1.0
Botswana				
Burundi				
Cameroon (b)				
Cape Verde Islands				
Central African Republic				
Chad (b)	0.2	0.2		
Comoros Islands (b)				
Congo				
Djibouti (a)				
Equatorial Guinea				
Ethiopia	0.2	0.2		
Gabon (b)	5.0	1.5	0	1.5
Gambia (b)				
Ghana				
Guinea (b)				
Guinea-Bissau (b)			1.0	1.0
Ivory Coast				
Kenya				
Lesotho				
Liberia				
Madagascar				
Malawi				
Mali (b)	1.0	1.0		
Mauritania (a)				
Mauritius				
Mozambique				
Niger (b)	1.0	0	0	1.0
Rwanda				
Sao Tome e Principe				
Senegal (b)				
Seychelles				
Sierra Leone				
Somalia (a)				
Sudan (a)				
Swaziland				

TABLE 30 (continued)

| | 1975 | | 1976 | |
	Commit-ments	Disburse-ments	Commit-ments	Disburse-ments
Tanzania				
Togo			0.9	0.9
Uganda (b)				
Upper Volta (b)	0.2	0.2	1.0	1.0
Zaire				
Zambia				
Zimbabwe				
Africa Unallocated or Unspecified				
Total Africa	7.6[1]	3.1	3.9	6.4
Total Sub-Saharan Africa (SSA)	7.6	3.1	3.9	6.4
SSA as % of Total Africa	100.0%	100.0%	100.0%	100.0%
Total Arab League Africa (a) (ALA)	0	0	0	0
ALA as % of Total Africa	0	0	0	0
Total Sub-Saharan Members of the Islamic Conference (b)	7.4	2.9	2.0	4.5
As % of Total SSA	97.4%	93.5%	51.3%	70.3%

TABLE 30 (continued)

| | 1977 | | 1978 | |
	Commit- ments	Disburse- ments	Commit- ments	Disburse- ments
Angola				
Benin				
Botswana				
Burundi				
Cameroon (b)				
Cape Verde Islands				
Central African Republic				
Chad (b)				
Comoros Islands (b)				
Congo				
Djibouti (a)				
Equatorial Guinea				
Ethiopia				
Gabon (b)				
Gambia (b)				
Ghana				
Guinea (b)				
Guinea-Bissau (b)				
Ivory Coast				
Kenya				
Lesotho				
Liberia				
Madagascar				
Malawi				
Mali (b)				
Mauritania (a)				
Mauritius				
Mozambique				
Niger (b)			0.5	0.5
Rwanda				
Sao Tome e Principe				
Senegal (b)				
Seychelles				
Sierra Leone				
Somalia (a)				
Sudan (a)				
Swaziland				

TABLE 30 (continued)

	1977		1978	
	Commit-ments	Disburse-ments	Commit-ments	Disburse-ments
Tanzania				
Togo				
Uganda (b)				
Upper Volta (b)				
Zaire				
Zambia				
Zimbabwe				
Africa Unallocated or Unspecified			5.0	5.0
Total Africa	0	0	5.5[2]	5.5[2]
Total Sub-Saharan Africa (SSA)	0	0	5.5	5.5
SSA as % of Total Africa	0	0	100.0%	100.0%
Total Arab League Africa (a) (ALA)	0	0	0	0
ALA as % of Total Africa	0	0	0	0
Total Sub-Saharan Members of the Islamic Conference (b)	0	0	0.5	0.5
As % of Total SSA	0	0	100.0%	100.0%

TABLE 30 (continued)

	1979		1980[3]	
	Commit- ments	Disburse- ments	Commit- ments	Disburse- ments
Angola				
Benin				
Botswana				
Burundi				
Cameroon (b)				
Cape Verde Islands				
Central African Republic				
Chad (b)				
Comoros Islands (b)				
Congo				
Djibouti (a)				
Equatorial Guinea				
Ethiopia				
Gabon (b)				
Gambia (b)				
Ghana				
Guinea (b)				
Guinea-Bissau (b)				
Ivory Coast				
Kenya				
Lesotho				
Liberia				
Madagascar				
Malawi				
Mali (b)				
Mauritania (a)				2.0
Mauritius				
Mozambique				
Niger (b)				
Rwanda				
Sao Tome e Principe				
Senegal (b)				
Seychelles				
Sierra Leone	4.0	4.0		
Somalia (a)				
Sudan (a)				
Swaziland				

TABLE 30 (continued)

| | 1979 | | 1980[3] | |
	Commit-ments	Disburse-ments	Commit-ments	Disburse-ments
Tanzania				
Togo				
Uganda (b)				
Upper Volta (b)				
Zaire				
Zambia				
Zimbabwe				
Africa Unallocated or Unspecified	0	3.0		
Total Africa	4.0	7.0		2.0
Total Sub-Saharan Africa (SSA)	4.0	7.0		0
SSA as % of Total Africa	100.0%	100.0%		0
Total Arab League Africa (a) (ALA)	0	0		2.0
ALA as % of Total Africa	0	0		100.0%
Total Sub-Saharan Members of the Islamic Conference (b)	0	0		0
As % of Total SSA	0	0		0

TABLE 30 (continued)

	Total Commitments	Total Disbursements
Angola	0	0
Benin	2.3	2.3
Botswana	0	0
Burundi	0	0
Cameroon (b)	0	0
Cape Verde Islands	0	0
Central African Republic	0	0
Chad (b)	0.3	0.3
Comoros Islands (b)	0	0
Congo	0	0
Djibouti (a)	0	0
Equatorial Guinea	0	0
Ethiopia	0.2	0.2
Gabon (b)	5.0	3.0
Gambia (b)	0	0
Ghana	0	0
Guinea (b)	0.7	1.2
Guinea-Bissau (b)	1.0	1.0
Ivory Coast	0	0
Kenya	0	0
Lesotho	0	0
Liberia	0	0
Madagascar	0	0
Malawi	0	0
Mali (b)	3.1	3.1
Mauritania (a)	0.7	2.7
Mauritius	0	0
Mozambique	0	0
Niger (b)	2.4	2.4
Rwanda	0	0
Sao Tome e Principe	0	0
Senegal (b)	0.4	0.4
Seychelles	0	0
Sierra Leone	4.0	4.0
Somalia (a)	0	0
Sudan (a)	0	0
Swaziland	0	0
Tanzania	0	0

TABLE 30 (continued)

	Total Commitments	Total Disbursements
Togo	0.9	0.9
Uganda (b)	0	0
Upper Volta (b)	1.3	1.3
Zaire	0	0
Zambia	0.8	0.8
Zimbabwe	0	0
Africa Unallocated or Unspecified	5.0	8.0
Total Africa	28.1	31.6
Total Sub-Saharan Africa (SSA)	27.4	28.9
SSA as % of Total Africa	97.5%	91.5%
Total Arab League Africa (a) (ALA)	0.7	2.7
ALA as % of Total Africa	2.5%	8.5%
Total Sub-Saharan Members of the Islamic Conference (b)	14.2	12.7
As % of Total SSA	63.4%	60.8%

1   In addition, there were scholarships worth $ 15.6 million for unspecified ldc's.
2   It is expected that a portion of Algeria's "unspecified" bilateral aid also went to African countries.
3   Data for Algeria's bilateral aid to Africa in 1980 were unavailable at the time of publication.

Source: OECD

TABLE 31
Geographic Distribution of Commitments of Official Bilateral Aid: 1973–1979: Iraq
($ Million)

| | Arab Countries | | Sub-Saharan Africa | | Asia | | Other Countries* | | Total |
	$	%	$	%	$	%	$	%	$
1973	50.5	44.9	12.0	10.7	50.0	44.4	0	0	112.5
1974	294.0	62.3	0	0	178.0	37.7	0	0	472.0
1975	305.7	88.9	12.3	3.6	26.1	7.6	0	0	344.1
1976	76.2	35.1	20.0	9.2	121.0	55.7	0	0	217.2
1977	33.6	27.2	0	0	90.0	72.8	0	0	123.6
1978	545.5	96.0	12.0	2.1	11.2	2.0	0	0	568.7
1979	709.8	59.4	115.7	9.7	0	0	368.9	30.9	1,194.4
Total	$2,015.3	66.4%	$172.0	5.7%	$476.3	15.7%	$368.9	12.2%	$3,032.5

* Includes unallocated or unspecific amounts

Source: OECD

TABLE 32
Iraqi Fund for External Development
Geographic Distribution of Aid Commitments: 1975–1980
($ Million)

	Arab Countries		Sub-Saharan Africa		Asia		Other		Total
	$	%	$	%	$	%	$	%	$
1975–1978									593.3[1]
1979	57.0	53.4	6.5	6.1	0	0	43.2	40.5	106.7
1980	95.8	37.9	19.6	7.7	137.6	54.4	0	0	253.0
Total[2]	$152.8	42.5%	$26.1	7.3%	$137.6	38.3%	$43.2	12.0%	$359.7[3]

1 Based on official estimates of total IFED commitments from 1975 to 1979 of $ 700 million.
2 Includes 1979 and 1980 only.
3 Cumulative commitments by the IFED amounted to $ 1,744 million by October 1980. Disbursements were expected to reach $ 340 million by the end of 1980. (OECD, *1980 Review*, p. 136) However, no more detailed statistics have been released.

Source: Fund Annual Reports and Coordination Secretariat at the Arab Fund for Economic and Social Development, "Summary Loans and Technical Assistance Extended to Developing Countries" (Quarterly).

TABLE 33

Geographic Distribution of Bilateral Aid by Country: 1973–1980: *Iraq*

($ Million)

	1973		1974	
	Commit-ments	Disburse-ments	Commit-ments	Disburse-ments
Angola				
Benin				
Botswana				
Burundi				
Cameroon (b)				
Cape Verde Islands				
Central African Republic				
Chad (b)	12.0	0		
Comoros Islands (b)				
Congo				
Djibouti (a)				
Equatorial Guinea				
Ethiopia				
Gabon (b)				
Gambia (b)				
Ghana				
Guinea (b)				
Guinea-Bissau (b)				
Ivory Coast				
Kenya				
Lesotho				
Liberia				
Madagascar				
Malawi				
Mali (b)				
Mauritania (a)				
Mauritius				
Mozambique				
Niger (b)				
Rwanda				
Sao Tome e Principe				
Senegal (b)				
Seychelles				
Sierra Leone				
Somalia (a)			49.0	22.4

TABLE 33 (continued)

| | 1973 | | 1974 | |
	Commit-ments	Disburse-ments	Commit-ments	Disburse-ments
Sudan (a)			10.0	10.0
Swaziland				
Tanzania				
Togo				
Uganda (b)				
Upper Volta (b)				
Zaire				
Zambia				
Zimbabwe				
Africa Unallocated or Unspecified				
Total Africa	12.0	0	59.0	32.4
Total Sub-Saharan Africa (SSA)	12.0	0	0	0
SSA as % of Total Africa	100.0%	0	0	0
Total Arab League Africa (a) (ALA)	0	0	59.0	32.4
ALA as % of Total Africa	0	0	100.0%	100.0%
Total Sub-Saharan Members of the Islamic Conference (b)	12.0	0	0	0
As % of Total SSA	100.0%	0	0	0

TABLE 33 (continued)

| | 1975 | | 1976 | |
	Commit-ments	Disburse-ments	Commit-ments	Disburse-ments
Angola				
Benin				
Botswana				
Burundi				
Cameroon (b)				
Cape Verde Islands				
Central African Republic	0.2	0.2		
Chad (b)			10.0	0
Comoros Islands (b)				
Congo				
Djibouti (a)				
Equatorial Guinea				
Ethiopia				
Gabon (b)				
Gambia (b)				
Ghana				
Guinea (b)			10.0	0
Guinea-Bissau (b)				
Ivory Coast				
Kenya				
Lesotho				
Liberia				
Madagascar				
Malawi				
Mali (b)	0.9	0.9		
Mauritania (a)				
Mauritius				
Mozambique				
Niger (b)				
Rwanda				
Sao Tome e Principe				
Senegal (b)	0.03	0.03		
Seychelles				
Sierra Leone				
Somalia (a)	11.1	33.7	0	7.5
Sudan (a)			29.0	29.0
Swaziland				

TABLE 33 (continued)

	1975		1976	
	Commit-ments	Disburse-ments	Commit-ments	Disburse-ments
Tanzania	0.2	0.2		
Togo				
Uganda (b)	10.0	0	0	3.0
Upper Volta (b)				
Zaire				
Zambia				
Zimbabwe				
Africa Unallocated or Unspecified	1.1	1.1		
Total Africa	23.5	36.1	49.0	39.5
Total Sub-Saharan Africa (SSA)	12.4	2.4	20.0	3.0
SSA as % of Total Africa	52.8%	6.7%	40.8%	7.6%
Total Arab League Africa (a) (ALA)	11.1	33.7	29.0	36.5
ALA as % of Total Africa	47.2%	93.3%	59.2%	92.4%
Total Sub-Saharan Members of the Islamic Conference (b)	10.9	0.9	20.0	3.0
As % of Total SSA	96.5%	69.2%	100.0%	100.0%

TABLE 33 (continued)

	1977		1978	
	Commit-ments	Disburse-ments	Commit-ments	Disburse-ments
Angola				
Benin				
Botswana				
Burundi				
Cameroon (b)				
Cape Verde Islands				
Central African Republic			0	6.0
Chad (b)			12.0	0
Comoros Islands (b)				
Congo				
Djibouti (a)				
Equatorial Guinea				
Ethiopia				
Gabon (b)				
Gambia (b)				
Ghana				
Guinea (b)				
Guinea-Bissau (b)				
Ivory Coast				
Kenya				
Lesotho				
Liberia				
Madagascar				
Malawi				
Mali (b)				
Mauritania (a)			9.8	9.8
Mauritius				
Mozambique				
Niger (b)				
Rwanda				
Sao Tome e Principe				
Senegal (b)				
Seychelles				
Sierra Leone				
Somalia (a)			15.0	15.0
Sudan (a)			2.0	2.0
Swaziland				

TABLE 33 (continued)

| | 1977 | | 1978 | |
	Commit- ments	Disburse- ments	Commit- ments	Disburse- ments
Tanzania				
Togo				
Uganda (b)				
Upper Volta (b)				
Zaire				
Zambia				
Zimbabwe				
Africa Unallocated or Unspecified				
Total Africa	0	0	38.8	32.8
Total Sub-Saharan Africa (SSA)	0	0	12.0	6.0
SSA as % of Total Africa	0	0	30.9 %	18.3 %
Total Arab League Africa (a) (ALA)	0	0	26.8	26.8
ALA as % of Total Africa	0	0	69.1 %	81.7 %
Total Sub-Saharan Members of the Islamic Conference (b)	0	0	12.0	0
As % of Total SSA	0	0	100.0 %	100.0 %

TABLE 33 (continued)

	1979[1]		1980[2]	
	Commit- ments	Disburse- ments	Commit- ments	Disburse- ments
Angola				
Benin				
Botswana				
Burundi				
Cameroon (b)				
Cape Verde Islands			0	2.0
Central African Republic	0.2	0.2		
Chad (b)				
Comoros Islands (b)				
Congo				
Djibouti (a)			1.1	0
Equatorial Guinea				
Ethiopia				
Gabon (b)				
Gambia (b)				
Ghana				
Guinea (b)	6.5	0		
Guinea-Bissau (b)				
Ivory Coast				
Kenya				
Lesotho				
Liberia				
Madagascar	30.0	0	7.7	9.4
Malawi				
Mali (b)				
Mauritania (a)	57.0	49.0	0	4.6
Mauritius				
Mozambique	10.0	10.0	10.3	10.3
Niger (b)				
Rwanda				
Sao Tome e Principe				
Senegal (b)				
Seychelles				
Sierra Leone				
Somalia (a)	20.0	0	0	21.5
Sudan (a)				
Swaziland				

TABLE 33 (continued)

	1979[1]		1980[2]	
	Commit- ments	Disburse- ments	Commit- ments	Disburse- ments
Tanzania	30.0	0		
Togo				
Uganda (b)				1.3
Upper Volta (b)				
Zaire				
Zambia	39.0	9.0		
Zimbabwe				
Africa Unallocated or Unspecified				
Total Africa	192.7	68.2	19.1	49.1
Total Sub-Saharan Africa (SSA)	115.7	19.2	18.0	23.0
SSA as % of Total Africa	60.0 %	28.2 %	94.2 %	46.8 %
Total Arab League Africa (a) (ALA)	77.0	49.0	1.1	26.1
ALA as % of Total Africa	40.0 %	71.8 %	5.8 %	53.2 %
Total Sub-Saharan Members of the Islamic Conference (b)	6.5	0	0	1.3
As % of Total SSA	5.6 %	0	0	5.7 %

TABLE 33 (continued)

	Total Commitments	Disbursements
Angola	0	0
Benin	0	0
Botswana	0	0
Burundi	0	0
Cameroon (b)	0	0
Cape Verde Islands	0	2.0
Central African Republic	0.4	6.4
Chad (b)	34.0	0
Comoros Islands (b)	0	0
Congo	0	0
Djibouti (a)	1.1	0
Equatorial Guinea	0	0
Ethiopia	0	0
Gabon (b)	0	0
Gambia (b)	0	0
Ghana	0	0
Guinea (b)	16.5	0
Guinea-Bissau (b)	0	0
Ivory Coast	0	0
Kenya	0	0
Lesotho	0	0
Liberia	0	0
Madagascar	37.7	9.4
Malawi	0	0
Mali (b)	0.9	0.9
Mauritania (a)	66.8	63.4
Mauritius	0	0
Mozambique	20.3	20.3
Niger (b)	0	0
Rwanda	0	0
Sao Tome e Principe	0	0
Senegal (b)	0.03	0.03
Seychelles	0	0
Sierra Leone	0	0
Somalia (a)	95.1	100.1
Sudan (a)	41.0	41.0
Swaziland	0	0
Tanzania	30.2	0.2

TABLE 33 (continued)

	Commitments	Total Disbursements
Togo	0	0
Uganda (b)	10.0	4.3
Upper Volta (b)	0	0
Zaire	0	0
Zambia	39.0	9.0
Zimbabwe	0	0
Africa Unallocated or Unspecified	1.1	1.1
Total Africa	394.1	258.1
Total Sub-Saharan Africa (SSA)	190.1	53.6
SSA as % of Total Africa	48.2%	20.8%
Total Arab League Africa (a) (ALA)	204.0	204.5
ALA as % of Total Africa	51.8%	79.2%
Total Sub-Saharan Members of the Islamic Conference (b)	61.4	5.2
As % of Total SSA	32.5%	9.9%

1   In addition, there were oil credits of $ 215 million for unspecified ldc's in 1979.
2   Preliminary Data for 1980 refer only to commitments of the Iraq Fund for External Development.

Source: OECD and Fund Annual Reports as compiled by the Arab Fund for Economic and Social Development, Coordination Secretariat

TABLE 34

Geographic Distribution of Commitments of Official Bilateral Aid: 1973–1979: Kuwait

($ Million)

	Arab Countries $	%	Sub-Saharan Africa $	%	Asia $	%	Other Countries* $	%	Total $
1973	614.3	97.4	16.7	2.6	0	0	0	0	631.0
1974	970.8	74.7	108.0	8.3	71.8	5.5	148.9	11.5	1,299.5
1975	2,386.7	88.8	48.5	1.8	98.6	3.7	153.2	5.7	2,687.0
1976	1,433.7	82.2	88.2	5.1	180.5	10.3	42.8	2.5	1,745.2
1977	1,269.1	72.8	81.7	4.7	133.4	7.7	259.3	14.9	1,743.5
1978	1,005.2	79.1	49.0	3.9	85.0	6.7	131.2	10.3	1,270.4
1979	531.1	65.0	27.3	3.3	116.8	14.3	142.5	17.4	817.7
Total	$ 8,210.9	80.5%	$ 419.4	4.1%	$ 686.1	6.7%	$ 877.9	8.6%	$ 10,194.3

* Includes unallocated or unspecified amounts

Source: OECD

223

TABLE 35
Kuwait Fund for Arab Economic Development
Geographic Distribution of Aid Commitments: 1962–1980
($ Million)

	Arab Countries		Sub-Saharan Africa		Asia[1]		Other		Total
	$	%	$	%	$	%	$	%	$
1962–1974	545.0[2]	100.0	0	0	0	0	0	0	545.0
1975	215.2	63.5	42.6	12.6	80.9	23.9	0	0	338.7
1976	125.8	43.3	39.9	13.7	124.0	42.7	0.9	0.3	290.6
1977	243.9	51.7	96.3	19.6	131.2	27.8	4.0	0.8	475.4
1978	94.5	46.1	42.5	20.7	63.5	31.0	4.4	2.1	204.9
1979	249.4	69.7	17.8	5.0	76.2	21.3	14.5	4.1	357.9
1980	97.9	36.5	99.0	37.0	61.6	23.0	9.3	3.5	267.8
Total	$1,571.7	63.4%	$338.1	13.6%	$537.4	21.7%	$33.1	1.3%	$2,480.3

1 Includes Turkey.
2 Approximate figure. Actual commitment KD158.

Source: Fund Annual Reports and Coordination Secretariat at the Arab Fund for Economic and Social Development, "Summary of Loans and Technical Assistance Extended to Developing Countries" (Quarterly)

TABLE 36
Geographic Distribution of Bilateral Aid by Country: 1973–1980: *Kuwait*
($ Million)

| | 1973 | | 1974 | |
	Commit-ments	Disburse-ments	Commit-ments	Disburse-ments
Angola				
Benin				
Botswana				
Burundi			2.0	2.0
Cameroon (b)				
Cape Verde Islands				
Central African Republic				
Chad (b)	16.1	13.5	0	2.6
Comoros Islands (b)				
Congo				
Djibouti (a)				
Equatorial Guinea			15.0	15.0
Ethiopia			0.01	0.01
Gabon (b)				
Gambia (b)				
Ghana				
Guinea (b)			15.0	15.0
Guinea-Bissau (b)			0.5	0.5
Ivory Coast				
Kenya				
Lesotho				
Liberia				
Madagascar			6.8	7.3
Malawi				
Mali (b)				
Mauritania (a)	10.2	10.2	0.8	0.2
Mauritius				
Mozambique				
Niger (b)			0.4	0.4
Rwanda				
Sao Tome e Principe				
Senegal (b)	0.6	0.6	37.8	37.8
Seychelles				
Sierra Leone				
Somalia (a)			24.2	24.2

TABLE 36 (continued)

| | 1973 | | 1974 | |
	Commitments	Disbursements	Commitments	Disbursements
Sudan (a)	65.7	20.0	171.0	114.7
Swaziland				
Tanzania				
Togo				
Uganda (b)			7.4	1.1
Upper Volta (b)				
Zaire				
Zambia				
Zimbabwe				
Africa Unallocated or Unspecified			22.0	6.6
Total Africa	92.6	44.3	302.9	227.4
Total Sub-Saharan Africa (SSA)	16.7	14.1	106.9	88.3
SSA as % of Total Africa	18.0%	31.8%	35.3%	38.0%
Total Arab League Africa (a) (ALA)	75.9	30.2	196.0	139.1
ALA as % of Total Africa	82.0%	68.2%	64.7%	61.0%
Total Sub-Saharan Members of the Islamic Conference (b)	16.7	14.1	61.1	57.4
As % of Total SSA	100.0%	100.0%	72.0%	70.3%

TABLE 36 (continued)

	1975		1976	
	Commit-ments	Disburse-ments	Commit-ments	Disburse-ments
Angola				
Benin				
Botswana				
Burundi			1.2	0.1
Cameroon (b)	0.6	0		
Cape Verde Islands				
Central African Republic				
Chad (b)	0.8	0.8		
Comoros Islands (b)			6.5	1.4
Congo			13.7	0
Djibouti (a)				
Equatorial Guinea				
Ethiopia				
Gabon (b) .			0.1	0.1
Gambia (b)			1.0	1.0
Ghana			0.01	0.01
Guinea (b)	0.5	0.5	9.2	0
Guinea-Bissau (b)	1.2	1.2	0.5	0.5
Ivory Coast				
Kenya			0.01	0.01
Lesotho				
Liberia				
Madagascar				
Malawi				
Mali (b)	0.7	0.7	17.1	0
Mauritania (a)	29.3	7.2	48.9	41.3
Mauritius				
Mozambique				
Niger (b)				
Rwanda	3.4	0.3		
Sao Tome e Principe				
Senegal (b)	1.5	1.0	16.4	0
Seychelles				
Sierra Leone				
Somalia (a)	26.8	5.6	23.3	20.5
Sudan (a)	87.4	61.0	206.3	78.8
Swaziland				

TABLE 36 (continued)

| | 1975 | | 1976 | |
	Commit-ments	Disburse-ments	Commit-ments	Disburse-ments
Tanzania	15.5	0		
Togo				
Uganda (b)	20.6	0.8	0	0.5
Upper Volta (b)				
Zaire			10.0	10.0
Zambia				
Zimbabwe				
Africa Unallocated or Unspecified	1.0	6.3	12.4	12.4
Total Africa	189.3	85.4	366.6	166.6
Total Sub-Saharan Africa (SSA)	45.8	11.6	88.1	26.0
SSA as % of Total Africa	24.2%	13.6%	24.0%	15.6%
Total Arab League Africa (a) (ALA)	143.5	73.8	278.5	140.6
ALA as % of Total Africa	75.8%	86.4%	76.0%	84.4%
Total Sub-Saharan Members of the Islamic Conference (b)	25.9	5.0	50.8	3.5
As % of Total SSA	57.8%	94.3%	67.1%	25.7%

TABLE 36 (continued)

| | 1977 | | 1978 | |
	Commit-ments	Disburse-ments	Commit-ments	Disburse-ments
Angola				
Benin			8.2	0
Botswana				
Burundi	6.1	0.4	0	1.9
Cameroon (b)	15.7	2.9	0	0.8
Cape Verde Islands				
Central African Republic				
Chad (b)				
Comoros Islands (b)	5.2	2.6	2.0	3.6
Congo	0	3.0	3.6	5.0
Djibouti (a)				
Equatorial Guinea				
Ethiopia				
Gabon (b)				
Gambia (b)	15.7	0.1	0	1.4
Ghana	31.3	0	0	9.0
Guinea (b)	0.4	2.6	0	4.6
Guinea-Bissau (b)			7.3	0
Ivory Coast				
Kenya				
Lesotho			4.3	0
Liberia			8.0	0
Madagascar	7.3	0	10.6	0
Malawi				
Mali (b)	0	3.0	0	1.5
Mauritania (a)	2.5	16.0	18.9	7.4
Mauritius				
Mozambique				
Niger (b)				
Rwanda	0	0.5	0	0.7
Sao Tome e Principe				
Senegal (b)			3.0	0
Seychelles				
Sierra Leone				
Somalia (a)	2.5	10.1	0	6.1
Sudan (a)	34.7	29.5	18.2	11.4
Swaziland				

TABLE 36 (continued)

| | 1977 | | 1978 | |
	Commit-ments	Disburse-ments	Commit-ments	Disburse-ments
Tanzania	0	6.9	0	1.0
Togo				
Uganda (b)				
Upper Volta (b)				
Zaire				
Zambia				
Zimbabwe				
Africa Unallocated or Unspecified			2.0[1]	0
Total Africa	121.4	77.6	86.1[1]	54.4
Total Sub-Saharan Africa (SSA)	81.7	22.0	49.0[1]	29.5
SSA as % of Total Africa	67.3 %	28.4 %	56.9 %	54.2 %
Total Arab League Africa (a) (ALA)	39.7	55.6	37.1	24.9
ALA as % of Total Africa	32.7 %	71.6 %	43.1 %	45.8 %
Total Sub-Saharan Members of the Islamic Conference (b)	37.0	11.2	12.3	11.9
As % of Total SSA	45.3 %	50.9 %	25.1 %	40.3 %

TABLE 36 (continued)

| | 1979 | | 1980[2] | |
	Commit-ments	Disburse-ments	Commit-ments	Disburse-ments
Angola				
Benin	0	2.1	0	1.8
Botswana			7.3	0
Burundi	0	1.5	1.8	3.5
Cameroon (b)	0	3.7	0	8.3
Cape Verde Islands				
Central African Republic	3.6	1.3	0	2.1
Chad (b)				
Comoros Islands (b)	6.4	2.8	0.4	3.8
Congo	0	4.5	20.9	4.9
Djibouti (a)	0.5	0	5.6	3.0
Equatorial Guinea				
Ethiopia				
Gabon (b)				
Gambia (b)	0.6	3.4	16.6	5.4
Ghana	0	8.1	0	12.3
Guinea (b)	0.4	1.3		
Guinea-Bissau (b)	0	0.2	0	1.2
Ivory Coast				
Kenya				
Lesotho				
Liberia	0	3.6	0	3.2
Madagascar	0	9.0	0	3.6
Malawi				
Mali (b)	1.0	5.5	15.6	3.8
Mauritania (a)	69.0	37.1	0	22.1
Mauritius			5.6	0
Mozambique	1.3	0		
Niger (b)			11.2	1.0
Rwanda	0.4	0.6	0	1.3
Sao Tome e Principe				
Senegal (b)	5.8	1.0	0	0.8
Seychelles			1.1	0
Sierra Leone			0.5	0
Somalia (a)	2.2	9.9	0	17.7
Sudan (a)	25.1	30.7	4.7	14.2
Swaziland				

TABLE 36 (continued)

	1979		1980[2]	
	Commit-ments	Disburse-ments	Commit-ments	Disburse-ments
Tanzania	0	1.4	18.1	5.3
Togo				
Uganda (b)	0	0.1		
Upper Volta (b)				
Zaire				
Zambia				
Zimbabwe				
Africa Unallocated or Unspecified	7.8[1]	3.9		
Total Africa	124.1[1]	131.7	109.4	119.3
Total Sub-Saharan Africa (SSA)	27.3[1]	54.0	99.1	57.0
SSA as % of Total Africa	22.0%	41.0%	90.6%	47.8%
Total Arab League Africa (a) (ALA)	96.8	77.7	10.3	62.3
ALA as % of Total Africa	78.0%	59.0%	9.4%	52.2%
Total Sub-Saharan Members of the Islamic Conference (b)	14.2	18.0	43.8	24.3
As % of Total SSA	58.0%	35.9%	44.2%	42.6%

TABLE 36 (continued)

| | Total | |
	Commitments	Disbursements
Angola	0	0
Benin	2.2	3.9
Botswana	7.3	0
Burundi	11.1	9.4
Cameroon (b)	16.3	15.7
Cape Verde Islands	0	0
Central African Republic	3.6	3.4
Chad (b)	16.9	16.9
Comoros Islands (b)	20.5	14.2
Congo	38.2	17.4
Djibouti (a)	6.1	3.0
Equatorial Guinea	15.0	15.0
Ethiopia	0.01	0.01
Gabon (b)	0.1	0.1
Gambia (b)	33.9	11.3
Ghana	31.31	29.4
Guinea (b)	25.5	24.0
Guinea-Bissau (b)	9.5	3.6
Ivory Coast	0	0
Kenya	0.01	0.01
Lesotho	4.3	0
Liberia	8.0	6.8
Madagascar	24.7	19.9
Malawi	0	0
Mali (b)	34.4	14.5
Mauritania (a)	179.6	141.5
Mauritius	5.6	0
Mozambique	1.3	0
Niger (b)	11.6	1.4
Rwanda	3.8	3.4
Sao Tome e Principe	0	0
Senegal (b)	65.1	41.2
Seychelles	1.1	0
Sierra Leone	0.5	0
Somalia (a)	79.0	94.1
Sudan (a)	613.1	360.3
Swaziland	0	0
Tanzania	33.6	14.6

TABLE 36 (continued)

	Total Commitments	Total Disbursements
Togo	0	0
Uganda (b)	28.0	2.5
Upper Volta (b)	0	0
Zaire	10.0	10.0
Zambia	0	0
Zimbabwe	0	0
Africa Unallocated or Unspecified	45.2	29.2
Total Africa	$ 1,392.4[1]	$ 906.7
Total Sub-Saharan Africa (SSA)	$ 514.6	$ 302.5
SSA as % of Total Africa	37.0 %	33.4 %
Total Arab League Africa (a) (ALA)	$ 877.8	$ 604.2
ALA as % of Total Africa	63.0 %	66.6 %
Total Sub-Saharan Members of the Islamic Conference (b)	$ 261.8	$ 145.4
As % of Total SSA	55.8 %	53.2 %

1 Includes $ 2 million and $ 5 million to Nigeria in 1978 and 1979, respectively.
2 Preliminary data based on commitments of the Kuwait Fund.

Source: OECD and Fund Annual Reports as compiled by the Arab Fund for Economic and Social Development, Coordination Secretariat

TABLE 37

Geographic Distribution of Commitments of Official Bilateral Aid: 1973–1979: Libya

($ Million)

	Arab Countries $	%	Sub-Saharan Africa $	%	Asia $	%	Other Countries* $	%	Total $
1973	322.3	85.1	24.3	6.4	30.3	8.0	1.8	0.5	378.7
1974	88.0	21.1	56.9	13.6	60.5	14.5	212.5	50.9	417.9
1975	35.1	7.5	147.8	31.8	190.3	40.9	92.3	19.8	465.5
1976	9.5	3.9	37.2	15.3	93.0	38.3	103.0	42.4	242.7
1977	15.4	15.9	4.2	4.3	55.0	56.8	22.2	22.9	96.8
1978	522.6	65.8	106.9	13.5	55.0	6.9	109.5	13.8	794.0
1979	99.4	89.6	0	0	0	0	11.5	10.4	110.9
Total	$ 1,092.3	43.6 %	$ 377.3	15.1 %	$ 484.1	19.3 %	$ 552.8	22.1 %	$ 2,506.5

* Includes unallocated or unspecified amounts.

Source: OECD

TABLE 38
Geographic Distribution of Bilateral Aid by Country: 1973–1980: *Libya*
($ Million)

| | 1973 | | 1974 | |
	Commit-ments	Disburse-ments	Commit-ments	Disburse-ments
Angola				
Benin				
Botswana				
Burundi	3.4	0	0	1.0
Cameroon (b)				
Cape Verde Islands				
Central African Republic				
Chad (b)	8.7	3.6	4.2	9.1
Comoros Islands (b)				
Congo				
Djibouti (a)				
Equatorial Guinea			1.2	0
Ethiopia			1.0	1.0
Gabon (b)	3.4	0	10.1	0
Gambia (b)			1.1	1.1
Ghana				
Guinea (b)	2.0	0	11.1	11.0
Guinea-Bissau (b)			0.5	0.5
Ivory Coast				
Kenya				
Lesotho				
Liberia			2.0	0
Madagascar				
Malawi				
Mali (b)	1.8	0.3	4.0	5.5
Mauritania (a)	33.5	17.6	7.2	20.4
Mauritius				
Mozambique				
Niger (b)			3.2	0
Rwanda			0.1	0
Sao Tome e Principe				
Senegal (b)			1.0	1.0
Seychelles				
Sierra Leone				
Somalia (a)	1.5	1.5	19.0	0

TABLE 38 (continued)

| | 1973 | | 1974 | |
	Commit-ments	Disburse-ments	Commit-ments	Disburse-ments
Sudan (a)				
Swaziland				
Tanzania				
Togo			1.2	1.2
Uganda (b)	7.4	7.4	13.1	13.1
Upper Volta (b)			3.1	3.1
Zaire				
Zambia	0.3	0	0	0.3
Zimbabwe				
Afria Unallocated or Unspecified				
Total Africa	62.0	30.4	83.0	68.3
Total Sub-Saharan Africa (SSA)	27.0	11.3	56.8	47.9
SSA as % of Total Africa	43.5%	37.2%	68.4%	70.1%
Total Arab League Africa (a) (ALA)	35.0	19.1	26.2	20.4
ALA as % of Total Africa	56.5%	62.8%	31.6%	29.9%
Total Sub-Saharan Members of the Islamic Conference (b)	23.3	11.3	51.3	44.4
As % of Total SSA	86.3%	100.0%	90.3%	92.7%

TABLE 38 (continued)

	1975		1976	
	Commit- ments	Disburse- ments	Commit- ments	Disburse- ments
Angola				
Benin				
Botswana				
Burundi	0	1.2		
Cameroon (b)			8.0	8.0
Cape Verde Islands				
Central African Republic				
Chad (b)	8.2	1.0	0	1.3
Comoros Islands (b)				
Congo				
Djibouti (a)				
Equatorial Guinea	0	1.2		
Ethiopia				
Gabon (b)	0	11.8	20.0	0
Gambia (b)	0.4	0.4		
Ghana				
Guinea (b)	0	0.1	6.8	1.2
Guinea-Bissau (b)	3.0	0	0.1	3.0
Ivory Coast				
Kenya				
Lesotho				
Liberia	0	2.0		
Madagascar				
Malawi				
Mali (b)				
Mauritania (a)	0	2.0		
Mauritius				
Mozambique				
Niger (b)			0.8	3.0
Rwanda	4.5	3.2	0	0.9
Sao Tome e Principe				
Senegal (b)				
Seychelles				
Sierra Leone	0.2	0	0	0.2
Somalia (a)	0	12.0	0	6.8
Sudan (a)	0.3	0.3		
Swaziland				

TABLE 38 (continued)

| | 1975 | | 1976 | |
	Commit-ments	Disburse-ments	Commit-ments	Disburse-ments
Tanzania				
Togo			1.6	1.6
Uganda (b)	30.0	6.0	0.3	0
Upper Volta (b)				
Zaire	101.3	20.3	0	11.1
Zambia				
Zimbabwe				
Africa Unallocated or Unspecified	0.1	0.1		
Total Africa	148.0	61.8	37.3	37.1
Total Sub-Saharan Africa (SSA)	147.7	47.1	37.3	30.3
SSA as % of Total Africa	99.8%	76.2%	100.0%	81.7%
Total Arab League Africa (a) (ALA)	0.3	14.7	0	6.8
ALA as % of Total Africa	0.2%	23.8%	0	18.3%
Total Sub-Saharan Members of the Islamic Conference (b)	41.6	19.1	35.7	16.5
As % of Total SSA	28.2%	40.6%	95.7%	54.5%

TABLE 38 (continued)

	1977		1978	
	Commit-ments	Disburse-ments	Commit-ments	Disburse-ments
Angola				
Benin				
Botswana				
Burundi				
Cameroon (b)				
Cape Verde Islands				
Central African Republic				
Chad (b)				
Comoros Islands (b)				
Congo				
Djibouti (a)				
Equatorial Guinea				
Ethiopia				
Gabon (b)				
Gambia (b)				
Ghana				
Guinea (b)			58.0	58.0
Guinea-Bissau (b)				
Ivory Coast				
Kenya				
Lesotho				
Liberia				
Madagascar	4.0	1.0	1.0	4.0
Malawi				
Mali (b)			3.7	3.7
Mauritania (a)				
Mauritius				
Mozambique				
Niger (b)			16.3	11.5
Rwanda	0.1	0.1		
Sao Tome e Principe				
Senegal (b)				
Seychelles	0.1	0.1		
Sierra Leone				
Somalia (a)				
Sudan (a)				
Swaziland				

240

TABLE 38 (continued)

| | 1977 | | 1978 | |
	Commit-ments	Disburse-ments	Commit-ments	Disburse-ments
Tanzania				
Togo				
Uganda (b)			27.9	0
Upper Volta (b)				
Zaire				
Zambia				
Zimbabwe				
Africa Unallocated or Unspecified	2.0	2.0		
Total Africa	6.2	3.2	106.9	77.2
Total Sub-Saharan Africa (SSA)	6.2	3.2	106.9	77.2
SSA as % of Total Africa	100.0%	100.0%	100.0%	100.0%
Total Arab League Africa (a) (ALA)	0	0	0	0
ALA as % of Total Africa	0	0	0	0
Total Sub-Saharan Members of the Islamic Conference (b)	0	0	105.9	73.2
As % of Total SSA	0	0	99.1%	94.8%

TABLE 38 (continued)

| | 1979 | | 1980[1] | |
	Commit- ments	Disburse- ments	Commit- ments	Disburse- ments
Angola				
Benin				
Botswana				
Burundi				
Cameroon (b)				
Cape Verde Islands				
Central African Republic				
Chad (b)				
Comoros Islands (b)				
Congo				
Djibouti (a)				
Equatorial Guinea				
Ethiopia				
Gabon (b)				
Gambia (b)				
Ghana				
Guinea (b)				
Guinea-Bissau (b)				
Ivory Coast				
Kenya				
Lesotho				
Liberia				
Madagascar				
Malawi				
Mali (b)				
Mauritania (a)	25.0	12.5		
Mauritius				
Mozambique				
Niger (b)	0	5.0		
Rwanda				
Sao Tome e Principe				
Senegal (b)				
Seychelles				
Sierra Leone				
Somalia (a)				
Sudan (a)				
Swaziland				

TABLE 38 (continued)

	1979		1980[1]	
	Commit-ments	Disburse-ments	Commit-ments	Disburse-ments
Tanzania				
Togo				
Uganda (b)				
Upper Volta (b)				
Zaire				
Zambia				
Zimbabwe				
Africa Unallocated or Unspecified				
Total Africa	25.0	17.5		
Total Sub-Saharan Africa (SSA)	0	5.0		
SSA as % of Total Africa	0	28.6%		
Total Arab League Africa (a) (ALA)	25.0	12.5		
ALA as % of Total Africa	100.0%	71.4%		
Total Sub-Saharan Members of the Islamic Conference (b)	0	5.0		
As % of Total SSA	0	100.0%		

TABLE 38 (continued)

	Total	
	Commitments	Disbursements
Angola	0	0
Benin	0	0
Botswana	0	0
Burundi	3.4	2.2
Cameroon (b)	8.0	8.0
Cape Verde Islands	0	0
Central African Republic	0	0
Chad (b)	21.1	15.0
Comoros Islands (b)	0	0
Congo	0	0
Djibouti (a)	0	0
Equatorial Guinea	1.2	1.2
Ethiopia	1.0	1.0
Gabon (b)	33.5	11.8
Gambia (b)	1.5	1.5
Ghana	0	0
Guinea (b)	77.8	70.3
Guinea-Bissau (b)	3.6	3.5
Ivory Coast	0	0
Kenya	0	0
Lesotho	0	0
Liberia	2.0	2.0
Madagascar	5.0	5.0
Malawi	0	0
Mali (b)	9.5	9.5
Mauritania (a)	65.7	52.5
Mauritius	0	0
Mozambique	0	0
Niger (b)	20.3	19.5
Rwanda	4.7	4.2
Sao Tome e Principe	0	0
Senegal (b)	1.0	1.0
Seychelles	0.1	0.1
Sierra Leone	0.2	0.2
Somalia (a)	20.5	20.5
Sudan (a)	0.3	0.3
Swaziland	0	0
Tanzania	0	0

TABLE 38 (continued)

	Total Commitments	Total Disbursements
Togo	2.8	2.8
Uganda (b)	78.4	26.5
Upper Volta (b)	3.1	3.1
Zaire	101.3	31.4
Zambia	0.3	0.3
Zimbabwe	0	0
Africa Unallocated or Unspecified	2.1	2.1
Total Africa	468.4	295.5
Total Sub-Saharan Africa (SSA)	381.9	222.0
SSA as % of Total Africa	81.5 %	75.1 %
Total Arab League Africa (a) (ALA)	86.5	73.5
ALA as % of Total Africa	18.5 %	24.9 %
Total Sub-Saharan Members of the Islamic Conference (b)	257.8	169.5
As % of Total SSA	67.9 %	77.1 %

1 Data for bilateral aid to Africa in 1980 were unavailable at the time of publication.

TABLE 39

Geographic Distribution of Commitments of Official Bilateral Aid: 1973–1979: Qatar
($ Million)

| | Arab Countries | | Sub-Saharan Africa | | Asia | | Other Countries* | | Total |
	$	%	$	%	$	%	$	%	$
1973	112.6	100.0	0	0	0	0	0	0	112.6
1974	196.3	92.9	3.5	1.7	11.5	5.4	0	0	211.3
1975	374.0	96.6	12.0	3.1	1.0	0.3	0	0	387.0
1976	91.4	87.9	12.6	12.1	0	0	0	0	104.0
1977	95.0	90.8	9.6	9.2	0	0	0	0	104.6
1978	235.6	98.7	0	0	3.0	1.3	0	0	238.6
1979	49.8	84.7	8.8	15.0	0	0	0.2	0.3	58.8
Total	$ 1,154.7	94.9%	$ 46.5	3.8%	$ 15.5	1.3%	$ 0.2	0%	$ 1,216.9

* Includes unallocated or unspecified amounts

Source: OECD

TABLE 40
Geographic Distribution of Bilateral Aid by Country: 1973–1980: *Qatar*
($ Million)

| | 1973 | | 1974 | |
	Commit-ments	Disburse-ments	Commit-ments	Disburse-ments
Angola				
Benin				
Botswana				
Burundi				
Cameroon (b)				
Cape Verde Islands				
Central African Republic				
Chad (b)			1.0	1.0
Comoros Islands (b)				
Congo				
Djibouti (a)				
Equatorial Guinea				
Ethiopia				
Gabon (b)				
Gambia (b)				
Ghana				
Guinea (b)				
Guinea-Bissau (b)			1.0	1.0
Ivory Coast				
Kenya				
Lesotho				
Liberia				
Madagascar				
Malawi				
Mali (b)			1.5	1.5
Mauritania (a)			12.0	12.0
Mauritius				
Mozambique				
Niger (b)				
Rwanda				
Sao Tome e Principe				
Senegal (b)				
Seychelles				
Sierra Leone				
Somalia (a)	1.0	1.0	16.0	16.0

TABLE 40 (continued)

| | 1973 | | 1974 | |
	Commit-ments	Disburse-ments	Commit-ments	Disburse-ments
Sudan (a)			14.0	0
Swaziland				
Tanzania				
Togo				
Uganda (b)				
Upper Volta (b)				
Zaire				
Zambia				
Zimbabwe				
Africa Unallocated or Unspecified				
Total Africa	1.0	1.0	45.5	31.5
Total Sub-Saharan Africa (SSA)	0	0	3.5	3.5
SSA as % of Total Africa	0	0	7.7%	11.1%
Total Arab League Africa (a) (ALA)	1.0	1.0	42.0	28.0
ALA as % of Total Africa	100.0%	100.0%	92.3%	88.9%
Total Sub-Saharan Members of the Islamic Conference (b)	0	0	3.5	3.5
As % of Total SSA	0	0	100.0%	100.0%

TABLE 40 (continued)

	1975		1976	
	Commit-ments	Disburse-ments	Commit-ments	Disburse-ments
Angola				
Benin				
Botswana				
Burundi				
Cameroon (b)				
Cape Verde Islands			0.5	0.5
Central African Republic				
Chad (b)				
Comoros Islands (b)				
Congo				
Djibouti (a)				
Equatorial Guinea				
Ethiopia				
Gabon (b)			1.5	1.5
Gambia (b)			1.1	1.1
Ghana				
Guinea (b)	4.0	4.0		
Guinea-Bissau (b)				
Ivory Coast				
Kenya				
Lesotho				
Liberia				
Madagascar				
Malawi				
Mali (b)	1.0	1.0	6.0	2.0
Mauritania (a)	1.5	1.5	1.5	1.5
Mauritius				
Mozambique				
Niger (b)				
Rwanda				
Sao Tome e Principe				
Senegal (b)	3.0	3.0	1.5	1.5
Seychelles				
Sierra Leone				
Somalia (a)	2.8	2.8	0.003	0.003
Sudan (a)	2.0	16.0	0.6	0.6
Swaziland				

TABLE 40 (continued)

| | 1975 | | 1976 | |
	Commit-ments	Disburse-ments	Commit-ments	Disburse-ments
Tanzania				
Togo				
Uganda (b)	4.0	4.0	2.0	2.0
Upper Volta (b)				
Zaire				
Zambia				
Zimbabwe				
Africa Unallocated or Unspecified				
Total Africa	18.3	32.3	14.7	10.7
Total Sub-Saharan Africa (SSA)	12.0	12.0	12.6	8.6
SSA as % of Total Africa	59.1%	37.2%	85.7%	80.4%
Total Arab League Africa (a) (ALA)	6.3	20.3	2.1	2.1
ALA as % of Total Africa	40.9%	60.8%	14.3%	19.6%
Total Sub-Saharan Members of the Islamic Conference (b)	12.0	12.0	12.1	8.1
As % of Total SSA	100.0%	100.0%	96.0%	94.2%

TABLE 40 (continued)

| | 1977 | | 1978 | |
	Commit-ments	Disburse-ments	Commit-ments	Disburse-ments
Angola				
Benin				
Botswana				
Burundi				
Cameroon (b)	3.0	0		
Cape Verde Islands	0.5	0.5		
Central African Republic				
Chad (b)				
Comoros Islands (b)				
Congo				
Djibouti (a)				
Equatorial Guinea				
Ethiopia				
Gabon (b)				
Gambia (b)	1.1	1.1		
Ghana				
Guinea (b)				
Guinea-Bissau (b)				
Ivory Coast				
Kenya				
Lesotho				
Liberia				
Madagascar				
Malawi				
Mali (b)				
Mauritania (a)				
Mauritius				
Mozambique				
Niger (b)				
Rwanda				
Sao Tome e Principe				
Senegal (b)				
Seychelles				
Sierra Leone				
Somalia (a)				
Sudan (a)			1.0	1.0
Swaziland				

TABLE 40 (continued)

| | 1977 | | 1978 | |
	Commit-ments	Disburse-ments	Commit-ments	Disburse-ments
Tanzania				
Togo				
Uganda (b)	5.0	2.5		
Upper Volta (b)				
Zaire				
Zambia				
Zimbabwe				
Africa Unallocated or Unspecified				
Total Africa	9.6	4.1	1.0	1.0
Total Sub-Saharan Africa (SSA)	9.6	4.1	0	0
SSA as % of Total Africa	100.0%	100.0%	0	0
Total Arab League Africa (a) (ALA)	0	0	1.0	1.0
ALA as % of Total Africa	0	0	100.0%	100.0%
Total Sub-Saharan Members of the Islamic Conference (b)	9.1	3.6	0	0
As % of Total SSA	94.8%	87.8%	0	0

TABLE 40 (continued)

	1979		1980[1]	
	Commit-ments	Disburse-ments	Commit-ments	Disburse-ments
Angola				0.6
Benin				
Botswana				
Burundi				
Cameroon (b)				3.0
Cape Verde Islands				
Central African Republic				
Chad (b)				
Comoros Islands (b)				
Congo				
Djibouti (a)				2.0
Equatorial Guinea				
Ethiopia				
Gabon (b)				
Gambia (b)				
Ghana				
Guinea (b)				
Guinea-Bissau (b)				
Ivory Coast				
Kenya				
Lesotho				
Liberia				
Madagascar				
Malawi				
Mali (b)	4.0	0		
Mauritania (a)	1.7	1.8		3.3
Mauritius				
Mozambique				
Niger (b)				
Rwanda				
Sao Tome e Principe				
Senegal (b)				
Seychelles				
Sierra Leone				2.0
Somalia (a)	1.5	1.5		8.4
Sudan (a)	0.6	0.6		10.0
Swaziland				

TABLE 40 (continued)

| | 1979 | | 1980[1] | |
	Commit-ments	Disburse-ments	Commit-ments	Disburse-ments
Tanzania				
Togo				
Uganda (b)				
Upper Volta (b)				
Zaire	4.8	4.8		
Zambia				
Zimbabwe				
Africa Unallocated or Unspecified				
Total Africa	12.6	8.7		29.3
Total Sub-Saharan Africa (SSA)	8.8	4.8		5.6
SSA as % of Total Africa	69.8%	55.2%		19.1%
Total Arab League Africa (a) (ALA)	3.8	3.9		23.7
ALA as % of Total Africa	30.2%	44.8%		80.9%
Total Sub-Saharan Members of the Islamic Conference (b)	4.0	0		3.0
As % of Total SSA	45.5%	0		53.6%

TABLE 40 (continued)

	Total[2]	
	Commitments	Disbursements
Angola	0	0.6
Benin	0	0
Botswana	0	0
Burundi	0	0
Cameroon (b)	3.0	3.0
Cape Verde Islands	1.0	1.0
Central African Republic	0	0
Chad (b)	1.0	1.0
Comoros Islands (b)	0	0
Congo	0	0
Djibouti (a)	0	2.0
Equatorial Guinea	0	0
Ethiopia	0	0
Gabon (b)	1.5	1.5
Gambia (b)	2.2	2.2
Ghana	0	0
Guinea (b)	4.0	4.0
Guinea-Bissau (b)	1.0	1.0
Ivory Coast	0	0
Kenya	0	0
Lesotho	0	0
Liberia	0	0
Madagascar	0	0
Malawi	0	0
Mali (b)	12.5	4.5
Mauritania (a)	16.7	20.1
Mauritius	0	0
Mozambique	0	0
Niger (b)	0	0
Rwanda	0	0
Sao Tome e Principe	0	0
Senegal (b)	4.5	4.5
Seychelles	0	0
Sierra Leone	0	2.0
Somalia (a)	21.3	29.7
Sudan (a)	18.2	28.2
Swaziland	0	0
Tanzania	0	0

TABLE 40 (continued)

| | Total[2] | |
	Commitments	Disbursements
Togo	0	0
Uganda (b)	11.0	8.5
Upper Volta (b)	0	0
Zaire	4.8	4.8
Zambia	0	0
Zimbabwe	0	0
Africa Unallocated or Unspecified	0	0
Total Africa	102.7	118.6
Total Sub-Saharan Africa (SSA)	46.5	38.6
SSA as % of Total Africa	45.3%	32.5%
Total Arab League Africa (a) (ALA)	56.2	80.0
ALA as % of Total Africa	54.7%	67.5%
Total Sub-Saharan Members of the Islamic Conference (b)	40.7	30.2
As % of Total SSA	87.5%	78.2%

1 Preliminary. Data about Qatar's bilateral commitments to Africa in 1980 were unavailable at the time of publication.

2 Includes only disbursements for 1980. Because Qatar has historically disbursed its commitments promptly, one might assume that the funds disbursed in 1980 were largely committed in the same year.

Source: OECD

TABLE 41
Geographic Distribution of Commitments of Official Bilateral Aid: 1973–1979: Saudi Arabia
($ Million)

	Arab Countries		Sub-Saharan Africa		Asia		Other Countries*		Total
	$	%	$	%	$	%	$	%	$
1973	578.5	90.0	7.0	1.1	57.0	8.9	0	0	642.5
1974	1,057.6	83.6	16.6	1.3	110.5	8.7	80.5	6.4	1,265.2
1975	2,359.1	90.2	102.9	3.9	151.5	5.8	0.7	0.1	2,614.2
1976	1,694.6	65.9	42.3	1.6	836.4	32.5	0	0	2,573.3
1977	1,882.6	64.3	91.0	3.1	516.0	17.6	438.5	15.0	2,928.1
1978	2,608.5	79.6	143.6	4.4	502.1	15.3	21.7	0.7	3,275.9
1979	1,171.5	79.6	33.7	2.3	151.9	10.3	114.2	7.8	1,471.3
Total	$11,352.4	76.9%	$437.1	3.0%	$2,325.4	15.7%	$655.6	4.4%	$14,770.5

* Includes unallocated or unspecified amounts

Source: OECD

TABLE 42
Geographic Distribution of Bilateral Aid by Country: 1973–1980:
Saudi Arabia
($ Million)

| | 1973 | | 1974 | |
	Commit-ments	Disburse-ments	Commit-ments	Disburse-ments
Angola				
Benin				
Botswana				
Burundi				
Cameroon (b)				
Cape Verde Islands				
Central African Republic				
Chad (b)				
Comoros Islands (b)				
Congo				
Djibouti (a)				
Equatorial Guinea				
Ethiopia				
Gabon (b)	5.0	5.0		
Gambia (b)				
Ghana				
Guinea (b)			10.0	10.0
Guinea-Bissau (b)				
Ivory Coast				
Kenya				
Lesotho				
Liberia				
Madagascar				
Malawi				
Mali (b)			1.0	1.0
Mauritania (a)	2.0	0	31.5	21.5
Mauritius				
Mozambique				
Niger (b)	2.0	0		
Rwanda				
Sao Tome e Principe				
Senegal (b)			5.0	0
Seychelles				
Sierra Leone				

258

TABLE 42 (continued)

| | 1973 | | 1974 | |
	Commit- ments	Disburse- ments	Commit- ments	Disburse- ments
Somalia (a)			10.0	10.0
Sudan (a)	15.0	15.0	14.4	14.4
Swaziland				
Tanzania				
Togo			0.6	0.6
Uganda (b)				
Upper Volta (b)				
Zaire				
Zambia				
Zimbabwe				
Africa Unallocated or Unspecified				
Total Africa	24.0	20.0	72.5	54.0
Total Sub-Saharan Africa (SSA)	7.0	5.0	16.6	11.6
SSA as % of Total Africa	29.2%	25.0%	22.9%	21.5%
Total Arab League Africa (a) (ALA)	17.0	15.0	55.9	42.4
ALA as % of Total Africa	70.8%	75.0%	77.1%	78.5%
Total Sub-Saharan Members of the Islamic Conference (b)	7.0	5.0	16.0	11.0
As % of Total SSA	100.0%	100.0%	96.4%	94.8%

TABLE 42 (continued)

| | 1975 | | 1976 | |
	Commit-ments	Disburse-ments	Commit-ments	Disburse-ments
Angola				
Benin				
Botswana				
Burundi				
Cameroon (b)	17.4	17.4		
Cape Verde Islands				
Central African Republic				
Chad (b)	1.8	1.8	0.01	0.01
Comoros Islands (b)			2.1	2.1
Congo			20.0	4.2
Djibouti (a)				
Equatorial Guinea				
Ethiopia	1.0	1.0		
Gabon (b)	10.0	10.0		
Gambia (b)				
Ghana				
Guinea (b)	1.4	1.4	0.2	0.2
Guinea-Bissau (b)				
Ivory Coast				
Kenya				
Lesotho				
Liberia				
Madagascar				
Malawi				
Mali (b)	16.0	16.0	5.9	0
Mauritania (a)			116.6	94.1
Mauritius				
Mozambique				
Niger (b)	13.2	13.2	7.9	2.1
Rwanda	5.0	5.0	5.0	0
Sao Tome e Principe				
Senegal (b)				
Seychelles				
Sierra Leone				
Somalia (a)	34.6	17.2	11.7	22.8
Sudan (a)	123.1	95.3	159.0	167.0
Swaziland				

TABLE 42 (continued)

	1975		1976	
	Commit-ments	Disburse-ments	Commit-ments	Disburse-ments
Tanzania				
Togo	2.0	2.0	1.1	1.1
Uganda (b)	35.2	15.3	0.04	0.04
Upper Volta (b)				
Zaire				
Zambia				
Zimbabwe				
Africa Unallocated or Unspecified				
Total Africa	260.7	195.6	329.6	293.2
Total Sub-Saharan Africa (SSA)	103.0	83.1	42.3	9.8
SSA as % of Total Africa	39.5 %	42.5 %	12.8 %	3.3 %
Total Arab League Africa (a) (ALA)	157.7	112.5	287.3	283.9
ALA as % of Total Africa	60.5 %	57.5 %	87.2 %	96.7 %
Total Sub-Saharan Members of the Islamic Conference (b)	95.0	75.1	16.2	4.5
As % of Total SSA	92.2 %	90.4 %	38.8 %	45.9 %

TABLE 42 (continued)

| | 1977 | | 1978 | |
	Commit-ments	Disburse-ments	Commit-ments	Disburse-ments
Angola				
Benin				
Botswana				
Burundi				
Cameroon (b)	30.0	6.2	0	2.5
Cape Verde Islands				
Central African Republic				
Chad (b)				
Comoros Islands (b)				
Congo	0	0.4	0	5.6
Djibouti (a)	10.0	10.0	60.0	60.0
Equatorial Guinea				
Ethiopia				
Gabon (b)			20.7	0
Gambia (b)	6.6	0	0	5.2
Ghana	32.5	0	0	9.4
Guinea (b)	1.7	0	0	0.5
Guinea-Bissau (b)			4.6	1.9
Ivory Coast				
Kenya			25.6	0
Lesotho				
Liberia			20.7	0
Madagascar			12.4	0
Malawi				
Mali (b)	20.0	7.7	13.8	1.5
Mauritania (a)	80.0	80.0	129.4	100.0
Mauritius	0.1	0		
Mozambique	0.1	0.1		
Niger (b)	0	2.9	5.0	5.3
Rwanda	0	3.9	0	0.5
Sao Tome e Principe				
Senegal (b)			40.8	0
Seychelles				
Sierra Leone				
Somalia (a)	221.1	161.2	0	5.6
Sudan (a)	140.1	86.2	353.3	37.3
Swaziland				

262

TABLE 42 (continued)

	1977		1978	
	Commit-ments	Disburse-ments	Commit-ments	Disburse-ments
Tanzania				
Togo				
Uganda (b)	0	0.4	0	0.02
Upper Volta (b)				
Zaire				
Zambia				
Zimbabwe				
Africa Unallocated or Unspecified				
Total Africa	542.2	359.0	686.3	235.3
Total Sub-Saharan Africa (SSA)	91.0	21.6	143.6	32.4
SSA as % of Total Africa	16.8%	6.0%	20.9%	13.8%
Total Arab League Africa (a) (ALA)	451.2	337.4	542.7	202.9
ALA as % of Total Africa	83.2%	94.0%	79.1%	86.2%
Total Sub-Saharan Members of the Islamic Conference (b)	58.3	17.1	84.9	16.9
As % of Total SSA	64.1%	79.2%	59.1%	52.2%

TABLE 42 (continued)

	1979		1980[1]	
	Commit-ments	Disburse-ments	Commit-ments	Disburse-ments
Angola				
Benin				
Botswana			11.0	0
Burundi			2.6	0
Cameroon (b)	3.6	8.5		12.8
Cape Verde Islands			2.6	0
Central African Republic	0	5.3		
Chad (b)				
Comoros Islands (b)	24.6	0		9.7
Congo				10.0
Djibouti (a)				
Equatorial Guinea				
Ethiopia				
Gabon (b)			2.7	0
Gambia (b)	0	0.7	8.9	1.0
Ghana	0	8.5		13.0
Guinea (b)	0	0.4	30.0	0.1
Guinea-Bissau (b)	0	1.7		0.22
Ivory Coast				
Kenya	0.02	0.02	19.8	0
Lesotho			4.5	0
Liberia	0	11.2		5.9
Madagascar	0	4.8		3.1
Malawi				
Mali (b)	0	3.9	10.1	8.5
Mauritania (a)	116.7	18.5		37.4
Mauritius				
Mozambique				
Niger (b)	0	0.1		
Rwanda				
Sao Tome e Principe				
Senegal (b)				
Seychelles				
Sierra Leone				
Somalia (a)	20.0	29.7	11.7	32.3
Sudan (a)	135.7	243.3	6.0	125.2
Swaziland				

TABLE 42 (continued)

	1979		1980[1]	
	Commit-ments	Disburse-ments	Commit-ments	Disburse-ments
Tanzania				
Togo	4.9	0.04	10.6	0.04
Uganda (b)	0	0.5		
Upper Volta (b)				
Zaire			0	0
Zambia	0.5	0.5	69.2	
Zimbabwe	0.1	0.1		5.0
Africa Unallocated or Unspecified				
Total Africa	306.1	337.8	189.7	264.3
Total Sub-Saharan Africa (SSA)	33.7	46.3	172.0	69.4
SSA as % of Total Africa	11.0%	13.7%	90.7%	26.2%
Total Arab League Africa (a) (ALA)	272.4	291.5	17.7	194.9
ALA as % of Total Africa	89.0%	86.3%	9.3%	73.7%
Total Sub-Saharan Members of the Islamic Conference (b)	28.2	15.8	51.7	32.4
As % of Total SSA	83.7%	34.1%	30.1%	46.6%

TABLE 42 (continued)

	Total Commitments	Total Disbursements
Angola	0	0
Benin	0	0
Botswana	11.0	0
Burundi	2.6	0
Cameroon (b)	51.0	47.4
Cape Verde Islands	2.6	0
Central African Republic	0	5.3
Chad (b)	1.81	1.81
Comoros Islands (b)	26.7	11.8
Congo	20.0	20.2
Djibouti (a)	70.0	70.0
Equatorial Guina	0	0
Ethiopia	1.0	1.0
Gabon (b)	38.4	15.0
Gambia (b)	15.5	6.9
Ghana	32.5	30.9
Guinea (b)	43.3	12.6
Guinea-Bissau (b)	4.6	3.8
Ivory Coast	0	0
Kenya	45.4	0
Lesotho	4.5	0
Liberia	20.7	17.1
Madagascar	12.4	7.9
Malawi	0	0
Mali (b)	66.8	38.6
Mauritania (a)	476.2	351.5
Mauritius	0.1	0
Mozambique	0.1	0.1
Niger (b)	28.1	23.6
Rwanda	10.0	9.4
Sao Tome e Principe	0	0
Senegal (b)	45.8	0
Seychelles	0	0
Sierra Leone	0	0
Somalia (a)	309.1	278.8
Sudan (a)	946.6	783.7
Swaziland	0	0
Tanzania	0	0

TABLE 42 (continued)

	Commitments	Total Disbursements
Togo	19.2	3.7
Uganda (b)	35.2	16.3
Upper Volta (b)	0	0
Zaire	0	0
Zambia	69.7	0.5
Zimbabwe	0.1	5.1
African Unallocated or Unspecified	0	0
Total Africa	$ 2,411.1	$ 1.763.1
Total Sub-Saharan Africa (SSA)	609.2	279.1
SSA as % of Total Africa	25.3 %	15.8 %
Total Arab League Africa (a) (ALA)	1,801.9	1,484.0
ALA as % of Total Africa	74.7 %	84.2 %
Total Sub-Saharan Members of the Islamic Conference (b)	357.2	177.9
As % of Total SSA	58.6 %	63.7 %

1 Preliminary. Data for 1980 commitments relate to the Saudi Fund for Development only.

Source: OECD and Fund Annual Reports as compiled by the Arab Fund for Economic and Social Development, Coordination Secretariat

TABLE 43
Saudi Fund for Development[1]
Geographic Distribution of Aid Commitments: 1975–1980
($ Million)

	Arab Countries		Sub-Saharan Africa		Asia[2]		Other		Total
	$	%	$	%	$	%	$	%	$
1975	176.1	62.5	29.7	10.5	75.9	26.9	0	0	281.7
1976	140.1	32.9	36.7	8.6	249.3	58.5	0	0	426.1
1977	425.8	55.4	86.3	11.2	201.1	26.2	55.3	7.2	768.5
1978	231.4	27.7	95.8	11.5	277.0	33.2	230.8	27.6	835.0
1979	187.0	40.0	23.6	5.0	151.0	32.0	110.4	23.0	472.0
1980	55.3	16.7	125.5	37.9	150.4	30.8	0	0	331.2
Total	$ 1,215.7	39.0%	$ 397.6	12.8%	$ 1,104.7	35.5%	$ 396.5	12.7%	$ 3,114.5

1 All figures are for signed loan commitments.
2 Includes Turkey.

Source: Fund Annual Reports, Coordination Secretariat at the Arab Fund for Economic and Social Development, "Summary of Loans and Technical Assistance Extended to Developing Countries" (Quarterly), and for 1979, OECD, *Development Cooperation 1980 Review*, p. 132

TABLE 44

Geographic Distribution of Commitments of Official Bilateral Aid: 1973–1979: United Arab Emirates
($ Million)

	Arab Countries		Sub-Saharan Africa		Asia		Other Countries*		Total
	$	%	$	%	$	%	$	%	$
1973	370.4	88.0	3.6	0.9	46.8	11.1	0.1	0.02	420.9
1974	564.0	77.5	53.4	7.3	79.6	10.9	30.4	4.2	727.4
1975	948.9	81.3	11.5	1.0	164.2	14.1	42.0	3.6	1,166.6
1976	1,007.3	91.3	6.6	0.6	78.9	7.2	9.9	0.9	1,102.7
1977	751.7	64.2	21.8	1.9	22.3	1.9	375.9	32.1	1,171.7
1978	850.9	87.3	8.1	0.8	38.5	3.9	77.5	7.9	975.0
1979	1,019.2	85.6	8.3	0.7	8.3	0.7	155.4	13.1	1,191.2
Total	$5,512.4	81.6%	$113.3	1.7%	$438.6	6.5%	$691.2	10.2%	$6,755.5

* Includes unallocated or unspecified amounts

Source: OECD

TABLE 45
Geographic Distribution of Bilateral Aid by Country: 1973–1980:
United Arab Emirates
($ Million)

| | 1973 | | 1974 | |
	Commit-ments	Disburse-ments	Commit-ments	Disburse-ments
Angola				
Benin				
Botswana				
Burundi				
Cameroon (b)				
Cape Verde Islands				
Central African Republic				
Chad (b)				
Comoros Islands (b)				
Congo				
Djibouti (a)				
Equatorial Guinea				
Ethiopia				
Gabon (b)				
Gambia (b)				
Ghana				
Guinea (b)				
Guinea-Bissau (b)				
Ivory Coast				
Kenya				
Lesotho				
Liberia				
Madagascar				
Malawi				
Mali (b)				
Mauritania (a)			5.6	0
Mauritius				
Mozambique				
Niger (b)	0.1	0.1		
Rwanda				
Sao Tome e Principe				
Senegal (b)				
Seychelles				
Sierra Leone				

270

TABLE 45 (continued)

	1973		1974	
	Commit-ments	Disburse-ments	Commit-ments	Disburse-ments
Somalia (a)	3.0	3.0	5.5	5.5
Sudan (a)	3.0	0	12.0	15.1
Swaziland				
Tanzania				
Togo				
Uganda (b)				
Upper Volta (b)			3.0	3.0
Zaire			50.3	50.3
Zambia				
Zimbabwe				
Africa Unallocated or Unspecified	3.5	3.5	0.1	0.1
Total Africa	9.6	6.6	76.5	74.0
Total Sub-Saharan Africa (SSA)	3.6	3.6	53.4	53.4
SSA as % of Total Africa	37.5%	54.5%	69.8%	72.2%
Total Arab League Africa (a) (ALA)	6.0	3.0	23.1	20.6
ALA as % of Total Africa	62.5%	45.5%	30.2%	27.8%
Total Sub-Saharan Members of the Islamic Conference (b)	0.1	0.1	3.0	3.0
As % of Total SSA	100.0%	100.0%	5.6%	5.6%

TABLE 45 (continued)

	1975		1976	
	Commit-ments	Disburse-ments	Commit-ments	Disburse-ments
Angola				
Benin				
Botswana				
Burundi			1.0	0.01
Cameroon (b)				
Cape Verde Islands				
Central African Republic				
Chad (b)				
Comoros Islands (b)			0.5	0.01
Congo				
Djibouti (a)				
Equatorial Guinea				
Ethiopia				
Gabon (b)				
Gambia (b)				
Ghana				
Guinea (b)				
Guinea-Bissau (b)	2.0	2.0		
Ivory Coast				
Kenya				
Lesotho				
Liberia				
Madagascar				
Malawi				
Mali (b)	4.0	4.0	5.1	1.0
Mauritania (a)	10.0	15.1	10.0	10.0
Mauritius			0.01	0.01
Mozambique				
Niger (b)				
Rwanda				
Sao Tome e Principe				
Senegal (b)				
Seychelles				
Sierra Leone				
Somalia (a)	15.5	15.5	6.1	0.1
Sudan (a)	64.5	59.3	59.8	25.4
Swaziland				

TABLE 45 (continued)

	1975		1976	
	Commit-ments	Disburse-ments	Commit-ments	Disburse-ments
Tanzania				
Togo				
Uganda (b)	4.0	15.3		
Upper Volta (b)				
Zaire				
Zambia				
Zimbabwe				
Africa Unallocated or Unspecified	1.5	1.5		
Total Africa	101.5	112.7	82.5	36.5
Total Sub-Saharan Africa (SSA)	11.5	22.8	6.6	1.0
SSA as % of Total Africa	9.9 %	18.9 %	8.0 %	2.8 %
Total Arab League Africa (a) (ALA)	90.0	89.9	75.9	35.5
ALA as % of Total Africa	88.7 %	79.8 %	92.0 %	97.2 %
Total Sub-Saharan Members of the Islamic Conference (b)	10.0	21.3	5.5	0.9
As % of Total SSA	100.0 %	100.0 %	83.3 %	90.0 %

TABLE 45 (continued)

| | 1977 | | 1978 | |
	Commit- ments	Disburse- ments	Commit- ments	Disburse- ments
Angola				
Benin				
Botswana				
Burundi			0	0.1
Cameroon (b)				
Cape Verde Islands				
Central African Republic				
Chad (b)				
Comoros Islands (b)				
Congo				
Djibouti (a)				
Equatorial Guinea				
Ethiopia				
Gabon (b)				
Gambia (b)	1.3	0.7	0	0.6
Ghana				
Guinea (b)	4.1	0	0	1.9
Guinea-Bissau (b)				
Ivory Coast				
Kenya				
Lesotho			0.7	0.1
Liberia				
Madagascar				
Malawi				
Mali (b)	0	0.5	0	0.6
Mauritania (a)	14.1	10.0		
Mauritius				
Mozambique				
Niger (b)				
Rwanda				
Sao Tome e Principe				
Senegal (b)			1.0	0
Seychelles				
Sierra Leone				
Somalia (a)	122.3	9.4		
Sudan (a)	93.3	13.0	2.5	10.5
Swaziland				

274

TABLE 45 (continued)

	1977		1978	
	Commit-ments	Disburse-ments	Commit-ments	Disburse-ments
Tanzania	6.2	0		
Togo				
Uganda (b)	10.3	0	6.4	0
Upper Volta (b)				
Zaire				
Zambia				
Zimbabwe				
Africa Unallocated or Unspecified				
Total Africa	251.6	33.6	10.6	13.8
Total Sub-Saharan Africa (SSA)	21.9	1.2	8.1	3.3
SSA as % of Total Africa	8.7%	3.6%	76.4%	23.9%
Total Arab League Africa (a) (ALA)	229.7	32.4	2.5	10.5
ALA as % of Total Africa	91.3%	96.4%	23.6%	76.1%
Total Sub-Saharan Members of the Islamic Conference (b)	15.7	1.2	7.4	3.1
As % of Total SSA	71.7%	100.0%	91.4%	93.9%

TABLE 45 (continued)

	1979		1980[1]	
	Commit-ments	Disburse-ments	Commit-ments	Disburse-ments
Angola				
Benin				
Botswana				
Burundi	0	0.2	0	0.2
Cameroon (b)				
Cape Verde Islands			1.1	0
Central African Republic				
Chad (b)				
Comoros Islands (b)	3.1	0.1		2.8
Congo				
Djibouti (a)				
Equatorial Guinea				
Ethiopia				
Gabon (b)				
Gambia (b)	0	0.04	1.0	0.6
Ghana				
Guinea (b)	0	1.3		0.5
Guinea-Bissau (b)			4.4	
Ivory Coast				
Kenya				
Lesotho	0	0.3	1.1	0.1
Liberia				
Madagascar	4.2	0		1.9
Malawi				
Mali (b)	0	0.9		5.0
Mauritania (a)	35.4	8.2	6.5	0.3
Mauritius				
Mozambique				
Niger (b)				
Rwanda				
Sao Tome e Principe				
Senegal (b)	0	0.4		1.3
Seychelles	1.0	0		0.8
Sierra Leone				
Somalia (a)	27.4	53.7		48.6
Sudan (a)	10.8	10.9	101.3	70.4
Swaziland				

TABLE 45 (continued)

| | 1979 | | 1980[1] | |
	Commit-ments	Disburse-ments	Commit-ments	Disburse-ments
Tanzania	0	2.2		2.1
Togo				
Uganda (b)	0	0.2		5.8
Upper Volta (b)				
Zaire				23.5
Zambia				
Zimbabwe				
Africa Unallocated or Unspecified				
Total Africa	81.9	78.4	115.4	163.9
Total Sub-Saharan Africa (SSA)	8.3	5.6	7.6	44.6
SSA as % of Total Africa	10.1%	7.2%	6.6%	27.2%
Total Arab League Africa (a) (ALA)	73.6	72.8	107.8	119.3
ALA as % of Total Africa	89.9%	92.8%	93.4%	72.8%
Total Sub-Saharan Members of the Islamic Conference (b)	3.1	2.9	5.4	16.0
As % of Total SSA	37.3%	52.5%	71.1%	35.9%

TABLE 45 (continued)

	Total	
	Commitments	Disbursements
Angola	0	0
Benin	0	0
Botswana	0	0
Burundi	1.0	0.5
Cameroon (b)	0	0
Cape Verde Islands	1.1	0
Central African Republic	0	0
Chad (b)	0	0
Comoros Islands (b)	3.6	2.9
Congo	0	0
Djibouti (a)	0	0
Equatorial Guinea	0	0
Ethiopia	0	0
Gabon (b)	0	0
Gambia (b)	2.3	1.9
Ghana	0	0
Guinea (b)	4.1	3.7
Guinea-Bissau (b)	6.4	2.0
Ivory Coast	0	0
Kenya	0	0
Lesotho	1.8	0.5
Liberia	0	0
Madagascar	4.2	1.9
Malawi	0	0
Mali (b)	9.1	12.0
Mauritania (a)	81.6	43.6
Mauritius	0.01	0.01
Mozambique	0	0
Niger (b)	0.1	0.1
Rwanda	0	0
Sao Tome e Principe	0	0
Senegal (b)	1.0	1.7
Seychelles	1.0	0.8
Sierra Leone	0	0
Somalia (a)	179.8	135.8
Sudan (a)	347.2	207.6
Swaziland	0	0
Tanzania	6.2	4.3

TABLE 45 (continued)

	Commitments	Total Disbursements
Togo	0	0
Uganda (b)	20.7	21.3
Upper Volta (b)	3.0	3.0
Zaire	50.3	73.8
Zambia	0	0
Zimbabwe	0	0
Africa Unallocated or Unspecified	5.1	5.1
Total Africa	$ 729.6	$ 522.5
Total Sub-Saharan Africa (SSA)	121.0	135.5
SSA as % of Total Africa	16.6 %	25.9 %
Total Arab League Africa (a) (ALA)	608.6	387.0
ALA as % of Total Africa	83.4 %	74.1 %
Total Sub-Saharan Members of the Islamic Conference (b)	50.3	48.6
As % of Total SSA	43.4 %	37.3 %

1 Preliminary. Data for 1980 commitments relate to the Abu Dhabi Fund only.

Source: OECD and Fund Annual Reports as compiled by the Arab Fund for Economic and Social Development, Coordination Secretariat

TABLE 46
Abu Dhabi Fund for Arab Economic Development
Geographic Distribution of Aid Commitments: 1975–1980
($ Million)

	Arab Countries		Sub-Saharan Africa		Asia		Other		Total
	$	%	$	%	$	%	$	%	$
1975	45.8	100.0	0	0	0	0	0	0	45.8
1976	120.9	71.8	5.0	3.0	42.5	25.2	0	0	168.4
1977	104.4	75.5	11.5	8.3	22.3	16.1	0	0	138.2
1978	185.5	84.8	8.3	3.8	17.7	8.1	7.3	3.3	218.8
1979	127.2	95.1	6.6	4.9	0	0	0	0	133.8
1980	169.6	83.7	6.1	3.0	0	0	27.0	13.3	202.7
Total	$753.4	83.0%	$37.5	4.1%	$82.5	9.1%	$34.3	3.8%	$907.7

Source: Fund Annual Reports and Coordination Secretariat at the Arab Fund for Economic and Social Development, "Summary of Loans and Technical Assistance Extended to Developing Countries" (Quarterly)

TABLE 47
Consolidated Bilateral Aid Commitments by Recipient Country:
1973-1980
($ Million)

	1973	1974	1975	1976	1977
Angola	0	0	0	0	0
Benin	0	1.3	0	1.0	0
Botswana	0	0	0	0	0
Burundi	3.4	2.0	0	2.2	6.1
Cameroon (b)	0	0	18.0	8.0	48.7
Cape Verde Islands	0	0	0	0.5	0.5
Central African Republic	0	0	0.2	0	0
Chad (b)	36.9	5.2	11.0	10.0	0
Comoros Islands (b)	0	0	0	9.1	5.2
Congo	0	0	0	33.7	0
Djibouti (a)	0	0	0	0	10.0
Equatorial Guinea	0	16.2	0	0	0
Ethiopia	0	1.0	1.2	0	0
Gabon (b)	8.4	10.1	15.0	21.6	0
Gambia (b)	0	1.1	0.4	2.1	24.7
Ghana	0	0	0	0	63.8
Guinea (b)	2.0	36.7	5.9	26.2	6.2
Guinea-Bissau (b)	0	2.0	6.2	1.6	0
Ivory Coast	0	0	0	0	0
Kenya	0	0	0	0.01	0
Lesotho	0	0	0	0	0
Liberia	0	2.0	0	0	0
Madagascar	0	6.8	0	0	11.3
Malawi	0	0	0	0	0
Mali (b)	2.2	8.2	23.6	34.1	20.0
Mauritania (a)	46.1	57.4	40.8	177.0	96.6
Mauritius	0	0	0	0.1	0.1
Mozambique	0	0	0	0	0.1
Niger (b)	2.5	4.1	14.2	8.7	0
Rwanda	0	0.1	12.9	5.0	0.1
Sao Tome e Principe	0	0	0	0	0
Senegal (b)	0.7	44.1	4.5	17.9	0
Seychelles	0	0	0	0	0.1
Sierra Leone	0	0	0.2	0	0
Somalia (a)	5.5	123.7	90.8	41.1	345.9
Sudan (a)	83.7	221.4	277.3	454.7	268.1

281

TABLE 47 (continued)

	1973	1974	1975	1976	1977
Swaziland	0	0	0	0	0
Tanzania	0	0	15.7	0	6.2
Togo	0	1.8	2.0	3.6	0
Uganda (b)	7.4	20.5	103.8	2.0	15.3
Upper Volta (b)	0.1	6.1	0.2	1.0	0
Zaire	0	50.3	101.3	10.0	0
Zambia	0.3	0.8	0	0	0
Zimbabwe	0	0	0	0	0
Africa Unallocated or Unspecified	3.5	22.1	3.7	12.4	2.0
Total Africa	202.7	645.0	748.9	883.6	931.0
Total Arab League Africa (a)	135.3	402.5	408.9	672.9	720.6
As % of Total Africa	66.7	62.4	54.6	76.1	77.4
Total Members of the Islamic Conference (a + b)	195.5	540.6	611.7	815.1	840.7
As % of Total Africa	96.4	83.8	81.7	92.2	90.3
Total Sub-Saharan Africa	67.4	242.5	340.0	210.8	210.4
As % of Total Africa	33.3	37.6	45.4	23.9	22.6
Sub-Saharan Members of the Islamic Conference (b)	60.2	138.1	202.8	142.3	120.1
As % of Total SSA	89.3	56.9	60.3	71.7	57.1

TABLE 47 (continued)

	1978	1979	1980p	Total
Angola	0	0	0	0
Benin	8.2	0	0	10.5
Botswana	0	0	18.3	18.3
Burundi	0	0	4.4	18.1
Cameroon (b)	0	3.6	0	78.3
Cape Verde Islands	0	0	3.7	4.7
Central African Republic	0	3.8	0	4.0
Chad (b)	12.0	0	0	75.1
Comoros Islands (b)	2.0	34.1	0.4	50.8
Congo	3.6	0	20.9	58.2
Djibouti (a)	60.0	0.5	6.7	77.2
Equatorial Guinea	0	0	0	16.2
Ethiopia	0	0	0	2.2
Gabon (b)	20.7	0	2.7	75.8
Gambia (b)	0	0.6	26.5	55.4
Ghana	0	0	0	63.8
Guinea (b)	58.0	6.9	30.0	171.9
Guinea-Bissau (b)	11.9	0	4.4	26.1
Ivory Coast	0	0	0	0
Kenya	25.6	0.02	19.8	45.4
Lesotho	5.0	0	5.6	10.6
Liberia	28.7	0	0	30.7
Madagascar	24.0	34.2	7.7	84.0
Malawi	0	0	0	0
Mali (b)	17.5	5.0	25.7	136.3
Mauritania (a)	158.1	304.8	6.5	887.3
Mauritius	0	0	5.6	5.8
Mozambique	0	11.3	10.3	21.2
Niger (b)	21.8	0	11.2	62.5
Rwanda	0	0.4	0	18.5
Sao Tome e Principe	0	0	0	0
Senegal (b)	44.8	5.8	0	117.8
Seychelles	0	1.0	1.1	2.2
Sierra Leone	0	4.0	0.5	4.7
Somalia (a)	15.0	71.1	11.7	704.8
Sudan (a)	377.0	172.2	112.0	1,966.4
Swaziland	0	0	0	0
Tanzania	0	30.0	18.1	70.0
Togo	0	4.9	10.6	22.9

TABLE 47 (continued)

	1978	1979	1980p	Total
Uganda (b)	34.3	0	0	183.3
Upper Volta (b)	0	0	0	7.4
Zaire	0	4.8	69.2	235.6
Zambia	0	39.5	0	40.6
Zimbabwe	0	0.1	0	0.1
Africa Unallocated or Unspecified	7.0	7.8	0	58.5
Total Africa	935.2	746.4	433.6	$ 5,526.4
Total Arab League Africa (a)	610.1	548.6	136.9	$ 3,635.7
As % of Total Africa	65.2	73.5	31.6	65.8 %
Total Members of the Islamic Conference (a + b)	833.1	604.6	237.8	$ 4,679.1
As % of Total Africa	89.1	81.0	54.8	84.7 %
Total Sub-Saharan Africa	325.1	197.8	296.7	$ 1,890.7
As % of Total Africa	34.8	26.5	68.4	34.2 %
Sub-Saharan Members of the Islamic Conference (b)	223.0	56.0	100.9	$ 1,043.4
As % of Total SSA	70.1	29.5	34.0	56.9 %

P = Preliminary and partial data. Does not include commitments by Algeria, Libya or Qatar.

Source: OECD

TABLE 48

Aggregate Bilateral Commitments to Different Groups of Recipients: 1973–1980[1]
(\$ Million)

	Arab League States[2]		Sub-Saharan Members of the Islamic Conference		Least Developed Countries		Most Seriously Affected Countries		Total Africa	Total Sub-Saharan Africa
	\$	%[3]	\$	%[3]	\$	%[3]	\$	%[3]	\$	\$
Algeria	0.7	2.5	14.2	63.4	10.3	46.0	15.7	70.1	28.1	27.4
Iraq	204.0	51.8	61.4	32.5	92.0	48.7	150.0	79.4	394.1	190.1
Kuwait	877.8	63.0	261.8	55.8	242.7	47.2	363.6	77.5	1,392.4	514.6
Libya	86.5	18.5	257.8	67.9	220.8	58.1	238.6	62.8	468.4	381.9
Qatar	56.2	54.7	40.7	87.5	31.7	68.2	40.2	86.5	102.7	46.5
Saudi Arabia	1,801.9	74.7	357.2	58.6	249.1	40.9	403.2	66.2	2,411.1	609.2
United Arab Emirates	608.9	83.4	50.3	43.4	53.0	45.7	61.0	52.6	729.6	121.0
Total	\$3,635.7	65.8%	\$1,043.4	57.0%	\$899.6	49.1%	\$1,272.3	69.4%	\$5,526.4	\$1,890.7

1 Partial data for 1980. Includes only information on the commitments of the national funds of Abu Dhabi, Iraq, Kuwait and Saudi Arabia.

2 Includes Djibouti, Mauritania, Somalia and Sudan.

3 As a percent of total aid to Sub-Saharan Africa, except in the case of the Arab League States where the calculation refers to total aid to Africa.

Source: OECD

TABLE 49
Major African Recipients of Bilateral Assistance Ranked by Country:
1973–1980
($ Million)

Algeria		Iraq	
1. Gabon (b)	$ 5	1. Somalia (a b)	95.1
2. Sierra Leone	4	2. Mauritania (a b)	66.8
3. Mali (b)	3.1	3. Sudan (a b)	41
4. Niger (b)	2.4	4. Zambia	39
5. Benin	2.3	5. Madagascar	37.7
6. Upper Volta (b)	1.3	6. Chad (b)	34
7. Guinea Bissau (b)	1.0	7. Tanzania	30.2
8. Togo	0.9	8. Mozambique	20.3
9. Zambia	0.8	9. Guinea (b)	16.5
10. Guinea (b)	0.7	10. Uganda (b)	10.0
11. Mauritania (a b)	0.7		

Kuwait		Libya	
1. Sudan (a b)	613.1	1. Zaire	101.3
2. Mauritania (a b)	179.6	2. Uganda (b)	78.4
3. Somalia (a b)	79.0	3. Guinea (b)	77.8
4. Senegal (b)	65.1	4. Mauritania (a b)	65.7
5. Congo	38.2	5. Gabon (b)	33.5
6. Mali (b)	34.4	6. Chad (b)	21.1
7. Gambia (b)	33.9	7. Somalia (a b)	20.5
8. Tanzania	33.6	8. Niger (b)	20.3
9. Ghana	31.3	9. Mali (b)	9.5
10. Uganda (b)	28.0	10. Cameroon (b)	8.0

TABLE 49 (continued)

Qatar		Saudi Arabia	
1. Somalia (a b)	21.3	1. Sudan (a b)	946.6
2. Sudan (a b)	18.2	2. Mauritania (a b)	476.2
3. Mauritania (a b)	16.7	3. Somalia (a b)	310.1
4. Mali (b)	12.5	4. Djibouti (a b)	70.0
5. Uganda (b)	11.0	5. Zaire	69.2
6. Zaire	4.8	6. Mali (b)	66.8
7. Senegal (b)	4.5	7. Cameroon (b)	51.0
8. Guinea (b)	4.0	8. Senegal (b)	45.8
9. Cameroon (b)	3.0	9. Kenya	45.4
10. Gambia (b)	2.2	10. Guinea (b)	43.3

U.A.E.	
1. Sudan (a b)	347.2
2. Somalia (a b)	179.8
3. Mauritania (a b)	81.6
4. Zaire	50.3
5. Uganda (b)	20.7
6. Mali (b)	9.1
7. Guinea-Bissau (b)	6.4
8. Tanzania	6.2
9. Madagascar	4.2
10. Guinea (b)	4.1

(a) Member of the Arab League
(b) Member of the Islamic Conference